THE THEOLOGY OF THE BOOKS OF NAHUM, HABAKKUK, AND ZEPHANIAH

The books of Nahum, Habakkuk, and Zephaniah address problems in and around ancient Judah in ways that are as incisive and critical as they are optimistic and constructive. Daniel C. Timmer's *The Theology of the Books of Nahum, Habakkuk, and Zephaniah* situates these books in their social and political contexts, examining the unique theology of each as it engages thorny problems in Judah and beyond. In dialogue with recent scholarship, this study focuses on these books' analysis and evaluation of the world as it is, examining both human beings and their actions, and God's commitment to purify, restore, and perfect the world. Timmer also surveys these books' later theological use and cultural reception. His study brings their theology into dialogue with concerns as varied as ecology, nationalism, and widespread injustice. It highlights the enduring significance of divine justice and grace for solid hope and effective service in our world.

Daniel C. Timmer is Professor of Biblical Studies at Puritan Reformed Theological Seminary (Grand Rapids) and Professeur adjoint d'Ancien Testament at the Faculté de théologie évangelique (Montreal). He is the author of *The Non-Israelite Nations in the Book of the Twelve* and coeditor, with Steed V. Davidson, of *Prophetic Otherness: Constructions of Otherness in Prophetic Literature.*

OLD TESTAMENT THEOLOGY

GENERAL EDITORS

Brent A. Strawn
*D. Moody Smith Distinguished Professor of Old Testament
and Professor of Law
Duke Divinity School and Duke University School of Law*

Stephen B. Chapman
*Associate Professor of Old Testament
Duke Divinity School, Duke University*

Patrick D. Miller[†]
*Charles T. Haley Professor of Old Testament Theology, Emeritus
Princeton Theological Seminary*

This series aims to remedy the deficiency of available published material on the theological concerns of the Old Testament books. Here, specialists explore the theological richness of a given book at greater length than is usually possible in the introductions to commentaries or as part of other Old Testament theologies. They are also able to investigate the theological themes and issues of their chosen books without being tied to a commentary format or to a thematic structure provided from elsewhere. When complete, the series will cover all the Old Testament writings and will thus provide an attractive, and timely, range of short texts around which courses can be developed.

PUBLISHED VOLUMES

The Theology of the Book of Proverbs, Katharine J. Dell
The Theology of the Books of Haggai and Zechariah, Robert L. Foster
The Theology of the Book of Kings, Keith Bodner
The Theology of the Book of Amos, John Barton
The Theology of the Book of Genesis, R. W. L. Moberly
The Theology of the Book of Jeremiah, Walter Brueggemann

THE THEOLOGY OF THE BOOKS OF NAHUM, HABAKKUK, AND ZEPHANIAH

DANIEL C. TIMMER

Puritan Reformed Theological Seminary, Grand Rapids
Faculté de théologie évangélique, Montreal

CAMBRIDGE
UNIVERSITY PRESS

Shaftesbury Road, Cambridge CB2 8EA, United Kingdom

One Liberty Plaza, 20th Floor, New York, NY 10006, USA

477 Williamstown Road, Port Melbourne, VIC 3207, Australia

314–321, 3rd Floor, Plot 3, Splendor Forum, Jasola District Centre,
New Delhi – 110025, India

103 Penang Road, #05–06/07, Visioncrest Commercial, Singapore 238467

Cambridge University Press is part of Cambridge University Press & Assessment,
a department of the University of Cambridge.

We share the University's mission to contribute to society through the pursuit of
education, learning and research at the highest international levels of excellence.

www.cambridge.org
Information on this title: www.cambridge.org/9781108475594

DOI: 10.1017/9781108651943

© Cambridge University Press & Assessment 2024

This publication is in copyright. Subject to statutory exception and to the provisions
of relevant collective licensing agreements, no reproduction of any part may take
place without the written permission of Cambridge University Press & Assessment.

First published 2024

A catalogue record for this publication is available from the British Library

*A Cataloging-in-Publication data record for this book is available from
the Library of Congress*

ISBN 978-1-108-47559-4 Hardback
ISBN 978-1-108-46869-5 Paperback

Cambridge University Press & Assessment has no responsibility for the persistence
or accuracy of URLs for external or third-party internet websites referred to in this
publication and does not guarantee that any content on such websites is, or will
remain, accurate or appropriate.

Contents

General Editors' Preface	*page* ix
Preface	xiii
Acknowledgments	xvi
List of Abbreviations	xviii

1 READING ANCIENT ISRAELITE PROPHETIC
   BOOKS 1
   Israelite Prophets and Prophecy in Their Ancient
   Near Eastern Context   2
   The Book of the Twelve (Minor Prophets)   9
   Approaching the Theology of Prophetic Books   14
   Engaging Israelite Prophecy and Its Claims
   in the Twenty-First Century   19

2 THE THEOLOGY OF THE BOOK OF NAHUM 24
   Issues in the Interpretation of Nahum   26
   A Theological Exploration of Nahum   37
   A Theology of Nahum   75
   Nahum's Contribution to Jewish and Christian
   Traditions   78
   Past and Present Reception of Nahum   91

3 THE THEOLOGY OF THE BOOK OF HABAKKUK 104

Issues in the Interpretation of Habakkuk   106
A Theological Exploration of Habakkuk   126
A Theology of Habakkuk   154
Habakkuk's Contribution to Jewish and Christian
Traditions   158
Past and Present Reception of Habakkuk   169

4 THE THEOLOGY OF THE BOOK OF ZEPHANIAH 173

Issues in the Interpretation of Zephaniah   174
A Theological Exploration of Zephaniah   186
A Theology of Zephaniah   216
Zephaniah's Contribution to Jewish
and Christian Traditions   223
Past and Present Reception of Zephaniah   233

5 CONCLUSION: THE PROPHETIC MESSAGE
AS PARADIGM FOR CHANGE 239

The Human Drama: On the Way to...   239
The Essence of the Change for Which the Prophets Call   242

Further Reading   247
Select Bibliography   255
Scripture Index   262
Author Index   269
Subject Index   276

General Editors' Preface

Some years ago, Cambridge University Press, under the editorship of James D. G. Dunn, initiated a series entitled *New Testament Theology*. The first volumes appeared in 1991 and the series was brought to completion in 2003. For whatever reason, a companion series that would focus on the Old Testament/Hebrew Bible was never planned or executed. The present series, *Old Testament Theology*, is intended to rectify this need.

The reasons for publishing *Old Testament Theology* are not, however, confined solely to a desire to match *New Testament Theology*. Instead, the reasons delineated by Dunn that justified the publication of *New Testament Theology* continue to hold true for *Old Testament Theology*. These include, among other things, the facts that: (1) Given faculty and curricular structures in many schools, the theological study of individual Old Testament writings is often spotty at best; (2) most exegetical approaches (and commentaries) proceed verse by verse such that theological interests are in competition with, if not completely eclipsed by, other important issues, whether historical, grammatical, or literary; and (3) commentaries often confine their discussion of a book's theology to just a few pages in the introduction. The dearth of materials focused exclusively on a particular book's theology may be seen as a result of factors like these; or, perhaps, it is the cause of such factors. Regardless, as Dunn concluded, without adequate theological resources, there is little incentive for teachers or students to engage the theology of specific books; they must be content with what are mostly general overviews. Perhaps the most serious problem resulting from all this is that students are at a disadvantage, even incapacitated, when it comes to the matter of integrating their study of the Bible with other courses in religion and theology. There is, therefore, an urgent need for a series to bridge the gap between the too-slim theological précis and the too-full commentary where theological concerns are lost among many others.

All of these factors commend the publication of *Old Testament Theology* now, just as they did for *New Testament Theology* more than three decades ago. Like its sister series, *Old Testament Theology* is a place where Old Testament scholars can write at greater length on the theology of individual biblical books and may do so without being tied to the linear, verse-by-verse format of the commentary genre or a thematic structure of some sort imposed on the text from outside. Each volume in the series seeks to describe the biblical book's theology as well as to engage the book theologically – that is, each volume intends to *do* theology through and with the biblical book under discussion, as well as delineate the theology contained within it. Among other things, theological engagement with the composition includes paying attention to its contribution to the canon and appraising its influence on and reception by later communities of faith. In these ways, *Old Testament Theology* seeks to emulate its New Testament counterpart.

In the intervening years since *New Testament Theology* was first conceived, however, developments have taken place in the field that provide still further reasons for the existence of *Old Testament Theology*; these have impact on how the series is envisioned and implemented and also serve to distinguish it, however slightly, from its companion series. Three developments in particular are noteworthy:

1. *The present hermeneutical climate*, often identified (rightly or wrongly) as "postmodern," is rife with possibility and potential for new ways of theologizing about scripture and its constituent parts. Theologizing in this new climate will of necessity look (and be) different from how it has ever looked (or been) before.
2. *The ethos change in the study of religion, broadly, and in biblical studies in particular.* No longer are the leading scholars in the field only Christian clergy, whether Catholic priests or mainline Protestant ministers. Jewish scholars and scholars of other Christian traditions are every bit as prominent, as are scholars of a non- or even anti-confessional stripe. In short, now is a time when "Old Testament Theology" must be conducted without the benefits of many of the old consensuses and certainties, even the most basic ones relating to epistemological framework and agreed-upon interpretative communities along with their respective traditions.
3. Finally, recent years have witnessed *a long-overdue rapprochement among biblical scholars, ethicists, and systematic theologians.* Interdisciplinary studies between these groups are now regularly published, thus furthering and facilitating the need for books that make the theology of scripture widely available for diverse publics.

In brief, the time is ripe for a series of books that will engage the theology of specific books of the Old Testament in a new climate for a new day. The result will not be programmatic, settled, or altogether certain. Despite that – or, in some ways, *because* of that – it is hoped that *Old Testament Theology* will contain highly useful volumes that are ideally poised to make significant contributions on a number of fronts including (1) the ongoing discussion of biblical theology in confessional and nonconfessional modes as well as in postmodern and canonical contexts, (2) the theological exchange between Old Testament scholars and those working in cognate and disparate disciplines, and (3) the always pressing task of introducing students to the theology of the discrete canonical unit: the biblical books themselves.

Brent A. Strawn
D. Moody Smith Distinguished Professor of Old Testament and Professor of Law, Duke Divinity School and Duke University School of Law

Stephen B. Chapman
Associate Professor of Old Testament, Duke Divinity School, Duke University

Patrick D. Miller[†]
Princeton Theological Seminary, Emeritus

Preface

The prophetic books of the Old Testament do not make for easy reading. Even when they are as short as are Nahum, Habakkuk, and Zephaniah, a fair appreciation of their messages requires the reader to reckon with interpretative challenges of all sorts. At the same time, these books present in relatively few words robust theologies that tackle problems that are perennial to human existence: the abuse of power, the myriad forms of sin and injustice in and around us, and the ever-present temptation to pride and self-justification at the expense of those around us.

Reading these prophetic books thus has the potential to be even more rewarding than it is demanding. The early twenty-first century, moreover, is a most opportune time to undertake this task. Many older paradigms inspired by the Enlightenment have been dethroned, making it easier for the reader to appreciate the unity of individual books and their relation to the canon of which they are part. At the same time, newer approaches have highlighted the involvement of the reader in the process of interpretation, and this promotes the contemporary reader's personal engagement with the text as both necessary and laden with significance. Finally, a renewed awareness of the integrity of the authorial voice brings both the reader and her or his methods into dialogue with an "other" that challenges one to look at oneself and one's world from another (often radically different) vantage point.

These welcome developments have facilitated my happy task of sketching the theologies of Nahum, Habakkuk, and Zephaniah without compromising their urgency and conviction. At the same time, I have tried to make these books as accessible as possible to readers of diverse epistemological backgrounds. While these two paths might seem destined to diverge, an articulation of these books' theologies from within their authors' conceptual worlds makes possible an unlimited variety of productive conversations about the relationship between these books' theologies and contemporary readers and their worlds. With this dialogical hearing of the text in mind, I have situated discussion of these books in relation to ethical, conceptual, and theological discussions that impact human existence; our knowledge, values, and priorities; our use of the environment; our valuation of material wealth; and the degree of hope we place in the power of individuals or political and social structures to effect lasting change in individuals and societies.

Several other emphases support the endeavor to read the prophets theologically and responsively. First, the theological description of these prophetic books is closely tied to their literary and historical dimensions. While this helps prevent the imposition of extraneous concepts and frameworks on these ancient compositions, I hope that it also makes their theology more concrete, palpable, and comprehensible. Yhwh's rejection of Babylon's grasping after absolute control as part of its program in the early sixth century is, in my judgment, far more interesting than abstract descriptions of God's sovereignty in history. Second, by regularly engaging with past and present secondary literature, I encourage the reader to evaluate both my arguments and those I review with a critical, generous spirit. (The impressive commentary of Thomas Renz, *The Books of Nahum, Habakkuk, and Zephaniah*, NICOT

[Grand Rapids, MI: Eerdmans, 2021] unfortunately appeared too late in the process for me to make use of it.) Finally, each chapter offers a broad overview of the reception history of the book at hand, with a parallel focus on the theological contribution of these compositions to the Jewish and Christian traditions (and canons). These vantage points should also prove helpful in connecting the ancient text with contemporary concerns even as they force readers to wrestle with the (relative) authority of Scripture, its privileged status in later theological traditions, and its wider reception (or rejection) in past and present culture.

Acknowledgments

The long gestation of this book is a testimony to the patience of Dr. Brent A. Strawn who, along with Dr. Stephen B. Chapman, shares responsibility for editing the *Old Testament Theology* series. I gratefully acknowledge Dr. Strawn's input, which has helped me improve this work in numerous ways. I happily express my debt to Dr. Jean Maurais and Dr. Dominique Angers, colleagues at the Faculté de théologie évangélique (FTE) in Montreal, for helping me obtain resources at a time when coronavirus-related restrictions made it impossible to use local libraries. In the same vein, Mrs. Laura Ladwig, Director of Library Services at the William Perkins Library, and Ms. Kim Dykema, then Assistant Librarian, tirelessly chased down articles and other resources that underlie this volume. My thanks are also due to Puritan Reformed Theological Seminary (PRTS), and especially Drs. Michael Barrett and Jonathon Beeke (former and present Academic Dean, respectively), Joel Beeke (Chancellor), and Adriaan Neele (President), for making research and writing an integral part of the learning, teaching, and spiritual formation that are at the heart of the seminary's mission. I am also indebted to the students at PRTS, FTE, Evangelical Theological Faculty (Leuven), and Reformed Theological Seminary (Jackson) whose questions, comments, and contributions enriched our shared exploration of these books over the past decade and more. Finally, I gratefully recognize the expert help of Nicola Maclean, Beatrice Rehl, Rosanna Barraclough, Joyce Reid, Dan Harding, and Veena Ramakrishnan at Cambridge University Press in preparing the manuscript for publication.

Much deeper gratitude goes to my wife, Andreea, for her indefatigable support, love, and encouragement. As a wife and mother she is a model of selfless love, persistence even when the winds are contrary, and constancy as a disciple of Jesus Christ. Our sons Nathan and Felix, so present in our daily lives, are daily reminders that we too have an audience. It is a great privilege to guide and accompany them on their way to adulthood – *je vous aime!* Finally, I express my gratitude to God for his grace to me in Jesus Christ that, as Nahum, Habakkuk, and Zephaniah demonstrate, gives unparalleled hope and joy even (especially!) when all other hopes fail.

Abbreviations

AB	Anchor Bible
ABD	*Anchor Bible Dictionary.* Edited by David Noel Freedman. 6 vols. New York: Doubleday, 1992
ABG	Arbeiten zur Bible und ihrer Geschichte
ABRL	Anchor Bible Reference Library
ABS	Archaeology and Biblical Studies
ACCS	Ancient Christian Commentary on Scripture
AIL	Ancient Israel and Its Literature
AJA	*American Journal of Archaeology*
ANEM	Ancient Near Eastern Monographs/Monografias sobre el Antiguo Cercano Oriente
ANET	*Ancient Near Eastern Texts Relating to the Old Testament.* Edited by James B. Pritchard. 3rd ed. Princeton: Princeton University Press, 1969
ATD	Das Alte Testament Deutsch
AThR	*Anglican Theological Review*
ATJ	*Ashland Theological Journal*
AYBC	Anchor Yale Bible Commentary
BBC	Blackwell Bible Commentaries
BBR	*Bulletin for Biblical Research*

BBRSup	Bulletin for Biblical Research Supplement
BETL	Bibliotheca Ephemeridum Theologicarum Lovaniensium
BHQ	*Biblica Hebraica Quinta*. Edited by Adrian Schenker et al. Stuttgart: Deutsche Bibelgesellschaft, 2004–
BI	*Biblical Interpretation*
Bib	*Biblica*
BibInt	Biblical Interpretation Series
BSac	*Bibliotheca Sacra*
BSAH	Blackwell Sourcebooks in Ancient History
BWA(N)T	Beiträge zur Wissenschaft vom Alten (und Neuen) Testament
BZABR	Beihefte zur Zeitschrift für altorientalische und biblische Rechtsgeschichte
BZAW	Beihefte zur Zeitschrift für die alttestamentliche Wissenschaft
CAT	Commentaire de l'Ancien Testament
CAT	Cuneiform Alphabetic Texts from Ugarit, Ras Ihn Hani, and Other Places
CBQ	*Catholic Biblical Quarterly*
CEB	Commentaire évangélique biblique
CHANE	Culture and History of the Ancient Near East
CHJ	Cambridge History of Judaism
COS	*The Context of Scripture*. Edited by William W. Hallo and K. Lawson Younger, Jr. 4 vols. Leiden: Brill, 1997–2016
CTR	*Criswell Theological Review*

CurBR	*Currents in Biblical Research*
DDD	*Dictionary of Deities and Demons in the Bible.* Edited by Karel van der Toorn, Bob Becking, and Pieter W. van der Horst. Leiden: Brill, 1995, 2nd rev. ed. Grand Rapids, MI: Eerdmans, 1999
EBR	*Encyclopedia of the Bible and Its Reception.* Edited by Hans-Josef Klauck et al. Berlin: de Gruyter, 2009–
ECC	Eerdmans Critical Commentary
EDB	*Eerdmans Dictionary of the Bible.* Edited by David Noel Freedman. Grand Rapids, MI: Eerdmans, 2000
ExAud	*Ex Auditu*
FAT	*Forschungen zum Alten Testament*
FOTL	Forms of Old Testament Literature
FRLANT	Forschungen zur Religion und Literatur des Alten und Neuen Testaments
GMTR	Guides to the Mesopotamian Textual Record
HALOT	*The Hebrew and Aramaic Lexicon of the Old Testament.* Ludwig Koehler and Walter Baumgartner, translated and edited by M. E. J. Richardson. Study edition. 2 vols. Leiden: Brill, 2001
HBAI	*Hebrew Bible and Ancient Israel*
HBM	Hebrew Bible Monographs
HBS	Herders biblische Studien
HBT	*Horizons in Biblical Theology*
HCOT	Historical Commentary on the Old Testament

HdO	*Handbuch der Orientalistik*
HR	*History of Religions*
HSM	Harvard Semitic Monographs
HTKAT	Herders Theologischer Kommentar zum Alten Testament
HTR	*Harvard Theological Review*
HUCA	*Hebrew Union College Annual*
ICC	International Critical Commentary
IDB	*The Interpreter's Dictionary of the Bible.* Edited by George A. Buttrick. 4 vols. New York: Abingdon, 1962
IEKAT	Internationaler Exegetischer Kommentar zum Alten Testament
IJST	*International Journal of Systematic Theology*
Int	*Interpretation*
IRT	Issues in Religion and Theology
JAJS	Journal of Ancient Judaism – Supplements
JAOS	*Journal of the American Oriental Society*
JBL	*Journal of Biblical Literature*
JBQ	*Jewish Bible Quarterly*
JETS	*Journal of the Evangelical Theological Society*
JHebS	*Journal of Hebrew Scriptures*
JNES	*Journal of Near Eastern Studies*
JR	*Journal of Religion*
JSOT	*Journal for the Study of the Old Testament*
JSOTSup	Journal for the Study of Old Testament Supplement Series
JTI	*Journal for Theological Interpretation*

JTS	*Journal of Theological Studies*
LAI	Library of Ancient Israel
LHBOTS	Library of Hebrew Bible/Old Testament Studies
LNTS	Library of New Testament Studies
LSAWS	Linguistic Studies in Ancient West Semitic
NA^{28}	*Novum Testamentum Graece*. Edited by Barbara Aland et al. Stuttgart: Deutsche Bibelgesellschaft, 2012
NASB	New American Standard Bible (1995)
NICOT	New International Commentary on the Old Testament
NIDOTTE	*New International Dictionary of Old Testament Theology and Exegesis*. Edited by Willem A. VanGemeren. 5 vols. Grand Rapids, MI: Zondervan, 1997
NIGTC	New International Greek Testament Commentary
NJB	New Jerusalem Bible (1985)
NJPS	New Jewish Publication Society Version
NRSV	New Revised Standard Version
NSBT	New Studies in Biblical Theology
NTT	New Testament Theology
OBO	Orbis Biblicus et Orientalis
OBT	Overtures to Biblical Theology
OIS	Oriental Institute Seminars
OLA	Orientalia Lovaniensia Analecta
Or	*Orientalia*
ORA	*Orientalische Religionen in der Antike*

OSJCB	Osnabrücker Studien zur Jüdischen und Christlichen Bibel
OTE	Old Testament Essays
OTL	Old Testament Library
OTP	*The Old Testament Pseudepigrapha.* Edited by James H. Charlesworth. 2 vols. Garden City, NY: Doubleday, 1983
OtSt	*Oudtestamentische Studiën*
OTT	Old Testament Theology
PBM	Paternoster Biblical Monographs
PRSt	*Perspectives in Religious Studies*
RBS	Resources for Biblical Study
RevExp	*Review and Expositor*
RHR	*Revue de l'histoire des religions*
RINAP	Royal Inscriptions of the Neo-Assyrian Period
SAA	State Archives of Assyria
SANER	Studies in Ancient Near Eastern Records
SAOC	Studies in Ancient Oriental Civilizations
SB	Sources Bibliques
SBS	Stuttgarter Bibelstudien
SCS	Septuagint and Cognate Studies
SHS	Scripture and Hermeneutics Series
SJC	Studies in Jewish Civilization
SJOT	*Scandinavian Journal of the Old Testament*
SNTSMS	Society for New Testament Monograph Series
SOTSMS	Society for Old Testament Monograph Series
STDJ	Studies on the Texts of the Desert of Judah
SymS	Symposium Series

TDOT	*Theological Dictionary of the Old Testament.* Edited by G. Johannes Botterweck, Helmut Ringgren, and Heinz-Josef Fabry. Translated by John T. Willias et al. 17 vols. Grand Rapids, MI: Eerdmans, 1974–2021.
Them	*Themelios*
TynB	*Tyndale Bulletin*
UCOP	University of Cambridge Oriental Publications
VT	*Vetus Testamentum*
VTSup	Supplements to Vetus Testamentum
WAW	Writings from the Ancient World
WBC	Word Biblical Commentary
WMANT	Wissenschaftliche Monographien zum Alten und Neuen Testament
WUNT	Wissenschaftliche Untersuchungen zum Neuen Testament
WW	*Word and World*
ZAW	*Zeitschrift für die alttestamentliche Wissenschaft*
ZDPV	*Zeitschrift des deutschen Palästina-Vereins*
ZECOT	Zondervan Exegetical Commentary on the Old Testament

CHAPTER 1

Reading Ancient Israelite Prophetic Books

Perhaps no figure from the ancient Near East is more foreign to much of the twenty-first century world, especially the West, than the prophet. This is not to suggest that prophetic figures are absent from the contemporary scene.[1] Some individuals are "prophetic" due to their conviction and commitment to speak in such a way as to promote change on the part of their hearers (be they for or against them) with respect to an issue of major importance. A classic example is Martin Luther King Jr.'s longstanding opposition to racism in the United States.[2] In such cases, there is some overlap between contemporary uses of the adjective "prophetic" and the kinds of prophecy that this volume explores. Walter Brueggemann even proposes that contemporary efforts to understand and articulate the content of the Old Testament are inevitably prophetic and "countercultural" insofar as they follow prophecy's presentation of "alternatives in judgment and hope" against the backdrop of a world that "is marked by technological,

---

[1] Samuel H. Brody, "Prophecy and Powerlessness," *Political Theology* 21 (2020): 43–55, explores some of these contemporary uses of "prophetic" movements in relation to political power.
[2] Joseph Rosenbloom, "Martin Luther King's Last 31 Hours: The Story of His Final Prophetic Speech," *The Guardian*, 4 April 2018.

therapeutic, military, consumerist values that empty the world of abiding meaning and risky fidelity."[3]

ISRAELITE PROPHETS AND PROPHECY IN THEIR ANCIENT NEAR EASTERN CONTEXT

Regional Variations in Prophecy and Its Authority

Contemporary figures who speak out against what they perceive to be wrong, and in favor of a yet-unrealized ideal, do bear a certain resemblance to the Israelite prophets whose books are part of the Old Testament.[4] At the same time, there are fundamental differences between contemporary figures and their ancient predecessors. Foremost among them is the ancient prophets' *claim to speak on behalf of a deity.* In the ancient Near East, speech that claimed a divine origin and divine authority was typically taken seriously by its recipients, whether they were kings, officials, or commoners. At the same time, given the many cultures and long swaths of history that make up the ancient Near East, it is not surprising that prophecy's importance and authority vis-à-vis other means of determining the divine will or the future varied from one setting to another. This regional and temporal diversity is relevant to our study of the prophetic books of Nahum, Habakkuk, and Zephaniah, since they were produced in Judah during or shortly

---

[3] Walter Brueggemann, "Old Testament Theology," in *The Oxford Handbook of Biblical Studies*, ed. John W. Rogerson and Judith M. Lieu (Oxford: Oxford University Press, 2006), 675–97 (693–94).

[4] It is important to recognize cultural, regional, and chronological diversity in the phenomenon of prophecy in the ancient Near East. See Seth L. Sanders, "Why Prophecy Became a Biblical Genre," *HBAI* 6 (2017): 26–52; and the very diverse collection of texts in Martti Nissinen, *Prophets and Prophecy in the Ancient Near East*, 2nd ed., with contributions by C. L. Seow, Robert K. Ritner, and H. Craig Melchert, WAW 41 (Atlanta, GA: SBL, 2019).

after the seventh century BCE. A crucially important regional difference between the Levant (the eastern Mediterranean seaboard, from modern-day Israel to south-central Turkey) and Mesopotamia has to do with the level of authority that was typically attributed to the prophetic message: "Within Mesopotamian intellectual culture, the difference between prophecy and divination was a difference between both types and levels of knowledge. Prophecy represented a significant but low level."[5]

As a result, Mesopotamian prophecy was often subject to verification by divination, as was the case at Mari, particularly when female prophets were involved.[6] Most other cultures in the ancient Near East (i.e., outside the Levant) similarly privileged "highly developed 'sciences' like astronomy and divination" over prophetic messages.[7]

Without claiming that the audience of the Israelite prophets shared the convictions of the prophets themselves, the conceptual framework for Israelite prophecy was different from that in Mesopotamia. The prophetic books that eventually became part of the Old Testament claimed to be not merely one way that YHWH communicated with his people but the privileged channel for divine revelation in terms of frequency and authority.[8] Deuteronomy 18 presents prophecy as the normal, characteristic way in which Moses, the archetypal prophet, and dozens of prophets after him would communicate YHWH's word to his chosen people. With the introduction "Thus says YHWH," the prophetic

---

[5] Sanders, "Why Prophecy Became a Biblical Genre," 33.
[6] Nissinen, *Prophets and Prophecy*, 21; Esther J. Hamori, "Gender and the Verification of Prophecy at Mari," *Die Welt des Orients* 42 (2012): 1–22.
[7] Sanders, "Why Prophecy Became a Biblical Genre," 28.
[8] Here and throughout, masculine grammar is used of YHWH and God only to lighten the style.

speaker claimed to transmit a message from Israel's deity, and as such the message carried his unlimited authority (Deut 18:18).

In the worldview embraced by the biblical prophets, no other supernatural being had power, knowledge, or sovereignty comparable to YHWH's. On this view, no legitimate conflict of authority was possible between God's word and the proclamation of other supernatural beings.[9] There was also not supposed to be any conflict between prophecy that was in line with Israel's developing scriptures (Deut 13:1–5) and guidance offered by Israelite priests, since legitimate cultic divination in Israel was limited to particular questions of very narrow scope (Exod 28:30; Num 27:12–23).[10] And, of course, there were to be no conflicting authority claims on the part of Israel's or Judah's royal, religious, and social leaders when the divine message criticized or condemned them.[11] The prophets often indicted these groups for abandoning YHWH's law and misusing their power for their own gain rather than for the protection and advancement of the nation in covenant with YHWH.[12] This pattern stands in marked contrast to prophecy elsewhere in the

[9] Note Habakkuk's visceral reaction to YHWH's word, Hab 3:16; similarly Isa 6:5; Amos 7:2; 5, etc.
[10] Ryan O'Dowd observes that "[t]rue prophecy ... affirms the great commandment (Deut 6:4–9) by hermeneutically applying the first commandment (Deut 5:6–7) to the future world of international religious discourse," O'Dowd, *The Wisdom of Torah: Epistemology in Deuteronomy and the Wisdom Literature*, FRLANT 225 (Gröningen: Vandenhoeck & Ruprecht, 2009), 69, and again, "Deuteronomy-as-torah is the truth standard for future prophetic tests" (ibid., 72).
[11] The prophet Jonah is a very odd exception in this regard.
[12] This is not to say that prophets are never "friends" of the state, even when they are its critics; see the essays in Christopher A. Rollston, ed., *Enemies and Friends of the State: Ancient Prophecy in Context* (University Park, PA: Eisenbrauns, 2018). Criticism of the state, however, be it of Israel, Judah, or a foreign power, is characteristic of the Old Testament at large and of the prophetic books in particular. See Robert Gnuse, *No Tolerance for Tyrants:*

ancient Near East, which provides very few examples of criticism of kings in particular.¹³

Prophecy as Commentary on the Relationship between Yhwh and Israel
In conjunction with guiding, evaluating, and criticizing as necessary Israelites' behavior in relation to God and to each other, ancient Israel's prophets also gave immense attention to Yhwh as Israel's covenant partner. This attention regularly focused on Yhwh's continued compassion, patience, and faithfulness toward his people even when they failed to demonstrate a reciprocal faithful commitment to him.¹⁴ The earliest writing prophets, commonly thought to be Hosea and Amos in the eighth century BCE, announced that the northern kingdom of Israel had reached a critical low point in its relationship to God due to a variety of

---

The Biblical Assault on Kings and Kingship (Collegeville, MN: Liturgical, 2011); Michael Walzer, *In God's Shadow: Politics in the Hebrew Bible* (New Haven, CT: Yale University Press, 2012); J. Gordon McConville, *God and Earthly Power: An Old Testament Political Theology, Genesis–Kings* (London: T & T Clark, 2006); Collin Cornell, *Divine Aggression in Psalms and Inscriptions: Vengeful Gods and Loyal Kings*, SOTSMS (Cambridge: Cambridge University Press, 2021).

¹³ Jonathan Stökl, "A Royal Advisory Service: Prophecy and the State in Mesopotamia," in *Enemies and Friends of the State: Ancient Prophecy in Context*, ed. Christopher A. Rollston (University Park, PA: Eisenbrauns, 2018), 87–114 (107) concludes that "potential [prophetic] criticism is not geared toward the establishment of a new form of government or essentially critical of the king. Instead, its ultimate aim, just as all other forms of the cult and state, was to enable the king to establish and maintain ideal kingship."

¹⁴ Here I develop Robert P. Gordon's suggestion that "the difference between Israelite prophecy and the rest may simply have been expressed in terms of its conception of its God," in "'Where Have All the Prophets Gone?': The 'Disappearing' Israelite Prophet against the Background of Ancient Near Eastern Prophecy," *BBR* 5 (1995): 67–86 (86).

widespread social and religious sins. Since previous disciplinary actions by Yhwh had not interrupted these patterns of behavior, these prophets and others after them announced that exile, the heaviest divine sanction possible, was inevitable. Even so, some prophets interceded with Yhwh on behalf of their audience, and in the early stages of this process Yhwh sometimes relented (see Amos 7:1–6, in contrast to 7:7–9). Yet even when exile had become inevitable, God's commitment to his people meant that rather than destroying them completely, he promised to purify and transform them so that no future disobedience could again impede his saving will for them. This strong interest in the distant future probably contributed to the decision to preserve the prophets' oracles on a large scale, something attested only rarely in other cultures, notably during the reigns of Esarhaddon and Assurbanipal in seventh-century Assyria.[15]

Prophecy and Non-Israelite Nations
The understanding that the messages of Israelite and Judean prophets were of lasting significance was reinforced by their pronounced interest in the international scene. This global perspective on Yhwh's involvement with the larger world continued earlier traditions and scriptures according to which his election of and involvement with Israel was intended to benefit the world at large (e.g., Gen 12:1–3).[16] Despite the fact that these prophets focused primarily on Israel and Judah and delivered their message only to those audiences and never to foreign groups (Jonah is an

---

[15] Nissinen, *Prophets and Prophecy*, 7.
[16] See, for example, Jon D. Levenson, "The Universal Horizon of Biblical Particularism," in *Ethnicity and the Bible*, ed. Mark Brett, BibInt 19 (Leiden: Brill, 1996), 143–69.

exception), the prophets' messages included nations and events far beyond the borders of Israel and Judah.[17] Oracles dealing with non-Israelite nations, whether announcing judgment (usually) or salvation (less often), thus appear frequently in the prophetic books. Israelite prophets condemned non-Israelites for reasons not very different than those given to justify God's disciplinary punishment of his people. Israelites were held accountable to God's guidelines for their life and practice as embodied in the detailed covenant made with them at Sinai.[18] Similarly, non-Israelites were held accountable to less specific but equally binding moral norms that, although "traditional and conventional" to a degree, were woven into the human conscience and so had YHWH as their author and enforcer (Amos 1:2–2:3; Isa 10:5–19, etc.).[19] Much as YHWH's judgment of Israel and Judah was not an end in itself, his words of condemnation against the nations are often part of a larger perspective in which many non-Israelites will one day recognize his sovereignty, submit to him, and enjoy his blessing as part of his renewed people (e.g., Isa 19:18–25).

---

[17] Very few texts other than Jonah assert that an Israelite prophet directly addressed a non-Israelite audience; see 2 Kgs 8:7–15; Isa 14:32; 21:11–12.

[18] The dating of the Pentateuchal laws is hotly debated. For a representative argument for their relatively late creation, see Rainer Albertz, *A History of Israelite Religion in the Old Testament Period*, 2 vols., trans. J. Bowden, OTL (Louisville, KY: Westminster John Knox, 1994), 2:464–93. For arguments in favor of an earlier date, with a special focus on the prophetic books, see Gene M. Tucker, "The Law in the Eighth-Century Prophets," in *Canon, Theology, and Old Testament Interpretation: Essays in Honor of Brevard S. Childs*, ed. Gene M. Tucker et al. (Philadelphia, PA: Fortress, 1988), 201–16.

[19] John H. Hayes, "Amos's Oracles Against the Nations (1:2–2:16)," *RevExp* 92 (1995): 153–67 (166). Isaiah clearly assumes that pride and folly are sins of which both Israelites and non-Israelites can be guilty, per John Barton, "Ethics in the Book of Isaiah," in *Writing and Reading the Scroll of Isaiah: Studies of an Interpretive Tradition*, ed. Craig C. Broyles and Craig A. Evans, 2 vols., VTSup 70 (Leiden: Brill, 1997), 1:67–77.

Concluding Summary

Israelite prophecy can be summarized as the human mediation of authoritative divine messages to Israel in the context of her covenant relationship with Yhwh.[20] The development of biblical prophecy as independent of the monarchy and other forms of political and social power gave the prophets the greatest possible freedom to criticize, confront, and even condemn their audience when necessary. Since it was presented as God's own speech, prophetic discourse could be profoundly subversive of human misuse of power.[21] Yet even the most negative prophetic messages were not the final divine word to Israel and Judah or to the world beyond their borders. The prophets insisted that beyond the judgment that Yhwh would eventually bring on these groups, there was to be a future restoration that would transform and renew his people, bringing blessing to them and to non-Israelites. By offering hope through and beyond judgment, the prophetic books of the Old Testament dealt forthrightly with the grave problems their audiences faced. That same honesty allowed them to propose appropriately radical solutions to those problems. These books' theologies are thus both unwaveringly honest and surprisingly hopeful, focused on Israel and Judah yet deeply interested in the world as a whole. Finally, the scope of these books' perspective is comprehensive, since the environmental, social, and other

---

[20] Compare the definitions of ancient Near Eastern prophecy more broadly considered by Brad Kelle, "The Phenomenon of Israelite Prophecy in Contemporary Scholarship," *CurBR* 12 (2014): 275–320.

[21] See the related social-scientific study of Israelite prophecy helpfully surveyed by Kelle, "The Phenomenon of Israelite Prophecy." On the unique way that the ancient Near Eastern concept of covenant or treaty is developed in the Old Testament, see Robert P. Gordon, "'Comparativism' and the God of Israel," in *The Old Testament and Its World*, ed. J. C. de Moor and Robert P. Gordon, *OtSt* 52 (Leiden: Brill, 2005), 45–67 (49–51).

contextual features of human existence are as inseparable from humans' relationship to Yhwh as are issues of ethics and belief.[22]

THE BOOK OF THE TWELVE (MINOR PROPHETS)

Recent Research on the Minor Prophets/Book of the Twelve
The last few decades have witnessed a marked shift in how many scholars approach and interpret the Minor Prophets (Hosea–Malachi). Whereas centuries of interpretation had almost without exception approached these books as *books* (originally, of course, *scrolls*), that is, as independent literary compositions, over the last few decades a growing number of specialists have begun to understand this group of compositions as more or less unified by editorial redaction (post-authorial development and additions).[23] To some extent this avenue of research was simply an attempt to understand the otherwise curious, not to say obscure, rationale behind the arrangement of these twelve writings. The clearest overall logic for the order of the Twelve in the Hebrew text tradition is a chronological movement from books associated with earlier prophets to those attributed to later ones, but the placement of Joel and Obadiah is difficult to explain on this logic. An alternative

---

[22] See, for example, Patricia K. Tull, "Consumerism, Idolatry, and Environmental Limits in Isaiah," in *The Book of Isaiah: Enduring Questions Answered Anew*, ed. Richard J. Bautch and J. Todd Hibbard (Grand Rapids, MI: Eerdmans, 2014), 196–213. For a comprehensive survey of the recent history of interpretation of the Old Testament prophetic books, see Christopher R. Seitz, "Prophecy in the Nineteenth Century Reception," in *Hebrew Bible Old Testament III/1, the Nineteenth Century*, ed. Magne Sæbø (Göttingen: V&R, 2013), 556–81.

[23] A convenient overview can be found in Aaron Schart, "Twelve, Book of the: History of Interpretation," in *Dictionary of the Old Testament: Prophets*, ed. Mark J. Boda and J. Gordon McConville (Downers Grove, IL: IVP Academic, 2012), 806–17.

attempt to explain the organization and development of the corpus thus began to focus on the ways in which these books might have developed from their earlier forms to the final forms in which we have them, and how those processes might have impacted the formation of the Book of the Twelve as a whole.

The Book of the Twelve as a Redactional Unity
At present, there is both consensus and dissent with respect to how the Minor Prophets/Book of the Twelve came to be.[24] In terms of consensus, many scholars find evidence in the individual books of the Twelve that each book developed *in relation to one or more books elsewhere in the collection*. Following the lead of James Nogalski in particular, such arguments often depend on "catchwords" that appear at the end of one book and at the beginning of the immediately following book in the order most often preserved in the Hebrew textual tradition.[25] Other proposed motivations for the diachronic development of these books individually and as a collection include *changing theologies* in Israel and Judah, *social upheaval* of which the exiles of the Northern and Southern Kingdoms are the most evident examples, and *the influence of eschatological and apocalyptic thinking* on Israel's scriptures.

---

[24] Recent research on this corpus is surveyed briefly in Daniel C. Timmer, "Prophetic Literature: Book of the Twelve," in *The State of Old Testament Studies*, ed. H. H. Hardy II and M. Daniel Carroll R. (Rodas) (Grand Rapids, MI: Baker Academic, forthcoming), and exhaustively in Lena-Sofia Tiemeyer and Jakob Wöhrle (eds.), *The Book of the Twelve: Composition, Reception, and Interpretation*, VTSup 184 (Leiden: Brill, 2020) and Julia M. O'Brien (ed.), *The Oxford Handbook of the Minor Prophets* (Oxford: Oxford University Press, 2021).

[25] On the significance of the different order of some parts of the Twelve in the Greek Old Testament (LXX), see Marvin Sweeney, "Sequence and Interpretation in the Book of the Twelve," in *Reading and Hearing the Book of the Twelve*, ed. James D. Nogalski and Marvin A. Sweeney, SBL SymS 15 (Atlanta, GA: Scholars, 2000), 49–64.

More modest theories regarding the formation of the Twelve simply propose that it is a thematic anthology, without appealing to precise historical causes to explain its literary development.[26]

Alongside this consensus exists a current of dissent as to what elements of these books in fact bear witness to such developments and what paradigms offer the most convincing arrangement of these data.[27] It is not uncommon, for example, for two reconstructions of a book's redactional development to choose somewhat different textual features as data, to interpret those data differently, and to use their findings to reconstruct different social and religious histories of Israel and Judah.[28] The conflicting conclusions of investigations focused on the same data and guided by the same method suggest that the method lacks sufficient controls and clarity or that the data identified are ambivalent.[29]

---

[26] David Peterson, "A Book of the Twelve?" in *Reading and Hearing the Book of the Twelve*, ed. James D. Nogalski and Marvin A. Sweeney, SBL SymS 15 (Atlanta, GA: Scholars, 2000), 3–10; Martin Beck, "Das Dodekapropheton als Anthologie," *ZAW* 118 (2006): 558–83; and Paul R. House, *The Unity of the Twelve*, JSOTSup 97 (Sheffield: Almond, 1990), all propose different understandings of the Twelve as an anthology.

[27] The dialogue is conveniently summarized in James D. Nogalski and Ehud Ben Zvi, *Two Sides of a Coin: Juxtaposing Views on Interpreting the Book of the Twelve/the Twelve Prophetic Books*, ed. Thomas Römer, Analecta Gorgiana 201 (Piscataway, NJ: Gorgias, 2009). On questions of method, see further Marvin Sweeney, "Synchronic and Diachronic Concerns in Reading the Book of the Twelve Prophets," in *Perspectives on the Formation of the Book of the Twelve: Methodological Foundations – Redactional Processes – Historical Insights*, ed. Rainer Albertz et al., BZAW 433 (Berlin: de Gruyter, 2012), 21–33; John Van Seters, "Editing the Bible: The Romantic Myths about Authors and Editors," *HBAI* 3 (2014): 343–54; Francis Landy, "Three Sides of a Coin," *JHebS* 10 (2010), article 11.

[28] This is evident in the wide-ranging survey by Barry Jones, "The Seventh-Century Prophets in Recent Research," *CurBR* 14 (2016): 129–75.

[29] This point has been strongly argued by Reinhard Müller and Juha Pakkala, *Editorial Techniques in the Hebrew Bible*, RBS 97 (Atlanta: Society of Biblical Literature Press, 2022).

There is also a lack of agreement as to how these reconstructions of textual development should be weighed against textual data that seem to push in other directions. These data include, first, features that suggest that the books of the Twelve themselves were transmitted as self-contained, independent literary compositions. Ehud Ben Zvi and others stress the following points in support of this position: Each book of the Twelve has its own title; the Jewish sectarian community at Qumran interpreted each of the Twelve as an independent work even though the community preserved most or all of the books concerned on one scroll; and each book has a clear beginning and ending and exhibits appropriate levels of lexical and thematic coherence.[30]

In addition to these book-focused questions, other disputed points of method and analysis include: the relative priority of shared catchwords (which ostensibly would tie two books together); features that distinguish the individual books from one another (focus, historical context, etc.); the point at which a book's literary or theological complexity exceeds what an interpreter thinks a single author is capable of producing; and the plausibility of large-scale redactional activity in light of its complexity and the rarity of such processes as empirically attested in prophetic literature of the ancient Near East.

How This Volume Approaches the Book of the Twelve
There is no doubt that the books that make up the Minor Prophets/ Book of the Twelve are related to one another – but *how* and *why* are they related? Because language expresses meaning through

---

[30] See Ben Zvi, "Remembering Twelve Prophetic Characters from the Past," in *The Book of the Twelve: One Book or Many?*, ed. Elena Di Pede and Donatelle Scailoa, FAT 91 (Tübingen: Mohr Siebeck, 2016), 6–36.

combinations of words rather than through isolated words or phrases, the present study of prophetic books gives more weight to frequently attested thematic or semantic commonalities than to isolated words or expressions apart from such large-scale ties.[31] The significant uncertainty that accompanies most theories of redactional development at the level of individual books, and especially at the level of the collection as a whole, similarly dissuades us from venturing too far from the explicit claims of the text as to its formation, historical location, and so on.[32] For example, there is often a great deal of diachronic or other variety within the explicit statements of the texts themselves that allows the interpreter to distinguish, for example, between the context in which – or an audience for which – an oracle of salvation is announced and the context in which an oracle of judgment would have functioned.[33] All things considered, the evident diversity of the collection of the Twelve and its constituent books is complemented by a significant degree of literary and theological homogeneity. Careful attention to the fruitful interrelation of this unity and diversity promises to

---

[31] For provocative reflections on the limited unity that redaction can produce, see Hervé Tremblay, "Vox clamantis in deserto? L'enseignement d'Amos sur la justice sociale dans le contexte de la théorie de l'unité des douze," in *The Book of the Twelve: One Book or Many?*, ed. Elena Di Pede and Donatella Scaiola, FAT 2.91 (Tübingen: Mohr Siebeck, 2016), 107–33.

[32] See the essays in Raymond F. Person and Robert Rezetko, *Empirical Models Challenging Biblical Criticism*, AIL (Atlanta, GA: Society of Biblical Literature, 2016); Benjamin D. Sommer, "Dating Pentateuchal Texts and the Perils of Pseudo-Historicism," in *The Pentateuch: International Perspectives on Current Research*, ed. Thomas B. Dozeman, Konrad Schmid, and Baruch W. Schwartz, FAT 78 (Tübingen: Mohr Siebeck, 2011), 85–108, and Benjamin Ziemer, *Kritik der Wachstumsmodells: Die Grenzen alttestamentlicher Redaktionsgeschichte im Lichte empirischer Evidenz*, VTSup 182 (Leiden: Brill, 2019).

[33] This is argued by Daniel C. Timmer, *The Non-Israelite Nations in the Book of the Twelve: Thematic Coherence and the Diachronic–Synchronic Relationship in the Minor Prophets*, BibInt 135 (Leiden: Brill, 2015), esp. 1–20, 221–44.

preserve the distinct emphases and interests of each book while recognizing the shared beliefs and outlooks that led to their preservation as prophetic literature and their eventual inclusion in the canon.[34]

APPROACHING THE THEOLOGY OF PROPHETIC BOOKS

Discerning the theology of a biblical book is not a straightforward task. Although there is a wide variety of methods and approaches for doing so, not all are equally helpful in bringing the content of the book into recognizable categories without uprooting individual bits of content from their contexts. For example, a number of works on the theology of the Old Testament organize its content under the headings of Christian theology, such as God, humanity, salvation, and so on. However, this framework is selective and to some degree artificial, and consequently forces some of the text's content into ill-fitting molds while neglecting other elements. The challenge interpreters face is thus how to identify, organize, and interconnect the content of biblical literature in a way that is faithful to it and captures not only its semantic content but also its rhetorical or pragmatic force, all the while avoiding reductionism.

A more inductive approach, taking the Book of Nahum as an example (see Chapter 2), might focus on topics that are native to and prominent in the book itself: the nature of sin as exemplified by Assyria, the reasons for which God commits to punishing

---

[34] Stephen B. Chapman cogently argues that scriptural writings would "have been likely to gain religious authority even prior to the time at which they were officially recognized," in "What Are We Reading? Canonicity and the Old Testament," *WW* 29 (2009): 334–47 (341–42).

it, and his grace in delivering those who trust in him from that judgment. This sort of approach captures more of the book's content by focusing on theological issues that are explicitly present and salient in the text. Yet if concepts such as sin, retribution, and deliverance are treated as static categories, the interpreter will fail to grasp the dynamics of the text, that is, the ways that it *develops and interrelates* the subjects that it presents.[35] Approaches that recognize this dynamic, organic dimension of biblical literature promise to bring us still closer to our goal of reckoning with the text's content and meaning. William P. Brown has formulated two overarching questions that he argues "guide all other questions concerning the text's context and meaning" and that capture the dynamic and organic nature of the books we study here: First, "what can be ascertained from the text about *God's character* and *relationship to the world?*" (what Brown terms "theo-logic"); and second, "what can be ascertained from the text about the *world in its relationship to God* and *humanity's place within it?*" (what Brown calls its cosmo-logic).[36]

If we consider Nahum in light of these two questions, God's character is certainly complex, and his relationship to the world is clearly not static. Consequently, the world's relationship to God is also dynamic, as is the relationship between the different human groups that appear on the historical scene Nahum presents. One of the more promising ways to handle this dynamic

---

[35] Walter Brueggemann, *Theology of the Old Testament: Testimony, Dispute, Advocacy* (Minneapolis, MN: Fortress, 1997), 34.
[36] William P. Brown, "Theological Interpretation: A Proposal," in *Method Matters: Essays on the Interpretation of the Hebrew Bible in Honor of David L. Petersen*, ed. Joel M. LeMon and Kent Harold Richards (Atlanta, GA: Society of Biblical Literature, 2009), 387–405 (390–91), emphasis in original. Cf. W. E. Lemke, "Theology (OT)," *ABD* 6:448–73.

diversity is by using a thematic approach. Attention to a book's themes as developed in different contexts makes it possible for the interpreter to address the meta-questions Brown proposes without losing sight of the text's nuances and details.[37] Because they can develop across some or all of a text, themes can accommodate developments and changes, yet they also provide significant coherence. Since themes can be traced across multiple contexts, a thematic approach can also be text-intensive, preserving the greatest amount of detail possible in the contours of the theme by rooting the discourse to particular contexts.[38] A thematic approach does not assume that all the oracles preserved in a prophetic book were composed or delivered in the order in which the reader encounters them,[39] but rather reflects the fact that reading texts is generally a sequential exercise and the working hypothesis that each book has been arranged in an intentional manner.[40] Still, the reader may be required to mentally reorder some elements with respect to the book's internal chronology as he or she proceeds through the book (e.g., the flash-forward to Nineveh's fall in Nah 2:3–10[4–11]).[41] Similarly, nonadjacent

---

[37] D. J. A. Clines, *The Theme of the Pentateuch*, 2nd ed., JSOTSup 10 (Sheffield: Sheffield Academic, 1997), 19–22.

[38] The danger of subjugating "the specific theological data of the text" to static or rigid themes is noted by Brueggemann, *Theology*, 85.

[39] Cf. Michael Weigl, "Current Research on the Book of Nahum: Exegetical Methodologies in Turmoil," *CurBR* 9 (2001): 81–130 (90).

[40] Alexander Samely, *Profiling Jewish Literature in Antiquity: An Inventory, from Second Temple Texts to the Talmuds* (Oxford: Oxford University Press, 2013), 89–90, 324–26; Stephen Dawkins and Johanna Nordlie, "Processes of Anaphor Resolution," in *Sources of Coherence in Reading*, ed. Robert F. Lorch and Edward J. O'Brien (Hillsdale, NJ: Lawrence Erlbaum Associates, 1995), 145–57, esp. 156.

[41] T. A. Van Dijk, "Cognitive Processing of Literary Discourse," *Poetics Today* 1 (1979): 143–60, esp. 156–57.

units of a prophetic book may be treated together in light of their shared theme(s) without compromising due attention to their respective contexts.

Lastly, because a thematic approach is well suited to tracing developments of all sorts, it helps the reader attend to the different ways that the text engages or addresses the reader. The text's tone, rhetoric, and various speech-acts[42] mean that its themes address the reader in a considered way. Despite sustained pressure against this dimension of academic biblical interpretation, famously captured in Krister Stendahl's distinction between "what it meant" and "what it means," there are good reasons to remain attentive to each book's strategies of persuasion and other means of affecting the reader, past and present.[43] This is not to imagine that we are the original audience addressed by the prophet or his book, but it simply reflects a textually authorized interest in how the message transcends the historical circumstances in which it was first articulated. Walter Brueggemann's attention to "strong verbs of transformation" in Israel's "*narrative* portrayal of Yahweh" exemplifies the thematic approach to theological interpretation undertaken here.[44] This approach is well suited to the tracing the theological, literary, and historical threads that form the texts of Nahum, Habakkuk, and Zephaniah, and especially the dynamic crises and actions in which YHWH takes center stage as creator, judge, deliverer, and consummator.

---

[42] Mikhail Kissine, "Sentence, Utterances, and Speech Acts," in *The Cambridge Handbook of Pragmatics*, ed. Keith Allen and Kasia M. Jaszczolt (Cambridge: Cambridge University Press, 2012), 169–90.

[43] Krister Stendahl, "Biblical Theology: Comparative," *IDB* 1: 418–32.

[44] Brueggemann, *Theology*, 145, emphasis in original; he also grounds the "dramatic movement" that he sees in Old Testament theology in "the character of Yahweh" (Brueggemann, *Theology*, 552).

A Synthesis of Key Themes in Israelite Prophetic Literature
Before reflecting, last of all, on how prophetic books can reach their audiences, it will be helpful to summarize some of the key themes and dynamics that they draw upon to that end. Israelite prophets claim to present the world, whether in local detail or in international perspective, as God sees it. The meta-narrative that underlies the prophetic messages in all their variety is grounded in God's rule over the world he created, the consequential actions of the human beings who live under his rule (whether obediently or not), and the slow but sure movement of history toward the full establishment of his rule over a transformed, purified humanity and world.[45]

The prophets frequently connect Yhwh's judicial and royal roles to his identity as the creator (Isa 14; 41; Amos 5; Nah 1:3–5; Hab 1:12; Zeph 1:2–3, etc.). Even when this basis is not explicitly mentioned, Yhwh's rule is assumed to be universal. Human beings, as moral agents, are responsible to him, even though Israel's election entails a special level of obligation in this regard (Amos 3:2). Despite its emphasis on the sins of the various audiences addressed, the prophetic message is hardly limited to condemnation and regularly presents the possibility of deliverance, although these promises are limited to those who turn from their sinful patterns of behavior and commit to serving God before all else (Ezek 18:21–23; Zeph 2:1–3). Yhwh's identity as unrivaled creator

---

[45] Robert P. Gordon, "Comparativism," 58, affirms of the narrative tradition of the Old Testament that "[t]he idea that Israel's God was solely responsible for the created order, controlled and shaped history, and determined the whole course of Israelite national affairs, can justly be claimed as the dynamo that powered the narrative-historical tradition within the Old Testament." In light of what is said earlier, I would add "and international" after "national" in this quotation.

also makes possible what is perhaps the most striking feature of the prophets' message. Through superlative and final acts of judgment and deliverance, Yhwh will remove from his world both moral wrong and those who remain committed to practicing it, while transforming others so that they no longer pursue their own agendas, disregard God, or mistreat other human beings. Yhwh's plan to *restore and perfect the world* he created, in which Israel has a particular role as his elect people, guides history and ensures that evil will not triumph.[46] This is the foundation of the hope that regularly surges into what would otherwise be a monochromatic message of judgment and destruction.

ENGAGING ISRAELITE PROPHECY AND ITS CLAIMS IN THE TWENTY-FIRST CENTURY

Many if not all of these concepts and beliefs are rather distant from dominant discourses in the late modern West. Because the prophetic books of the Old Testament are based in a worldview quite different from much contemporary thinking, they can be difficult to understand. But rather than letting this difference impede engagement with these texts, it is far better to see it as a measure of the potential that a sympathetic reading of them holds for clarifying, challenging, and enriching the reader's own values, beliefs, and thinking. Exploring alternative explanations of the

---

[46] Jon D. Levenson, *Creation and the Persistence of Evil: The Jewish Drama of Divine Omnipotence* (Princeton: Princeton University Press, 1988), carefully considers the interrelation of Yhwh's mastery over creation and the place of chaos and evil in the world. On Israel's election in some of the prophetic books, see Daniel C. Timmer, "The Election of the Nations," in *T&T Clark Handbook of Election*, ed. Edwin C. van Driel (London: T & T Clark, 2023), 45–62.

world and of humanity that are rooted in history is also fruitful in light of the overdependence of religious studies and much of theological studies "on the comprehensive approach to human knowledge that was constructed and fashioned at the time of the Enlightenment" and on methods that presume the interpreter can engage the subject matter without becoming involved.[47] A meta-critical perspective on relevant features of Enlightenment epistemology has significant implications for the ways that readers engage with these texts.[48] For example, against the Enlightenment ideal of the objective, disinterested observer or subject, a long tradition of philosophical reflection suggests that:

> All knowledge is personal knowledge. It depends upon our personal commitment to and participation in relationships through which our prior conceptions of the world are transformed. Such a conception of the knowing process subverts what has sometimes been called an epistemology of spatial distance – the Modernist ideal of detached, objective inquiry that keeps the object to be known at arm's length.[49]

The goal of developing a critical perspective that does not unduly privilege some key features of contemporary hermeneutics is not to bring about a return to a supposedly pristine pre-Enlightenment or pre-critical outlook. Rather, it is an invitation to engage with the prophetic books of the Old Testament

---

[47] Walter H. Capps, *Religious Studies: The Making of a Discipline* (Minneapolis, MN: Fortress, 1995), 344.

[48] This includes the often binary juxtaposition of secular modernity and religious belief; see Craig Woelfel, "T. S. Eliot and Our Beliefs about Belief," *Religion & Literature* 44 (2012): 128–36.

[49] Murray Rae, "'Incline Your Ear So That You May Live': Principles of Biblical Epistemology," in *The Bible and Epistemology: Biblical Soundings in the Knowledge of God*, ed. Mary Healy and Robin Parry (Milton Keynes: Paternoster, 2007), 161–80 (169).

in such a way that their claims can be understood clearly and evaluated in a self-aware and self-critical manner. As part of this process, the interpreter is responsible for adopting methods and attitudes that are well suited to the object studied. In the case of the prophetic books of the Old Testament, this requires perhaps more than anything else a willingness to look at oneself and the world in a paradigm in which Yhwh, the God of Israel and the creator of the world, regularly intervenes: "There is no good reason to decide as a presupposition of biblical hermeneutics that God is not involved in history. To do so is to set the biblical writings in a conceptual framework that is alien to them and will, very likely, preclude our understanding them aright."[50]

The prophets' belief that Yhwh had intervened in world history and would do so again is inseparable from their belief that he was the sole creator of the world, simultaneously involved in it and incapable of being confined within it. One might even say that creation (the beginning), history, and eschatology (the end or goal of history) are intertwined, and for that reason all of these subjects figure prominently in the prophets' words:

> That the world should be brought forth by God "out of nothing" ... implies that God creates with some purpose in mind. The principle of *creatio ex nihilo* implies that the world is invested with a telos. There is a reason for its being: and history, in consequence, is to be understood as the space and time opened up for the world to become what it is intended to be. Second, the idea of creation out of nothing means that the world is fully God's world. ... Everything is held in God's hands so that, even in the face of evil and sinfulness, it is possible to affirm, along with the

---

[50] Murray Rae, "Creation and Promise," in *"Behind" the Text: History and Biblical Interpretation*, ed. Craig Bartholomew et al., SHS 4 (Grand Rapids, MI: Zondervan, 2003), 267–99 (295). Brueggemann, *Theology*, 104, makes this point with respect to historical-critical approaches in particular.

biblical writers, that all things happen under the will and purpose of God. History may be confessed to have an overall coherence under the creative, providential and redemptive care of God.[51]

Although this understanding of the world is quite different from much of recent Western thought, it is no less intriguing and valuable for that reason. For example, one crucial "constructive question" is how modern epistemology can be revised in order to include "aspects of perception that are not reducible to sense perception in the narrow sense of the term."[52] Thomas Pfau observes, for example, that Immanuel Kant's "overriding concern with disentangling reason from the notion of transcendence" led him (and many after him) to define reality as "a single, continuous, and anthropomorphic domain" in which grace and the definitive vanquishing of evil cannot exist.[53] Brought to bear on our reading of the Old Testament, this epistemological flexibility allows the reader to approach these books with "imaginative seriousness" that can prepare the reader "to hear [and understand]

---

[51] Rae, "Creation and Promise," 284-85. For robust discussion of this question in a larger context, see Alvin Plantinga, *Where the Conflict Really Lies: Science, Religion, and Naturalism* (Oxford: Oxford University Press, 2011). Regarding the relation of God's will and human actions and moral responsibility, Jewish and Christian thinkers have offered various proposals; see Netanel Wiederblank, *Illuminating Jewish Thought: Explorations of Free Will, the Afterlife, and the Messianic Era* (Jerusalem: Maggid, 2018); Charles M. Wood, "Providence," in *The Oxford Handbook of Systematic Theology*, ed. John Webster, Kathryn Tanner, and Iain Torrance (Oxford: Oxford University Press, 2007), 91-104.

[52] Christine Helmer, "Theology and the Study of Religion," in *The Cambridge Companion to Religious Studies*, ed. Robert A. Orsi (Cambridge: Cambridge University Press, 2012), 230-54 (249-50).

[53] Thomas Pfau, "Religion," *The Oxford Handbook of European Romanticism*, ed. Paul Hamilton (Oxford: Oxford University Press, 2016), 730-51 (739). For a magisterial treatment of this issue, see Charles Taylor, *A Secular Age* (Harvard: Belknap, 2007).

what people describe through the vocabulary of the ecstatic, of relationality with a transcendent other," or the like.⁵⁴ Similarly, with regard to the question of history and a world open to divine intervention, open-mindedness encourages us to leave open the questions of "transempirical realities" and Yʜᴡʜ's involvement in this world.⁵⁵ With these dispositions and perspectives supporting our attempt to read Nahum, Habakkuk, and Zephaniah on their own terms, we can more objectively and productively engage and evaluate these books and our response to them.

---

⁵⁴ Helmer, "Theology and the Study of Religion," 250. For arguments that press in the opposite direction, see Roland Boer (ed.), *Secularism and Biblical Studies*, Worldview (London: Routledge, 2009). The concept of "imaginative seriousness" is proposed by R. W. L. Moberly, *The Theology of the Book of Genesis*, OTT (Cambridge: Cambridge University Press, 2009), 28.

⁵⁵ Roland Deines, "God's Role in History as a Methodological Problem for Exegesis," in *Acts of God in History*, ed. Christoph Ochs and Peter Watts, WUNT 317 (Tübingen: Mohr Siebeck, 2013), 1–26 (12).

CHAPTER 2

The Theology of the Book of Nahum

At first glance, the message and theology of Nahum should receive a warm reception from readers of all times and places. Even a cursory awareness of the history of the Assyrian empire in the first millennium reveals an ideological behemoth that was able to take what it wanted almost anywhere in the ancient Near East in order to meet its growing needs for natural resources, ensure its political stability, and realize its imperial vision of dominating the world.[1] The violence and bombast that were part of its ideology and practice, and especially its tendency to dehumanize its opponents, fly in the face of widely held norms then and now. More recent iterations of the imperial project also demonstrate the book's relevance for contemporary readers. The "discovery" of the Americas by European explorers in the fifteenth and sixteenth centuries, until recently presented as a "self-admiring, heroic tale of explorers and conquerors," now "reads like a much more brutal story, with Europeans trampling across much of the planet rather like the Four Horsemen of the Apocalypse."[2] The "despotic utopias" that arose between the world wars likewise imposed their will by force,

---

[1] See the comprehensive analysis of Assyrian imperialism offered in Mario Liverani, *Assyria: The Imperial Mission*, trans. A. Trameri and J. Valk (Winona Lake, IN: Eisenbrauns, 2017).

[2] Andrew Marr, *A History of the World* (London: Pann, 2012), 252.

even upon their own citizens.³ The history of the late twentieth and early twenty-first centuries further demonstrates that the lust for power, resources, and domination continues to animate political entities large and small, even though its immediate manifestations are becoming increasingly diverse.⁴ Against this sobering backdrop, Nahum's critique of imperialism and its promises that God will intervene to curtail evil are both pertinent and attractive.

At the same time, the solutions to injustice, oppression, and moral disorder that Nahum presents are neither simple nor tidy. Its promise that Yhwh will intervene in history to liberate the oppressed is inseparable from deadly violence against the oppressor; its use of stereotypes to portray both Judah and Assyria raises concerns about the justice of punishing all for the offenses of some; and its absolute tone seems to discount the possibility that the oppressor might be corrected or change.⁵ Yet Nahum has been included in the Jewish and Christian Bibles from the very beginning, suggesting that both faith traditions have found it compatible with the rest of their scriptures and useful as a basis for theological reflection. These considerations encourage us not to shy away from the challenges Nahum poses on the one hand, and

---

³ The phrase is Paul Johnson's, and he refers to Lenin's Soviet Russia and Mussolini's Italy; Paul Johnson, *Modern Times: The World from the Twenties to the Nineties*, rev. ed. (New York: HarperPerennial, 1992), 49–103.
⁴ For an argument linking imperialism and capitalism, see John Smith, *Imperialism in the Twenty-First Century: Globalization, Super-Exploitation, and Capitalism's Final Crisis* (New York: New York University Press, 2016). For arguments that imperialism continues but has changed considerably in the later modern period, see Trevor R. Getz and Heather Streets-Salter, *Modern Imperialism and Colonialism: A Global Perspective* (Upper Saddle River, NJ: Prentice Hall, 2011).
⁵ I wrestle with these issues in Daniel C. Timmer, "'Ah, Assyria Is No More!' Retribution, Theodicy, and Hope in Nahum," in *Theodicy and Hope in the Book of the Twelve*, ed. George Athas, Beth Stovell, Daniel C. Timmer, and Colin Toffelmire, LHBOTS 705 (London: T & T Clark, 2021), 157–72.

not to cavalierly dismiss it as self-evidently flawed on the other, in our attempt to sketch the theology of this prickly book.

We begin with the preliminary question of how to approach the Book of Nahum. The book's various historical ties to an extratextual world as well as its location in the history of Israelite religion and culture oblige us to consider issues related to its origin and development, including the essential question of its coherence. Adopting the method sketched in Chapter 1 allows us to read the book with due attention to its historical and literary features while preserving a focus on its theology. After looking briefly at the historical context that the book presents, we take up the main task of exploring the theology of the Book of Nahum with an eye to the interrelation of its themes and to developments and connections (or tensions) within or between them. The chapter concludes with a survey of how readers past and present have interpreted Nahum as Scripture and an overview of its wider reception in various cultural contexts, with special attention to the issue of violence.

ISSUES IN THE INTERPRETATION OF NAHUM

Unity and Diversity

Readers of Nahum share the unanimous conviction that the book is set near the middle of the seventh century BCE. Not only does it refer to the fall of Thebes (663 BCE) as a past event in Nahum 3:8 and anticipate the fall of Nineveh (612 BCE) as still future, but the author shows significant awareness of Neo-Assyrian ideology and represents Assyria's power as being at its height (1:12).[6] It is

---

[6] G. H. Johnston, "Nahum's Rhetorical Allusions to the Neo-Assyrian Lion Motif," *BSac* 158 (2001): 287–307; G. H. Johnston, "Nahum's Rhetorical Allusions to Neo-Assyrian Treaty Curses," *BSac* 158 (2001): 415–36; Angelika Berlejung, "Erinnerungen an Assyrien in Nahum 2,4–3,19," in *Die*

one thing to agree on a seventh-century setting, however, and quite another to agree that the book as a coherent whole had its origins in the same period. In favor of a date of composition in harmony with its seventh-century setting, the book contains no instances of Late Biblical Hebrew or historical references that would betray a significantly later date of composition or compilation.[7] However, many scholars argue that the book developed in a series of distinguishable stages on its way toward its final form, pointing especially to distinctive literary and theological features in 1:2–8 and 1:9–2:2[3] that seem to fit poorly with the surrounding contexts. While much of the rest of the book is readily attributed to the prophet/author, these apparent instances of incohesion at the literary level or of incoherence at the conceptual level in 1:2–8 and 1:9–2:2[3] prompt a number of interpreters to attribute those sections to later hands. Since the ways in which these passages contribute to Nahum's theology depends on the degree to which they are of a piece with the rest of the book, these issues demand close attention.[8] Here we will take them up in a preliminary way and leave fuller responses for the more detailed treatment later.

Regarding the poem in 1:2–8, the partial, interrupted acrostic that spans the passage, its global perspective, and its related lack

unwiderstehliche Wahrheit: Studien zur alttestamentlichen Prophetie, ed. Rüdiger Lux and Ernst-Joachim Waschke, ABG 23 (Leipzig: Evangelische Verlagsanstalt, 2006); Daniel C. Timmer, "Nahum's Representation of and Response to Neo-Assyria: Imperialism as a Multifaceted Point of Contact in Nahum," *BBR* 24 (2014): 349–62.

[7] See Ronald Hendel and Jan Joosten, *How Old Is the Hebrew Bible? A Linguistic, Textual, and Historical Study* (New Haven, CT: Yale University Press, 2018), identify the Hebrew of the Book of Nahum as Classical, and so locate it in the "monarchial period" of Israel Judah (108; cf. 36–38).

[8] For arguments for the plausibility of a seventh-century date, see Bob Becking, "Divine Wrath and the Conceptual Coherence of the Book of Nahum," *SJOT* 9 (1995): 277–96 (294–95).

of geopolitical specifics have prompted some readers to see it as a later addition.⁹ Accepting for the moment that the acrostic is indeed present in the text,¹⁰ one must first determine whether the juxtaposition of different literary structures (here an acrostic that is distinct from 1:1 and 1:9 and following) and the incomplete nature of the acrostic (which contains only the first eleven of the Hebrew alphabet's twenty-two letters) warrant the conclusion that it is not only structurally distinct but fundamentally different from its context and therefore is the work of another author. Because it is very difficult to deny to a single author the ability to compose a text using various styles and structures, the broken and incomplete acrostic is the more significant of these concerns. While a full acrostic covers a topic "from A to Z," a partial one is emphatically incomplete. This incompleteness is apparently at odds with the message of the poem, which presents a comprehensive, global divine intervention. Yet a closer look cautions against such a conclusion, since other acrostics in the Old Testament are also incomplete or broken.¹¹ Further, noting Benun's suggestion that many acrostics convey a sense of order, one might agree with Renz that the incomplete acrostic of Nahum 1:2–8 intentionally conveys the lack of order brought about by YHWH's earthshattering entry into the created order.¹²

---

⁹ For example, Klaus Seybold, *Profane Prophetie: Studien zum Buch Nahum*, SBS 135 (Stuttgart: Katholisches Bibelwerk, 1989); and Anselm Hagedorn, *Die Anderen im Spiegel: Israels Auseinandersetzung mit den Völkern in den Büchern Nahum, Zefanja, Obadja und Joel*, BZAW 414 (Berlin: de Gruyter, 2011).

¹⁰ Thomas Renz argues convincingly for its presence in "A Perfectly Broken Acrostic in Nahum 1?," *JHebS* 9 (2009): article 23. Contrast Michael Floyd, "The Chimerical Acrostic of Nahum 1:2–10," *JBL* 113 (1994): 421–37.

¹¹ See Ronald Benun, "Evil and the Disruption of Order: A Structural Analysis of the Acrostics in the First Book of Psalms," *JHebS* 6 (2006): article 5, who observes that five of the eight acrostics in the first book of the Psalter have at least one letter missing or added.

¹² Renz, "Perfectly Broken Acrostic," 22–26.

A second feature of 1:2–8 often thought to indicate its supplemental rather than original nature is its vision of divine intervention on a global scale.¹³ This feature is often evaluated with the assumption that earlier Israelite prophets spoke against specific nations, while only post-exilic prophets typically addressed the entire international scene in general terms.¹⁴ While most of Nahum is focused on Assyria, and so is presumably early, this would mean that 1:2–8 is later. Others adopt the opposite premise, however, as when Jakob Wöhrle identifies an earlier layer in the Book of the Twelve by means of its focus on the "nations" as a generic category and a later layer by its mention of specific nations.¹⁵ These contradictory approaches suggest that there is no clear pattern of historical development for universalizing or particularizing in Israelite prophetic discourse.¹⁶ It is unwise, therefore, to make the distinction between specific and general foci of prophetic condemnations a criterion for distinguishing between earlier and later layers in Nahum.

Finally, Nahum 1:9–2:2[3] is also often thought to be inauthentic. Before considering arguments in favor of that conclusion, we should note that a number of interpreters see the opening poem continuing through 1:10 or 1:11 rather than ending with 1:8. For

---

[13] For example, Lothar Perlitt, *Die Propheten Nahum, Habakuk, Zephanja*, ATD 25.1 (Göttingen: Vandenhoeck & Ruprecht, 2005), 3; Hagedorn, *Die Anderen*, 224.

[14] For example, David L. Peterson, "Israel and the Nations in the Later Latter Prophets," in *Constructs of Prophecy in the Former and Latter Prophets and Other Texts*, ed. Lester L. Grabbe and Martti Nissinen, ANEM 4 (Atlanta, GA: Society of Biblical Literature, 2011), 157–64.

[15] See Jakob Wöhrle, *Der Abschluss des Zwölfprophetenbuches: Buchübergreifende Redaktionsprozesse in den späten Sammlungen*, BZAW 389 (Berlin: de Gruyter, 2008), 19, 161–64, 279–81, 351–54.

[16] Paul Raabe, "The Particularizing of Universal Judgment in Prophetic Discourse," *CBQ* 64 (2002): 652–74.

example, Spronk argues that 1:1–11 is a cohesive group of three poetic units whose end is marked in the Hebrew text by a *setumah* (a section break added by early rabbinic transmitters of the Hebrew text) following 1:11, and he sees the oracle announced in 1:1 spelled out in 1:12–14 and 2:14.[17] Alternatively, Floyd sees the shift from a plural subject in 1:10 to a singular one in 1:11–14 as indicating a break, so that 1:9–10 "is closely related in form and content to 1:2–8."[18] These links between the poem in 1:2–8 and its context suggest that the hymn is not as detached from the following context as some have claimed.

Over against these observations stand a variety of arguments for seeing 1:9–2:2[3] as having been added to the developing book later than 2:3[4]–3:19. These include variations in grammatical person or number between the various addressees of 1:9–14, the fact that in these verses YHWH is the speaker while in most other parts of the book the prophet himself speaks, and the possibly varied historical backgrounds of the statements addressed to Judah. The detailed nature of these arguments means that they are best considered in the context of an exploration of the book's theology, so I return to them in due course. Here, however, the general approach taken to Nahum's challenging mix of literary, historical, and theological aspects should be laid out.

The Present Approach to Nahum
In the absence of clear literary indications that Nahum is a collection of independent subunits (cf. the Book of Psalms, where all but a very few psalms have individual superscriptions), our approach

---

[17] Klaas Spronk, *Nahum*, HCOT (Kampen: Kok Pharos, 1997), 27, 61.
[18] Michael H. Floyd, *Minor Prophets: Part 2*, FOTL 22 (Grand Rapids, MI: Eerdmans, 2000), 26.

attempts to understand Nahum's literary, historical, and theological facets in the context of the book as a whole. This heuristic orientation is based especially on an understanding of literary texts as compositions consisting of surface-level features (word choice, grammar, syntax) and subsurface conceptual contents.[19] Surface-level features such as those just noted in the discussion of possibly later additions to or redactions of an older core of Nahum are clearly important but are subordinate to the semantics or conceptual content of the text. As Won Lee puts it, conceptual coherence "overrides compositional unity because the latter owes its existence to the former."[20] For example, the significance of a surface feature such as a change from feminine to masculine grammar is best understood not by itself but in the context of the conceptual content of the text. When surface-level incohesion and conceptual incoherence are both present, the interpreter is justified in concluding that the text does not hold together at that point.[21] By the same token, when the semantic or conceptual *coherence* of the text

---

[19] See H. Bussmann (ed.), *Routledge Dictionary of Language and Linguistics*, trans. and ed. Gregory P. Trauth and Kerstin Kazzasi (London: Routledge, 1996), 198: "[C]oherence is separate from grammatical cohesion and specifically signifies the semantic meaning and the cohesion of the basic interconnection of the meanings of the text, its content/semantic and cognitive structure. Semantic coherence can be represented as a sequence of propositions that form a constellation of abstract concepts and connected relations."

[20] Won W. Lee, *Punishment and Forgiveness in Israel's Migratory Campaign* (Grand Rapids, MI: Eerdmans, 2003), 59. Similarly, James Barr observed that "the linguistic bearer of the theological statement is usually the sentence and the still larger literary complex and not the word or the morphological and syntactical mechanisms"; James Barr, *The Semantics of Biblical Language* (Oxford: Oxford University Press, 1961), 269.

[21] See Paul Noble, "Synchronic and Diachronic Approaches to Biblical Interpretation," *Journal of Literature & Theology* 7 (1993): 130–48; and Koog P. Hong, "Synchrony and Diachrony in Contemporary Biblical Interpretation," *CBQ* 75 (2013): 521–39, on the inseparability of these two perspectives.

is not in question, one should attempt to understand surface-level problems of *cohesion* in light of aesthetic or other factors. This is especially true of poetic texts such as Nahum, which typically have less cohesion than narrative texts.[22] This theoretical basis allows us to pursue a heuristic approach to Nahum's theology, attempting to read the book as a coherent whole. Predictably, we encounter various degrees of tension in the text at both its semantic (coherence) and surface (cohesion) levels, and only as we appreciate those tensions will we be able to articulate a theology that is faithful to the book.[23]

Several additional, practical considerations favor attempts to understand the theology of the book as a whole. First, the evidence of the manuscript tradition is uniform in witnessing to Nahum as we now have it.[24] Second, the presence of two emphatic theological statements identifying YHWH as Assyria's enemy (2:13[14]; 3:5) in what compositional approaches identify as the book's oldest sections suggests that these units have much in common with the perspective already evident in 1:2–8. Since 2:13[14] and 3:5 are more clearly integrated in their contexts than is the poem of 1:2–8 and so cannot easily be dated to other times, one might argue that the logic by which 1:2–8 is judged late is open to question.

---

[22] Ernst Wendland, "The Discourse Analysis of Hebrew Poetry: A Procedural Outline," in Ernst Wendland, *Discourse Perspectives on Hebrew Poetry in the Scriptures*, UBS Monograph Series 7 (Reading: United Bible Societies, 1994), 1–27 (4).

[23] On the importance of reading the parts in light of the whole, see Anthony J. Campbell, "Form Criticism's Future," in *The Changing Face of Form Criticism for the Twenty-First Century*, ed. Marvin A. Sweeney and Ehud Ben Zvi (Grand Rapids, MI: Eerdmans, 2003), 15–31.

[24] Duane Christiansen, *Nahum: A New Translation with Introduction and Commentary*, AYB 24F (New Haven, CT: Yale University Press, 2009), 64–66, surveys the manuscript evidence.

Historical Setting

We noted earlier that the Book of Nahum is set between the fall of Thebes to the Assyrian king Ashurbanipal in 663 and the fall of Nineveh, which occurred in 612. While 1:12 assumes that Neo-Assyrian power was at its height at some point during that half-century, Assyrian might and presence in the Levant were already longstanding realities by the seventh century. The earlier histories of Israel and Judah bear witness to the highly effective imperialism of the Neo-Assyrian empire, and the centrality of that phenomenon in Nahum makes an overview of Neo-Assyria's rise helpful for understanding the book's theology.

The Neo-Assyrian empire emerged near the end of the tenth century BCE and expanded rapidly beyond its heartland on the Tigris to the south and west.[25] Its westward expansion began under Assur-nasirpal II (883–859), and, after repeated campaigns in the Levant, his successor Shalmaneser III (858–824) made Assyrian presence there so effective that the Israelite king Jehu voluntarily made Israel a client state of Assyria, promising to pay tribute, remain subordinate to the empire, and cooperate with it in various ways.[26] An image on the Black Obelisk of Shalmaneser III represents the Israelite king Jehu (or his emissary) kneeling before the Assyrian king as he pays his tribute and powerfully

---

[25] H. W. F. Saggs, *The Might That Was Assyria*, Sidgwick and Jackson Great Civilizations Series (London: Sidgwick & Jackson, 1984), 70–121, and Georges Roux, *Ancient Iraq*, 3rd ed. (London: Penguin, 1992), 282–354, offer accessible overviews of this period. Note also Brad E. Kelle and Brent A. Strawn, "History of Israel 5: Assyrian Period," in *Dictionary of the Old Testament: Historical Books*, ed. Bill T. Arnold and H. G. M. Williamson (Downers Grove, IL: InterVarsity, 2005), 458–78, on which this section occasionally draws.

[26] A. Kirk Grayson, "Assyria, Assyrians," in *Dictionary of the Old Testament: Historical Books*, ed. Bill T. Arnold and H. G. M. Williamson (Downers Grove, IL: InterVarsity, 2005), 97–105 (100–1).

conveys Israel's subordinate status to Assyria during this time.[27] Since Judah was effectively subordinate to Israel during much of this period (cf. 2 Kgs 14:8–14), Assyrian presence was doubtless felt there as well.

Although Assyrian control over Syria-Palestine waned near the end of the eighth century, it was briefly reestablished by Adad-nirari III (810–783) and then, after a longer interruption, was fully revived by Tiglath-Pileser III (747–727). As long as Israel and Judah fulfilled their responsibilities as client states of Assyria, the empire's protection of its client states and the more general *pax Assyriaca* that endured from the middle of the eighth century to the middle of the seventh afforded Israel and Judah stability and the opportunity to prosper.[28] Infidelity or rebellion of a vassal state was taken very seriously by the empire, however, and both Israel and Judah eventually experienced some or all of the progressively applied sanctions that the empire imposed upon insubordinate client states.

Israel's troubles began in earnest around 735 BCE, when it joined forces with Aram (Syria) in order to counter Assyria's resurgence in the Levant (cf. Isa 7). Judah, pressured by the Israel-Aram coalition to join them or face them in battle, appealed to its Assyrian overlord for help. Assyria responded in 734–732 by invading Israel, annexing significant portions of it, and deporting thousands of its inhabitants (2 Kgs 15:28–29; Tiglath-Pileser III Annals 18, 24). Judah's dependence on Assyria in that conflict

---

[27] See the photo by Steven G. Johnson, http://commons.wikimedia.org/wiki/File:Jehu-Obelisk-cropped.jpg.

[28] Frederick Mario Fales, "On Pax Assyriaca in the Eighth–Seventh Centuries BCE and Its Implications," in *Isaiah's Vision of Peace in Biblical and Modern International Relations: Swords into Plowshares*, ed. Raymond Cohen and Raymond Westbrook, Culture and Religion in International Relations (New York: Palgrave Macmillan, 2008), 17–35.

cemented its status as a vassal.²⁹ Israel under Hoshea (731–722) shifted its loyalty from Assyria to Egypt (2 Kgs 17:1–5), leading the Assyrian king Shalmaneser V (726–722) to take control of Samaria and imprison Hoshea, and later to conquer all that remained of the northern kingdom. Assyrian records document further deportations by Sargon II (721–705) shortly after the fall of Israel. In most of these cases Israelites were forcibly relocated to distant corners of the Assyrian empire in order to sever their ties to their homeland and to promote their full integration into the empire.

Judah's status as an Assyrian client state was temporarily undone not long after the start of Hezekiah's reign (715–686), with evidence suggesting that Judah participated in the anti-Assyrian revolt led by Ashdod in 714–712.³⁰ In any case, it is clear that a few years before 701 Hezekiah himself instigated a revolt against Assyria involving several city-states and took measures focused on surviving the anticipated Assyrian punishment. Most notable among these was the half-kilometer-long Siloam tunnel that brought water from the Gihon spring outside the city walls to a pool inside Jerusalem. Although the siege of Jerusalem laid by the Assyrian army in 701 ended without the city falling into Assyrian hands, the campaign, of which the siege was only part, destroyed numerous fortified towns in Judah. By its end, Assyria had annexed large areas of Judah, and Hezekiah apparently accepted once again Judah's client state status. Assyria's control of Judah continued during the reign of Hezekiah's son and successor, Manasseh (686–643). Manasseh contributed both forced labor and military conscripts to Assyrian endeavors at least as late as 669, and his general fidelity to Assyria allowed Judah to recover

---

²⁹ K. Lawson Younger, Jr., "The Deportations of the Israelites," *JBL* 117 (1998): 201–27, upon whom I draw occasionally here.

³⁰ Kelle and Strawn, "History of Israel," 471.

somewhat from Sennacherib's punitive attacks.[31] This brings us to the period in which the Book of Nahum is set, shortly after the fall of Thebes in 663.

As portrayed by the biblical sources, YHWH religion in seventh-century Judah was in poor, and sometimes critical, condition.[32] The curt assertion that Judah was currently under covenant discipline (Nah 1:12) offers no description or explanation of that situation, but other parts of the Old Testament are less laconic. In the historiographic sources, Manasseh is repeatedly characterized as the primary source of Judah's religious deviation (2 Kgs 21:1–18; cf. 2 Chr 33:10–17), in response to which God promised to do to Jerusalem what he had done to Samaria, the capital city of the now-fallen northern kingdom of Israel (2 Kgs 18:13). Some of the prophetic books provide additional data, particularly on popular religion and behavior. The Book of Isaiah critiques the majority of the Judean population for religious and social offenses roughly a half-century before Nahum (Isa 1), announcing that deliverance would come only through judgment. Isaiah's contemporary Micah also critiqued Judean and Israelite society, particularly its leaders, for engaging in behavior that included the oppression of the vulnerable and the perversion of justice (Mic 3). According to biblical sources these problems continued after Nahum's time, and Habakkuk and Zephaniah condemned Judah

---

[31] *ANET*, 291, 294. Lester Grabbe, "The Kingdom of Judah from Sennacherib's Invasion to the Fall of Jerusalem: If We Had Only the Bible...," in *Good Kings and Bad Kings: The Kingdom of Judah in the Seventh Century BCE*, ed. Lester Grabbe (London: T & T Clark, 2007), 78–122 (103).

[32] Cf. Jeremy M. Hutton, "Southern, Northern, and Transjordanian Perspectives," in *Religious Diversity in Ancient Israel and Judah*, ed. Francesca Stavrakopoulou and John Barton (London: T & T Clark, 2010), 149–74; and Patrick D. Miller, *The Religion of Ancient Israel*, LAI (Louisville: Westminster John Knox, 2000), esp. 46–105.

for its worship of other gods (Zeph 1:4–5) and violence (Hab 1:2–4; Zeph 3:1–7). Archaeological and other sources confirm the diversity of Judean religion prior to and during the seventh century.[33] The fact that this reality is largely passed over by Nahum, which contrasts polytheistic Assyria in the role of Yhwh's enemy with an idealized Judah as his covenant partner, soon to be delivered from covenant discipline, suggests that Nahum's portrayal of Judah is idealized, and that both Judah and Assyria are presented in stereotypic fashion. This phenomenon makes an important contribution to the book's theology and is explored further later in this chapter.

A THEOLOGICAL EXPLORATION OF NAHUM

With our method for theologically focused interpretation in mind, we are now in a position to explore Nahum's theology against the backdrop of the seventh-century geopolitical and religious scene in Judah.

A Paradigmatic Perspective on Yhwh's Vengeance and Deliverance (Nah 1:2–8)
Yhwh's Wrath and Vengeance: The Initial Salvo
The Book of Nahum requires its readers to jump in at the deep end, as it were. After its short superscription, the book launches immediately into repeated affirmations of Yhwh's avenging and wrathful disposition against his "adversaries" and "enemies." The

---

[33] Ziony Zevit, *The Religions of Ancient Israel: A Synthesis of Parallactic Approaches* (London: Continuum, 2001); Richard Hess, *Israelite Religions: An Archaeological and Biblical Survey* (Grand Rapids, MI: Baker Academic, 2007), 269–90, 297–332.

first term used to describe Yhwh, *qannô*', "zealous," often refers to his "fiery, angry reaction to the infringement of his rights vis-à-vis Israel." Here, the global horizon of this particular passage prevents the reader from limiting its scope to Judah alone.³⁴ More generally, *qannô*' involves God's commitment to maintaining his glory, honor, and holiness in the face of direct opposition, and this broader sense is preferable here.³⁵ Yhwh is also described as "avenging/vengeful" (*nōqēm*) no fewer than three times, and this is reinforced by a cluster of additional terms and expressions linked to divine wrath throughout the passage. This expression of the divine character is also tied to God's relationship to human beings, when it often expresses divine retribution against non-Israelite nations for their pursuit of unlimited power and their mistreatment of God's people.³⁶ Complementing the way that the global horizon of the opening poem extends the reach of divine zeal, this vengeance cannot be limited to the non-Israelite nations. The stage is thus set for a divine intervention that focuses primarily on humans in relation to Yhwh while ignoring all other distinctions, including gender, ethnic, and political difference.

Binary Identities and Binary Fates in the Face of Yhwh's Vengeance and Deliverance

The description of God's definitive future intervention in terms that include Israel/Judah and non-Israelite nations alike is part of this passage's precision regarding the identity of those who will meet with Yhwh's wrath and those who will benefit from his saving shelter. Eschewing both geopolitical and ethnic categories, the

---

³⁴ H. G. L. Peels, "קנא," *NIDOTTE* 3:938.
³⁵ Cf. Eleonore Reuter, "קנא," *TDOT* 13:53–55.
³⁶ H. G. L. Peels, "נקם," *NIDOTTE* 3:154.

text uses only theological concepts that define human beings *in relationship to* YHWH. The *first group* appears initially in 1:3, which identifies the human objects of divine vengeance as his adversaries and enemies who are guilty of some offense against him. The terms translated as "adversary" (*ṣār*) and "enemy" (*'ōyēb*) involve mutual antipathy, and prevent the reader from thinking that God would act aggressively against those who are not (in God's estimation, if not in theirs) opposed to him.[37] The concept of guilt also involves mutual relationship, presupposing that humans are accountable to YHWH for their actions. This accountability is the foundation for the case that Nahum builds against Assyria, whose actions toward God (cf. 1:9) and others (cf. 3:1–4) elicit divine punishment.

The *second group* present in the opening poem is also identified exclusively in terms of its relationship to YHWH. The possibility that some might not suffer YHWH's vengeance is first evoked by the affirmation that he is "slow to anger and of great power" (1:3). "Slow to anger" echoes the classic expression of YHWH's penchant for grace and mercy in the face of Israel's sin (Exod 34:6–7). Similarly, the recognition of God's "great power" evokes his actions as creator of the cosmos (Ps 147:5; Jer 27:5; 32:17) and as the one who delivered Israel, most characteristically in the exodus from Egypt (Exod 32:11; Deut 4:37; 9:29; 2 Kgs 17:36; Neh 1:10).

The identity of this second group comes more clearly into view near the end of the poem. While divine wrath poses a real threat on a global scale (cf. 1:6), God is not only vengeful but also good, specifically as a shelter to those who perceive the threat that his

---

[37] Biblical Hebrew uses other expressions to describe unwarranted or one-sided aggression against another, for example, Prov 1:11 (ambush), 16 (shed blood), 18 (lie in wait).

vengeance poses to them and "seek refuge in him."³⁸ This deliverance involves mutual relationship: humility and trust in YHWH on the part of human beings, and YHWH's relational "knowledge" of those who take refuge in him. This life-preserving relationship can be contrasted with the lethal nonrelationship implied by vengeance, which involves a semantic polarity that separates YHWH from those upon whom he takes vengeance.³⁹ YHWH as Creator is the source of all life, and human beings as made in his image are in a unique relation to him: "humanness is always Yahwistic humanness."⁴⁰ To live apart from him or against him is thus inevitably to move toward death, whereas living in faithfulness with him is to move toward life in its fullness.

Nahum's consistent depiction of human beings as defined primarily by their relationship to YHWH encourages us to relate these binary fates for individuals with the similarly bifocal characterization of God in the book's opening poem. Nahum 1:2–8 consistently emphasizes divine vengeance against those who oppose YHWH and act contrary to his will. Yet the poem's affirmation of his beneficent relationship with Israel/Judah and his willingness to deliver those who seek refuge in him prevent this emphasis from becoming exclusive. Despite all that is said in the text about the unlimited power and extent of YHWH's retributive wrath, YHWH himself is at the same time the only way to escape it.⁴¹

---

³⁸ Johann Gamberoni, "חסה," *TDOT* 5:70, argues that the participle used here (חסים, in construct) consistently refers to "the devout worshipper in the best sense."

³⁹ Ernst R. Wendland, "What's the 'Good News' – Check out the 'Feet'! Prophetic Rhetoric and the Salvific Centre of Nahum's 'Vision,'" *OTE* 11 (1998): 154–81 (166–67).

⁴⁰ Walter Brueggemann, *Theology of the Old Testament: Testimony, Dispute, Advocacy* (Fortress: Minneapolis, 1997), 450.

⁴¹ Cf. Michael Widmer, *Moses, God, and the Dynamics of Intercessory Prayer: A Study of Exodus 32–34 and Numbers 13–14*, FAT 2.8 (Tübingen: Mohr Siebeck,

How and why does Yhwh deliver some human beings from the judgment that apparently threatens all humanity? Exodus 34 poses that question with reference to Israel, as do other books in the collection of the Minor Prophets (e.g., Hos 1:2; Joel 2:13; Mic 7:18–20). Most of these passages explicitly connect human repentance and behavioral change (*šûb*) with the possibility or (most often) certainty that Yhwh will be gracious to such persons (Hos 14:1; Joel 2:13; Jon 3:10; Zeph 2:3; cf. Mic 7:7, 18–20).[42] While Joel 2 and Zephaniah 2 entertain only the *possibility* that Yhwh might relent in the case of repentance, the other passages, including Nahum 1, are less equivocal. Still, it would be unwarranted to understand Yhwh's gracious response as obligatory or automatic. Exodus 34 and the passages noted here argue, rather, that it is *characteristic* for God to react in such a way to those who turn to him, so much so that mercy is bound up with Yhwh's very name (Exod 33:19; cf. Exod 34:5).

Like Nahum 1:2–8, these passages make use of Exodus 34:6–7 to claim that the divine character includes both a commitment to justice in punishing offenders and a predilection for showing mercy to those who turn from their rebellion to Yhwh. The focus on the contrasting human behaviors related to these two outcomes is crucial to understanding what would otherwise be a "bipolar and ambiguous" divine character.[43] Ultimately, the

---

2004), 186: "Although mercy and grace mark YHWH's fundamental nature, the second half of YHWH's self-disclosure ... and the renewed covenant stipulations ([Exod] 34:11–28) make it absolutely evident that 'cheap grace' is not being offered. And yet it speaks volumes for God's nature that immediately following Israel's prime sin, God wants Moses to know that He is primarily a gracious and compassionate God."

[42] See Jason T. LeCureux, *The Thematic Unity of the Book of the Twelve*, HBM (Sheffield: Sheffield Phoenix, 2012), 99–107, 119–28, 139–43, 156–57.

[43] Jan P. Bosman, *Social Identity in Nahum: A Theological-Ethical Enquiry*, Biblical Intersections 1 (Piscataway: Gorgias, 2008), 233.

pair of divine punishment that incapacitates or removes the guilty and divine deliverance that preserves those who turn to YHWH restores a righteous moral order in the sphere of human existence.[44]

Creator, Past and Present Deliverer of Israel, Future Judge and Deliverer of Humanity

The description of the theophany (God's breaking into time and space; see the discussion of prophecy and history in Chapter 1) in Nahum 1:3b–5 makes clear the global reach and moral focus of the judgment and deliverance that constitute it. While the storm imagery suggests that God is coming to punish human wrongs, this theophany is also described in language used elsewhere to recount YHWH's deliverance of Israel at the Red/Reed Sea after its flight from Egypt ("rebukes the sea"), so that judgment and deliverance remain connected. The use of the generic "sea" here underlines the general, global significance of this theophany in comparison with its smaller-scale anticipation long ago in Israel's history. A similarly asymmetrical connection is made in 1:4b, which echoes the drying up of the Reed Sea (Josh 2:10) or the Jordan River (Josh 4:23; 5:1) but again removes the limited historical focus by shifting from particular bodies of water to generic "rivers" in order to express the unparalleled significance of this theophany.

A number of interpreters see here the influence of the *Ba'al Epic*, a late second millennium Canaanite literary work in which the elimination of primordial chaos leads to the formation of an

---

[44] See H. H. Schmid, "Creation, Righteousness, Salvation: 'Creation Theology' as the Broad Horizon of Biblical Theology," in *Creation in the Old Testament*, ed. Bernhard W. Anderson, IRT 6 (Philadelphia, PA: Fortress, 1984), 102–17 (106–7).

orderly cosmos.⁴⁵ In the *Ba'al Epic*, the ascent of the Canaanite deity Ba'al to kingship involves repeated conflict with the god Yamm ("Sea"), a chaotic force. Ultimately, Ba'al kills and dismembers Yamm on his way to a limited and tenuous kingship over the cosmos.⁴⁶ Although this *Chaoskampf* motif is present elsewhere in the Old Testament (e.g., Ps 29:10), its relevance in Nahum 1 must be determined in light of the immediate literary context, in which the drying up of seas and rivers is parallel to the drying up of vegetation and the dissolution of mountains and hills. The desiccation of bodies of water and rivers followed by the consequent wilting of vegetation are processes quite different from the decimation of a personified and divinized force of chaos. Further, in Nahum 1:3b–5 YHWH destabilizes various spheres of the created order by entering it in his role as judge of all humanity (see the earlier discussion of the broken acrostic in 1:2–8). Finally, the focus here on divine retribution for human wrongs (cf. 1:2–3b) rather than on the elimination of resurgent chaos confirms the passage's consistent focus on human behavior vis-à-vis YHWH (1:5).

The predominantly destructive tenor of God's intervention in the opening poem is well suited to the focus on Assyria in the rest of the book, where it is the guilty party whose punishment will be

---

⁴⁵ On the phenomenon in general, see John Day, *God's Conflict with the Dragon and the Sea: Echoes of a Canaanite Myth in the Old Testament*, UCOP 35 (Cambridge: Cambridge University Press, 1985). On this motif in Nahum 1, see Carly L. Crouch, *War and Ethics in the Ancient Near East: Military Violence in Light of Cosmology and History*, BZAW 407 (Berlin: de Gruyter, 2009), 158, 166–67.

⁴⁶ Mark S. Smith, "The Baal Cycle," in *Ugaritic Narrative Poetry*, ed. Simon B. Parker, WAW 9 (Atlanta: SBL/Scholars, 1997), 102–5 (CAT 1.2, col. iv). The theme also appears in *Enuma Elish*, where Tiamat, the sea, is killed by Marduk as part of his ascendancy to the summit of the pantheon; cf. Benjamin R. Foster (trans.), "Epic of Creation (1.111)," *COS* 1:390–402.

delayed no longer. The concomitant focus on Judah in the book does not limit deliverance solely to it, still less does it elevate Judah to a place of dominance over the other nations, thereby replacing one nationalism with another. Rather, as elsewhere in the Old Testament, Yahwism "is advocated in political weakness" and in the face of a dominant power, but "never takes the form of the domination of the weak by the strong."[47] The interconnected concerns for justice and deliverance predominate in both parts of the book, and both are dependent upon Yhwh's unlimited power and sovereignty as the sole creator. In this way, both nationalism and religious exclusivism are countered.

The Opening Poem, the Rest of the Book, and the Reader
The poem that begins the Book of Nahum provides its readers with a hermeneutical framework for what follows. Not only does this opening poem transcend the historical particulars of Assyria's often cruel domination of the nations within its orbit, but the frame also introduces significant discontinuity between that situation and the global denouement it announces. Ultimately, Yhwh will once and for all punish and do away with his enemies, defined here in terms of their opposition to him. Inseparably from that judicial action, God will also deliver those who take refuge in him from the wrath he threatens against sinners. This binary division of humanity into Yhwh's enemies and those who seek deliverance in him, coupled with equally binary fates of destruction and preservation, leaves the reader in a liminal position. The theophany that Nahum announces has evidently not yet taken place, and so the author stresses the importance of being on good terms

---

[47] Gordon J. McConville, *God and Earthly Power: An Old Testament Political Theology*, LHBOTS 454 (London: T & T Clark, 2006), 29.

with YHWH before the "day of trouble" dawns. His past saving actions on Israel's behalf give ample proof that he is willing and able to deliver, while the outcome of his future intervention will realize, globally and finally, the justice and deliverance prefigured by YHWH's covenant relationship with Israel and Nineveh's anticipated fall.

YHWH Takes Vengeance against Assyria and Delivers Judah (and Others) (Nah 1:9–3:19)
Although divine vengeance as a response to human wrongdoing remains the central theme, the bulk of the Book of Nahum reads quite differently than 1:2–8. Specific individuals and groups are addressed, divine punishment is connected to detailed moral condemnations, and references to historical events and situations help situate the reader in mid-seventh-century Judah, which currently suffers under the yoke of Assyrian vassalship. While passing mention is made of nations other than Judah and Assyria, this particular pairing is central outside 1:2–8. YHWH's vengeance against human opposition remains the driving force behind the events recounted and foretold on the historical stage just as it was for the theophany of the opening hymn. Likewise, critique and condemnation of Assyria continue, highlighting the restoration of the moral order that God's judgment and deliverance will bring.

YHWH's Condemnation and Punishment of Assyrian Imperialism
The consistently negative nature of Nahum's portrayal of Assyria reflects a clear intention to condemn it for its crimes and to announce an inescapable punishment because of them. The significance of Nahum's stereotype of Assyria is taken up in the section "Nahum's Stereotypical Representations of Assyria and Judah";

here a summary of the book's critique of Assyria and of the punishments pronounced against it on that basis will suffice.

Opposition to YHWH   Immediately after the opening hymn, 1:9 introduces a group that has "plotted against YHWH." The structure of this section allows us to infer that the addressee is Assyria, which is consistently addressed in masculine grammar (singular for the king, plural for the empire as a whole) while direct address in feminine singular grammar is reserved for Judah.[48] These distinct addressees correspond to diametrically opposed fates (deliverance or destruction) for the two groups (see Table 2.1).

By accusing Assyria of plotting against YHWH, 1:9 identifies Assyria as one of his enemies and sheds some light on what that role involves. Assyria's intentional resistance to YHWH is also alleged in 1:11, where the one primarily responsible for such plotting (masculine singular grammar, so presumably the Assyrian king) is a "counselor subversive of YHWH's order" whose plans are "evil" (note the only other use of *rāʿâ* in 3:19).[49] If the author has in mind a specific situation, it is most likely Sennacherib's attack of Judah in 701, which occurred only a few decades before the period in which Nahum is set. In the biblical accounts, the heart of this confrontation was Assyria's claim that YHWH, like the gods of other nations who had already fallen to Assyria, would not be

---

[48] So also Bob Becking, "Passion, Power and Protection: Interpreting the God of Nahum," in *On Reading Prophetic Texts: Gender-Specific and Related Studies in Memory of Fokkelien van Dijk-Hemmes*, ed. Bob Becking and Meindert Dijkstra, BibInt 18 (Leiden: Brill, 1996), 1–20; following Simon De Vries, "The Acrostic of Nahum in the Jerusalem Liturgy," *VT* 16 (1966): 476–81. Here and throughout this chapter I occasionally draw upon or develop the discussion in Daniel C. Timmer, *Nahum: A Discourse Analysis of the Hebrew Bible*, ZECOT (Grand Rapids, MI: Zondervan Academic, 2020), 100–14.

[49] See Theodore J. Lewis, "Belial," *ABD* 1:654–66.

The Theology of the Book of Nahum

TABLE 2.1 Alternating addressees in Nahum 1:9–15[2:1]

Reference	Addressee	Grammar of addressee	Message
1:9–10	Assyria	Masculine plural	Destruction
1:11–13	Judah	Feminine singular	Deliverance
1:14	Assyria	Masculine singular	Destruction
1:15[2:1]	Judah	Feminine singular	Deliverance

able to deliver Jerusalem from Sennacherib (Isa 36:4–20; 37:11–13). Indeed, the Assyrian commander even claimed that Yhwh had authorized Assyria's aggression (Isa 36:10; Kgs 18:25).

Nahum and other biblical echoes of Israelite interaction with Assyria reflect the Neo-Assyrian empire's consistent presentation of its imperialism as being in full accord with the will of the gods (its own and those of the states it attacked) and indeed made possible by their active involvement in its military campaigns. The Assyrian king was the designated agent for accomplishing this aspect of the divine will. In keeping with this belief, Esarhaddon and kings before and after him authored royal inscriptions that began with self-descriptions like the following:

> [G]reat king, mighty king, king of the world, king of Assyria, governor of Babylon, king of Sumer and Akkad, king of the four quarters [of the world], true shepherd, favorite of the great gods, whom from his childhood the gods Aššur, Šamaš, Bēl, and Nabû, Ištar of Nineveh, (and) Ištar of Arbela named for the kingship of Assyria.[50]

Because Aššur claimed global supremacy, "[i]t was the Assyrian monarch's sacred obligation to explore, overcome, and incorporate

---

[50] Erle Leichty, *The Royal Inscriptions of Esarhaddon, King of Assyria (680–669 BC)*, RINAP 4 (Winona Lake, IN: Eisenbrauns, 2011), 11.

[all non-Assyrian territories] into the realm of Ashur."[51] On the basis of this royal ideology, amply attested throughout the Neo-Assyrian period, foreign states who refused to submit to the "yoke" of vassalship to Assyria were (from the Assyrian point of view) unjustifiably and arrogantly refusing the will of the gods, and of Aššur in particular.[52]

In light of the important role that religion played in the foreign policy of both Assyria and Judah, it is no surprise that Nahum asserts that Assyria, while on one level dealing only with the insignificant Levantine kingdom of Judah, is involved in nothing less than a "plot against YHWH." Nahum affirms that YHWH is the creator and judge of all human beings, and that his power and prerogative are unlimited. When Assyria presents itself (with its gods) as the supreme or only power, YHWH's claims are rejected and his honor and glory are ignored. In response, YHWH commits to taking vengeance on those who oppose his exclusive claims to deity.

Given the close link between Assyria and its king, it is no surprise that part of Nahum's response to Assyria's imperialistic violence focuses on the distinctively royal elements of "posterity, temple, and tomb."[53] Not only is the king inseparable from the empire, but in the biblical accounts of the Assyrian siege of Jerusalem the Assyrian king sets himself against YHWH and the gods of the other

---

[51] Bradley J. Parker, "The Construction and Performance of Kingship in the Neo-Assyrian Empire," *Journal of Anthropological Research* 67 (2011): 357–86 (363). This project is rooted in a cosmology in which the formation of the cosmos "culminates the creation of kingship," the primary goal of which is to bring order to the entire world; Liverani, *Assyria: The Imperial Mission*, 13–14.

[52] See Markus Zehnder, *Umgang mit Fremden in Israel und Assyrien: Ein Beitrag zur Anthropologie des 'Fremden' im Licht antiker Quellen*, BWANT 168 (Stuttgart: Kohlhammer, 2005), 66–69, and Bustenay Oded, *War, Peace and Empire: Justifications for War in Assyrian Royal Inscriptions* (Wiesbaden: Ludwig Reichert Verlag, 1992).

[53] Floyd, *Minor Prophets: Part 2*, 49.

nations (2 Kgs 18:33, 35; Isa 36:18, 20). Of course, he does so as the one appointed and equipped by the Assyrian pantheon, so that the outcome of the siege of Jerusalem is ultimately a theological contest. By delivering Jerusalem, YHWH shows "all the kingdoms of the earth ... that you, YHWH, are God alone" (2 Kgs 19:19; Isa 37:20).

This background (or a similar situation if Sennacherib's 701 attack is not in view) helps explain why Nahum 1:14 bases the punishments it announces on the "insignificance" of the Assyrian king.[54] While being insignificant is hardly wrong in itself, the monarch's claims of excessive and even transcendent significance fly in the face of YHWH's supremacy and rule. The Assyrian kings' self-descriptions and their efforts to preserve their legacy and dynasty were diametrically opposed to the Old Testament's ideal in which kings serve as YHWH's vice-regents, in submission to his law and in service to his people. Even though there is no clear paradigm for non-Israelite kingship in the Old Testament (cf. Deut 17:14–20 for the Israelite paradigm, and Ps 2 for a model in which foreign kings are ideally subordinate to the Davidic ruler), from Nahum's point of view such inflated self-representations were tantamount to self-idolatry and constituted idolatry outright when coupled with dependence upon other deities. Over against the long tradition of Assyrian royal ideology affirming that "Assyrian kingship is the only one to legitimately exercise universal dominion," is without equal, and "is the only one endowed with those qualities which render legitimate the exercise of power,"[55] YHWH asserts

---

[54] The other pertinent uses of the Qal of √q-l-l have the sense of "to be despised; to be reckoned insignificant; to be small" (Gen 16:4, 5; 1 Sam 2:30; Job 40:4).

[55] Mario Liverani, "The Ideology of the Assyrian Empire," in *Power and Propaganda: A Symposium on Ancient Empires*, ed. Mogens T. Larsen, Copenhagen Studies in Assyriology 7 (Copenhagen: Akademisk Forlag, 1979), 297–317 (310).

his exclusive kingship in favor of the oppressed and dismisses the Assyrian monarch as nothing but a trifle.

Yhwh's first reprisal, "your name will no longer be sown," spells the end of the king's dynasty,[56] contradicting long and widespread tradition that pursued the preservation of the king's name both literally (on monuments) and figuratively (via a dynasty).[57] The second threat, "from the house of your gods I will eliminate idol and image," focuses on the religious foundations of the king's claim to universal dominion. While the cult statues of conquered deities were normally placed in the sanctuaries of the victor and were only very rarely destroyed, this threat asserts emphatically that Yhwh will destroy the gods of the Assyrian monarch.[58] Finally, Yhwh announces that he will do away with the Assyrian king himself. The assertion that the Assyrian king is insignificant is thus a blanket rejection of his claims to universal dominion, his lack of accountability to Yhwh, his dependence upon other gods, and his excessive interest in his own legacy. In addition to expressing God's vengeance against human beings who discount his claims to unique supremacy and pursue significance in ways contrary to his moral order, God's removal of the Assyrian king is a demonstration of his absolute supremacy.[59]

---

[56] See Spronk, *Nahum*, 75; and Johnston, "Nahum's Rhetorical Allusions to Neo-Assyrian Treaty Curses," esp. 424–25.

[57] Sarah C. Melville, "The Succession Treaty of Esarhaddon," in *The Ancient Near East: Historical Sources in Translation*, ed. Mark W. Chavalas, BSAH (Oxford: Blackwell, 2006), 356; Simo Parpola and Kazuko Watanabe, *Neo-Assyrian Treaties and Loyalty Oaths*, SAA 2 (Helsinki: University of Helsinki Press, 1988), 35.

[58] Steven W. Holloway, *Aššur Is King! Aššur Is King! Religion in the Exercise of Power in the Neo-Assyrian Empire*, CHANE 10 (Leiden: Brill, 2001), 118–22.

[59] Yhwh's royal and military roles are quite close to the role of Divine Warrior, which focuses on "the divine maintenance of justice in the world." Cf. Theodore Hiebert, "Warrior, Divine," *ABD* 6: 876–80. Patrick D. Miller, *The*

Violence against and Exploitation of Human Beings for the Empire's Purposes Nahum's critique of Assyrian imperialism is not limited to the empire's opposition to Yhwh, which is the focus of 1:9–15[2:1]. That section asserts in passing that Assyria's opposition to Yhwh was inseparable from its brutal domination of Judah (1:13); the rest of the book focuses on Assyria's oppression of other nations as equally terrible and as a further expression of its opposition to Yhwh. This latter critique underlines the way that Assyria developed its imperialism on the historical scene, with a focus on its ideology and its misuse of power for self-serving ends. The pertinent sections that implicate the king and the empire as a stereotyped whole in this pattern of self-serving violence are, respectively, 2:11–13[12–14] and 3:1–7.

The first passage, 2:11–13[12–14], begins with rhetorical questions that imply Assyria's disappearance from the historical scene (2:11[12]). This literary technique, known as prolepsis, presents a future event as if it had already taken place in order to convince the reader of its inevitability and so to shape the reader's imagination of the future (note the same phenomenon in 2:3–10[4–11]). Further, the questions in 2:11[12] dismiss Nineveh's impressive power and accomplishments in illocutive speech – speech, that is, that "is itself the deed that it effects."[60] This heightened rhetoric is proportional to the ideologically loaded image of the Neo-Assyrian monarch as a lion that the passage undermines. In keeping with Assyrian royal ideology, Nahum presents the king as a lion who successfully protects his lair, provides for his pride, and

Divine Warrior in Early Israel, HSM 5 (Harvard: Harvard University Press, 1973), 170, speaks of the "centrality" of this role for Yahweh "in the Old Testament."

[60] Judith Butler, *Excitable Speech: A Politics of the Performative* (New York: Routledge, 1997), 3.

exhibits unparalleled power and violence – all positive features.[61] This image was one of the strongest and most effective expressions of Assyrian royal ideology, and appeared frequently in royally sponsored artwork and annals. In their annals, for example, Adad-Nirari II (911–891) self-identified as "a potent lion,"[62] Sargon II (722–705) compared himself to "a wild lion who is lordly with frightfulness" on the battlefield,[63] and Esarhaddon (680–669) recounted that he "raged like a lion" against foreign and domestic enemies alike.[64]

Imperialism was also the context for the Assyrian king's use of the role of shepherd, in which he protected his flock of citizens from the threat of chaos represented by wild animals, of which the lion was the preferred representative.[65] The image of the king killing a lion in hand-to-hand combat was particularly prominent as the royal seal from the time of Shalmaneser III onward (858–824).[66] Moreover, various Assyrian monarchs, Assurbanipal in particular, engaged in real and staged lion hunts to demonstrate

---

[61] The "friend" and "enemy" valences of the lion metaphor that Brent A. Strawn has identified contribute to Nahum's condemnation of the Assyrian monarch's role here; Brent A. Strawn, *What Is Stronger than a Lion? Leonine Image and Metaphor in the Hebrew Bible and the Ancient Near East*, OBO 212 (Fribourg: Academic Press Fribourg; Göttingen: Vandenhoeck & Ruprecht, 2005), 47–54.

[62] Sarah C. Melville, "Adad-Nirari II," in *The Ancient Near East: Historical Sources in Translation*, ed. Mark W. Chavalas, BSAH (Oxford: Blackwell, 2006), 282.

[63] Sarah C. Melville, "Sargon II," in *The Ancient Near East: Historical Sources in Translation*, ed. Mark W. Chavalas, BSAH (Oxford: Blackwell, 2006), 340.

[64] Against the brothers who attempted to usurp his throne (Nineveh Prism A, Leichty, *Royal Inscriptions of Esarhaddon*, 13) and against Egypt in his 671 campaign (Nineveh Prism E = Prism S, Leichty, *Royal Inscriptions of Esarhaddon*, 53).

[65] Elena Cassin, "Le roi et le lion," *RHR* 198 (1981): 355–401 (375–85).

[66] Berlejung, "Erinnerungen," 333.

their ability to fulfill the role of shepherd. Their success in the royal hunt was recounted in detail in royal inscriptions and bas-reliefs, with claims of vast numbers of kills and extensive depictions of the various stages of the hunt. The lion hunt reliefs in Ashurbanipal's North Palace at Nineveh spanned several rooms and hallways, and include scenes from his victory over the Elamites to highlight the connection between the king's supremacy over actual lions and his ability to subdue external political threats on the battlefield.[67] Since in doing so the king was fulfilling the gods' will to extend his sovereignty far and wide, this connection gave the royal lion hunt a significance that was no less religious than military and ideological.

Taken together, the Assyrian king's protection of his people against leonine threats and his lion-like violence against his enemies express his unparalleled ability to establish and preserve order throughout his empire while defeating the chaos that predominated outside its boundaries.[68] Nahum 2:11–13[12–14] responds to this political and military ideology by developing a lion metaphor in which several key behaviors of lions are transferred to the Assyrian king. While the "tearing," "strangling," and stockpiling of the lion's numerous victims are inevitably continuous activities and quite natural for a lion, the projection of these activities onto the Assyrian king and empire constitutes a damning critique. Transferring to Assyria and its king the natural behavior

---

[67] Cf. Michael B. Dick, "The Neo-Assyrian Royal Lion Hunt and Yahweh's Answer to Job," *CBQ* 125 (2006): 243–70 (246–47, 255); and Elnathan Weissert, "Royal Hunt and Royal Triumph in a Prism Fragment of Ashurbanipal," in *Assyria 1995*, ed. Simo Parpola and Robert Whiting (Helsinki: Neo-Assyrian Text Corpus Project, 1997), 339–58 (349).

[68] These and other uses of lion imagery in the ancient Near East are helpfully surveyed in Strawn, *What Is Stronger than a Lion?*, 131–230.

of a powerful carnivorous predator that kills and consumes other animals creates the image of an empire whose predatory violence against *other human beings* serves only itself. This raises grave moral concerns regarding extreme self-interest, misanthropy, and the gross abuse of power.

Yhwh's direct, personal opposition to Assyrian oppression of the less powerful makes clear that such crimes are as serious as the empire's antagonism against him that 1:9–11 describes in religious terms. Both spheres of Assyrian activity, religious and political alike, are in direct opposition to Yhwh and his world order. Given the diametrical opposition of Yhwh's and Assyria's programs for humanity, Assyria must either change or be eliminated. Since the possibility of Assyrian repentance is never mentioned in Nahum, only the punitive aspect of the divine character announced in the opening poem is in evidence with respect to the empire. Ironically, God's defense of his people (and other nations) against Assyria casts him in a role similar to that of the Assyrian monarch as shepherd but leads to a radically different outcome, in which he as the lion par excellence defends the less powerful against the privations of the predatory militaristic empire.[69] The destruction of Assyria, which on the judicial level is retribution for its morally unacceptable, self-serving, and destructive treatment of other groups, makes God's vengeance inseparable from his deliverance, echoing the complexity of the divine character introduced already in 1:2–8.

---

[69] The opposition between a metaphoric divine lion (Yahweh) and the Assyrian king underlines the conclusion of Strawn, *What Is Stronger than a Lion?*, 65, that "there is simply no deliverance from the lion – especially when that lion happens to be Yahweh." The irony of the reversal of roles is all the more ironic if the biblical image of the lion-king has Neo-Assyrian origins, a possibility Strawn explores (ibid., esp. 268–70).

Nahum's critique and condemnation of Assyria's excessive violence and exploitation is further developed in 3:4–7. The description of Nineveh as "the bloody city" full of plunder and lies is followed by a graphic depiction of a typical Neo-Assyrian attack. These twin perspectives set the stage for the description of the empire's economic and diplomatic affairs under the metaphor of prostitution. This metaphor typically involves a source domain (the literal concept) of illicit sexual activity, and so at first glance characterizes the target domain (the thing to which the literal concept is applied) of Assyria's relations with other states as similarly out-of-bounds in a general way. However, the significance of the metaphor as used here is determined by three specific condemnations that invert its normal construal of power, advantage, and status. *First*, Nineveh's "graceful allure," especially when paired with the accusation of deceitfulness in 3:1, implies that the benefits Assyria promised and sometimes gave to its client states were outweighed by other, unstated costs. *Second*, in the context of Assyria's international relations, "mistress of sorceries" likely refers to the pervasive presence of divination in its warfare and diplomacy.[70] These attempts to discern and influence the future for one's own benefit are evidence of a lack of trust in God, and so contrast sharply with Nahum's emphasis on Yhwh's unique power and trustworthiness.[71]

---

[70] See Lorenzo Verderame, "Astronomy, Divination, and Politics in the Neo-Assyrian Empire," in *Handbook of Archaeoastronomy and Ethnoastronomy*, ed. Clive L. N. Ruggles (New York: Springer, 2014), 1847–53; and Paul-Alain Beaulieu, "Mesopotamia," in *Religions of the Ancient World*, ed. Sarah I. Johnston (Cambridge, MA: Belknap Press of Harvard University Press, 2004), 165–72 (171).

[71] I use Richard Bauckham's "transcendent uniqueness" to underline that Yhwh is *sui generis*; see his "Biblical Theology and the Problems of Monotheism," in *Out of Egypt: Biblical Theology and Biblical Interpretation*, ed. Craig Bartholomew et al., SHS 5 (Carlisle: Paternoster, 2004), 187–232 (210–11).

Third, two parallel lines present the heart of this critique of Assyria, "who sells nations by her debaucheries, and clans by her sorceries." Quite unlike literal instances of this phenomenon, the exploitation and abuse of the prostitute's client are essential to the metaphor as developed here. "Nineveh is not depicted as an ordinary prostitute making a living, let alone as a sexually liberated and self-confident woman. Rather, she is a source of ensnarement and thinks nothing of selling peoples for her pleasure."[72] There was only one winner in Assyria's imperial project: Assyria herself. The metaphor thus represents Assyria as the only one profiting from her relationship with others groups, who derive no real benefit (and indeed only loss) from their relationship.

The unique profile of the metaphorical prostitution described here focuses on Neo-Assyrian violence, deception, and exploitation of the weak in order to condemn the empire, with special emphasis on its violations of its victims' human dignity and value. Yhwh's response as defender of the weak deconstructs the metaphorical prostitute. By shaming Assyria, he exposes what it would rather keep hidden, whether stratagems or more concrete exploitative commercial arrangements. By covering the personified empire with filth, he undoes its attractiveness and makes it contemptible. Finally, God's destruction of Assyria contradicts its claims to uniqueness and invincibility, removing the basis and capability for its abuse of other states.

This punishment involves a strong communicative aspect, seen in Nahum's emphasis on the audience of nations who see Assyria's metaphorical nakedness (3:6b–7). Antony Duff explains communicative punishment in these terms:

---

[72] Thomas Renz, "Nahum, Book of," *Dictionary for Theological Interpretation of the Bible*, ed. Kevin J. Vanhoozer (Grand Rapids, MI: Baker Academic, 2005), 528.

What makes punishment intrinsically appropriate as a response to crime, on communicative accounts, is that crimes are public wrongs that merit censure, and punishment communicates that censure. This explains the justificatory relationship between crime and punishment: censure is something suffered by, and normally painful to, those who are censured; the criminal deserves that kind of suffering, and punishment inflicts it. It also shows why it should be the responsibility of the state to punish criminals: as public wrongs, crimes should be authoritatively censured by the state, through the criminal process.[73]

When Yhwh punishes the wrong committed by some of his creatures in the presence of those wronged, the punishment communicates its significance on two levels. First, as the one who inflicts the punishment (albeit through human agents), Yhwh rejects Assyria's arrogant elevation of its gods to the level of true, unique deity. Second, by bringing the empire down from its assumed status far above those outside its borders, Yhwh demonstrates its human, transitory nature. And since God's punishment is motivated in part by Assyria's not infrequent treatment of its enemies as less than human,[74] he reaffirms its victims' full humanity. Finally, Assyria's devastation eliminates the possibility of recidivism, which is presented as good news for everyone but Assyria.

In the context of seventh-century Judah and its suffering under the Assyrian yoke, this outcome does still more, undermining "all kinds of authorities which tend to establish themselves as worldly guarantees of salvation."[75] While this is clearest

---

[73] R. Antony Duff, "Punishment," in *Oxford Handbook of Practical Ethics*, ed. Hugh LaFollette (Oxford: Oxford University Press, 2003), 331–57 (343).
[74] See Zehnder, *Umgang mit Fremden*, 63–74; and Megan Cifarelli, "Gesture and Alterity in the Art of Ashurnasirpal II of Assyria," *The Art Bulletin* 80 (1998): 210–28, esp. 212–13.
[75] Christofer Frey, "The Biblical Tradition in the Perspective of Political Theology and Political Ethics," in *Politics and Theopolitics in the Bible and*

in Nahum's rejection of Assyria's claims to unbounded authority and prerogative, it is also evident in the book's reticence to attribute any military rule to Judah in opposition to Assyria. This is complemented by the consistent absence of the Davidic king from Nahum's vision for the future, presumably because in Nahum the Davidide's inherently limited role is absorbed in YHWH's exercise of his own universal kingship.

Two observations follow. First, YHWH delegates power to human beings with a view toward service, protection of the weak, and preservation of justice. This reflects God's own use of power in Nahum, which he exercises to punish human wrongs and to deliver the weak from the clutches of the strong. It is, moreover, the model for good governments, who serve their citizens and protect the "public interest."[76] Second, recent and contemporary examples of nationalism often share a striking resemblance to Neo-Assyrian imperialism. Given the latter's strong religious component, Nahum prompts fascinating questions with respect to the West, which often understands the variegated secularisms it has developed over the last two centuries as the result of subtracting or removing the religious, with nothing taking its place.[77] The cultural reality is more complicated, and the West's widespread nationalism resembles in many ways "a powerful religion of the people" that "draws much of its content from key elements of traditional religions, duly sifted and reinterpreted."[78]

Postbiblical Literature, ed. Henning Graf Reventlow, Yair Hoffman, and Benjamin Uffenheimer, JSOTSup 171 (Sheffield: JSOT, 1994), 55–65.

[76] Andrew Heywood, *Political Theory: An Introduction*, 3rd ed. (New York: Palgrave Macmillan, 2004), 244–45.

[77] See Charles Taylor, *A Secular Age* (Cambridge, MA: Belknap Press of Harvard University Press, 2007).

[78] Anthony D. Smith, *Chosen Peoples: Sacred Sources of National Identity* (Oxford: Oxford University Press, 2004), 42.

A sacred communion of the people; the elevation of the voice of the people; the return to nature and to roots; the cult of authenticity; and the sacrificial virtues of heroes and prophets; these are the main themes and beliefs of the belief-system of nationalism, or what we may term a new *religion of the people*. ... [T]he new religion arises on behalf of "*the* people" and of "*a* people"; its object of worship is all the people of every class and region ... but also the people as a specific culture community in its homeland. In this vision, it is not the constituent members as individuals that are felt to be sacred – that is, separated and privileged – but the community as a whole, or rather the image of an authentic (pure, pristine, natural, uncorrupted, and unique) nation in its own landscape.[79]

By reserving ultimate sovereignty for Yhwh, Nahum contests the legitimacy of unbounded human authority and power. Of course, the book rejects imperialism in particular, but its critique of Assyria's abuse of power condemns exploitation of the weak in all forms and regardless of ideology. This critique applies to contemporary secular democratic states, economic systems, and individual relationships as much as first-millennium ancient Near Eastern superpowers.[80]

Before leaving this passage we must consider its use of gender categories and especially the possibility that it countenances male sexual violence against women. While Nahum contains several passages that evoke the specter of gender bias, patriarchy, and androcentrism (e.g., the taunt in 3:13 that Neo-Assyrian warriors are "women" and therefore unable to defend the empire against

---

[79] Smith, *Chosen Peoples*, 42.
[80] On capitalism, see Richard H. Roberts, ed., *Religion and the Transformations of Capitalism: Comparative Approaches* (New York: Routledge, 1995). The articles in the *Journal of Markets & Morality* range much further. For an ethic that involves relationships that serve others and pursues transcendent ideals, see David Brooks, *The Road to Character* (New York: Random House, 2015).

attack), 3:4–7 is doubtless the most striking.[81] Nahum's atypical personification of Nineveh as an exploitative, violent prostitute who "thinks nothing of selling peoples for her pleasure" in 3:4 makes it logical to present her punishment under the same personification.[82] The precise nature of this punishment is disputed, however. Nahum 3:4 is usually translated as "lift up your skirts over your face, and show the nations your nakedness, and kingdoms your disgrace." However, interpreters are divided as to whether the Hebrew text simply refers to shame through exposure or to the horrendous act of rape. Julia M. O'Brien argues for the latter, concluding that Nahum presents "Yahweh … as a man who sexually assaults Nineveh."[83] Some elements of O'Brien's argument fail to convince, however, as when she understands consensual intercourse in Leviticus 18:8 and Ezekiel 16:36 as rape. However, the fact that the phrase "your skirts were removed" in Jeremiah 13:22 (similar enough to "lift up your skirt" in Nah 3:5) is followed by what may be a description of sexual violence in the Jeremiah passage ("your heels were uncovered/have suffered violence") obliges us to examine these two texts more closely.

---

[81] Julia M. O'Brien, *Nahum*, 2nd ed., Readings (Sheffield: Sheffield Phoenix, 2009), 85–88, traces gender ideology across much of the book.

[82] See Renz, "Nahum," 528; and Phyllis Bird, *Missing Persons and Mistaken Identities: Women and Gender in Ancient Israel*, OBT (Minneapolis, MN: Fortress, 1997), 198–202. The reasons for which the author of Nahum chose the metaphor of a prostitute are hard to determine. One that merits consideration is based on Ishtar's complex identity (by the seventh century) as a goddess of kingship, war, sexual attraction, and prostitutes. Enough of that identity is reflected in the description of Nineveh in Nah 3:4–7 to suggest that Nahum has responded to Nineveh in terms of the city's own self-representation as a worshipper of Ishtar, making the gendered representation almost inevitable even while highly sardonic. See Tvzi Abusch, "Ishtar," *DDD*, 452–53; and Rivkah Harris, "Inanna-Ishtar as Paradox and a Coincidence of Opposites," *HR* 30 (1991): 261–78.

[83] O'Brien, *Nahum*, 62.

As the disagreement over the translation of this clause suggests, interpreters dispute the sense of the crucial element in Jeremiah 13:22 ("your heels suffered violence"). The presence of similar actions in Jeremiah 13:26 ("I have stripped your skirts off over your face so that your shame might be seen") only complicates the discussion.[84] Accepting for the sake of the argument that "your heels suffered violence" in Jeremiah 13:22 does denote male sexual violence against a female victim, the crucial issue is the relation between that phrase and the preceding one. In Jeremiah 13:22, the phrase "lift up your skirt" is followed – again for the sake of argument – by a description of sexual violence, and the relationship between the phrases seems clear. In Nahum 3:5, however, "lifting your skirts over your face" is followed by a different action: "I will show the nations your nakedness, and the kingdoms your shame." Despite sharing the element of lifted skirts, Jeremiah 13:22 and Nahum 3:5 use that shared element differently, as part of two very different scenarios. Given the different semantics of the two verses, sexual violence should not be read into Nahum 3:5 on the basis of the only partial parallel in Jeremiah 13:22.[85] The result of

---

[84] See Leslie Allen, *Jeremiah*, OTL (Louisville, KY: Westminster John Knox, 2008), 162, 164; Peter C. Craigie et al., *Jeremiah 1–25*, WBC 26 (Dallas, TX: Word, 1991), 193; J. A. Emerton, "The Meaning of the Verb ḥāmas in Jeremiah 13,22," in *Prophet und Prophetenbuch: Festschrift für Otto Kaiser zum 65. Geburtstag*, ed. Volkmar Fritz, Karl-Friedrich Pohlmann, and Hans-Christoph Schmitt, BZAW 185 (Berlin: de Gruyter, 1989), 19–28; and William McKane, *A Critical and Exegetical Commentary on Jeremiah*, ICC, 2 vols. (Edinburgh: T & T Clark, 1986), 1:311.

[85] Cf. Spronk, *Nahum*, 123–24; Heinz-Josef Fabry, *Nahum*, HTKAT (Freiburg: Herder, 2006), 109–11; and Gregory Cook, "Nahum and the Question of Rape," *BBR* 26 (2006): 341–52. For unambiguous references to rape, see Gen 34:2; Deut 22:28; 2 Sam 13:12, 14. There is some ancient Near Eastern legal precedent for the public denuding of prostitutes who present themselves in public as married women by veiling their heads, and there is also at least one case law

the lifting of the metaphorical prostitute's garment in Nahum is thus public exposure and shame, which aligns well with the communicative dimensions of punishment noted earlier.[86] The potent image underlines the degree to which the empire's motives, goals, and self-evaluation are incompatible with Yhwh's moral norms, and denigrates it for that reason.[87] Assyria's definitive status as disgraced, a very undesirable social standing,[88] is communicated

> that calls for the rape of a rapist's wife as punishment for his crime. For the former, see Martha Roth, *Law Collections from Mesopotamia and Asia Minor*, 2nd ed., WAW 6 (Atlanta, GA: Scholars, 1997), 167–69 (Middle Assyrian Laws A¶40), and the Sefire treaty: "[And just as] a [har]lot is stripped naked], so may the wives of Mati'el be stripped naked" (Joseph A. Fitzmeyer, "The Inscriptions of Bar-Ga'yah and Mati'el From Sefire," COS 2.21 [2:214]). For the latter, see Roth, *Law Collections from Mesopotamia and Asia Minor*, 174-75 (Middle Assyrian Laws A¶55).
>
> [86] A comprehensive perspective on the role of gender in Nahum would require further study of 3:4-7 and of other relevant passages in Nahum. The latter include texts that appear to be biased against women (again, the taunt in 3:13) and others that appear to be biased against men (e.g., the positive portrayal of feminine Judah paired with the negative portrayal of masculine Assyria and her king in 1:11-14). Ideally, the contribution of gender difference to Nahum's message (especially its bipartite view of humanity) should be integrated with analyses of the book's use of other forms of difference, including the ungendered and uniquely important relationship of human beings to Yhwh. Further discussion can be found in Cynthia R. Chapman, *The Gendered Language of Warfare in the Israelite-Assyrian Encounter*, HSM 62 (Winona Lake, IN: Eisenbrauns, 2004), esp. 103–10, and Claudia Bergmann, "'We Have Seen the Enemy, and He Is Only a She': The Portrayal of Warriors as Women," in *Writing and Reading War: Rhetoric, Gender, and Ethics in Biblical and Modern Contexts*, ed. Brad E. Kelle and Frank Ritchel Ames, foreword by Susan Niditch, SBL SymS 42 (Atlanta, GA: Society of Biblical Literature, 2006), 129–42.
>
> [87] Ronald R. Mudge, "Yahweh's Counter-Cultural View of Honor and Shame," *Conversations with the Biblical World* 34 (2014): 118–35, stresses the radical difference between divine and human views of honor and shame in the Old Testament.
>
> [88] Joshua Moon, "Honor and Shame in Hosea's Marriages," *JSOT* 39 (2015): 335–51 (340).

to the surrounding nations through the very public nature of its fall and disintegration.

Yhwh's Restoration and Deliverance of Judah and Other Nations

At last we turn to consider the unambiguously positive facet of Yhwh's intervention against Assyria. However, the author spends relatively little time spelling out the benefits of Assyria's demise for Judah, perhaps because they were self-evident or perhaps to maintain the book's focus on justice and retribution. Our examination of deliverance is thus limited to a few short passages (1:12–13, 15; 2:2[3]). An important aspect of this material is the link between the end of Judah's covenant discipline (1:12) and its restoration (1:15, 2:2[3]). Yhwh's covenant with Israel (cf. Exod 19–24) included a prominent conditional component (cf. Exod 19:5–6; Lev 26; Deut 28) that promised blessings if Israel obeyed and progressive punishments if it did not. This dynamic lies behind Yhwh's "affliction" of Judah (Nah 1:12), which the text portrays as coming to an end. While the end of covenant discipline (at least in its extreme forms) is sometimes tied to Israel's repentance (Deut 30:1–10), here that element is not mentioned, so that the emphasis falls on Yhwh's gracious initiative. However, it is significant that the author assumes that his Judean audience is Yhwhistic, that it would accept the implication that its recent troubles were due to its sins, and that Yhwh is indeed able to liberate it from Assyrian oppression. On this basis the author calls the newly liberated Judah to recognize God's unique agency and supremacy in liberating it from Assyria and restoring its well-being (šālôm, 2:1[1:15]), probably in the belief that such blessing is inseparable from obedience.

The description of Yhwh's intervention on Judah's behalf in 2:2[3] as "restoring the majesty of Jacob like the majesty of Israel" makes a slightly different contribution to the book's view of Judah's deliverance. The juxtaposition of Jacob and Israel hints that this verse should be understood in light of Jacob's encounter with God in Genesis 32.[89] That passage and its preceding context characterize Jacob as deceitful and consequently often in trouble before he wrestled with God, while afterwards restored relationships (Gen 33) and divine blessing predominate in his life (Gen 35:1–15). This intertextual connection suggests that Nahum 2:2[3] contains a promise that through a similarly difficult but transformative experience, Judah will experience YHWH's blessing and the security it brings.[90]

Judah's liberation also entails the emancipation of various non-Israelite nations and groups under Assyrian oppression (3:7, 19). This links this material to the divine plan to bless all peoples through Abram's descendants (Gen 12:1–3; cf. also Exod 19:4–6).[91] This perspective seems to be contradicted by the immediate agency of Babylon in bringing down the Assyrian empire, however. If Babylon's agency is determinative, and if Judah's liberation is therefore an unintended consequence of Babylon's own imperial project, how can Judah's liberation be tied to YHWH's plan for his people? The answer to this question is that Nahum's

---

[89] The interpretative tradition is hardly in agreement in identifying the "man" as God, but that uncertainty has no effect on my argument here. See Robert Alter, *Genesis: Translation and Commentary* (New York: W. W. Norton, 1996), 180–83.

[90] Victor P. Hamilton, "Jacob/Israel (Person)," *New Dictionary of Biblical Theology*, ed. T. Desmond Alexander and Brian S. Rosner (Downers Grove, IL: InterVarsity, 2000), 587–89 (588).

[91] As R. W. L. Moberly argues, the sense of the last clause in Gen 12:3 may be that others will "recognize and invoke Abraham as a model of desirable existence"; R. W. L. Moberly, *The Theology of the Book of Genesis*, OTT (Cambridge: Cambridge University Press, 2009), 154. Here it suffices to note that God remains the source of all blessing in this text (cf. 12:3a–b).

fundamental claim that YHWH is sovereign over the world as a whole makes Babylon's instrumentality only incidental, while his commitment to bring down Assyria for its offenses against him and various nations makes his agency the determining factor (cf. Nah 1:12). It is perhaps for the same reason that the author of Nahum is content, as we have seen, to deny any role in these events to Judah and its Davidic king. The fact that YHWH's intervention on the world stage sees Judah and other vassal states benefit from an identical deliverance also parallels the perspective of the opening poem, in which those who trust in YHWH are delivered regardless of their nationality. Nahum's silence as to the religious or moral failings of the other nations that YHWH delivers by bringing an end to Assyria is intriguing but inevitably gives the interpreter nothing other than silence to work with. The same cannot be said for Nahum's use of stereotypes, to which we now turn.

Nahum's Stereotypical Representations of Assyria and Judah

The general unease that many readers feel when confronted with stereotypes, especially if they are linked to the exercise of power, is reason enough to give close attention to Nahum's use of them. This readerly motivation is paralleled by others that arise more directly from the book itself. For example, the consistency with which Nahum attributes culpable behaviors to Assyria and minimizes condemnation of Judah shows that these stereotypes are intentional. Yet the contrasting identities that they create are foundational to the contrasting fates the book assigns to Judah and Assyria, making them integral to Nahum's message.

Since their appearance in sociological study of group membership in the 1920s, stereotypes have often been associated with prejudice, bias, and competition.[92] Recent research, however, has focused on stereotyping as a cognitive process that is part of "normal information processing," and views stereotypes as energy-saving aids to explanation that are formed from shared beliefs.[93] While stereotypes can be misconstrued and misused, they can also create "useful and inescapable" explanatory meanings that should be evaluated in the context of the discourse that employs them.[94] A fundamental consideration for understanding stereotypes involves the way that they identify *some* of the subject's traits as more salient than *others*.[95] Nahum does not present blunt stereotypes that have no basis in reality but characterizes Assyria and Judah in ways that simultaneously reflect some aspects of their historical identities while leaving others aside. On the one hand, the book's depiction of the Assyrian king and empire is consistent with the ideology that Neo-Assyria developed and transmitted internationally, and its depiction of Judah recognizes Judah's past misdeeds. On the other hand, Nahum mentions no positive aspect of Assyria and no negative aspect of Judah (with the exception of the implication that its past sins merited punishment). These simplifications of the two groups' identities and

---

[92] Margo J. Monteith, Anna Woodcock, and Jill E. Gulker, "Automaticity and Control in Stereotyping and Prejudice: The Revolutionary Role of Social Cognition across Three Decades of Research," in *Oxford Handbook of Social Cognition*, ed. Donal E. Carlston (New York: Oxford University Press, 2013), 74–94 (74–75).

[93] Monteith, Woodcock, and Gulker, "Automaticity," 76; Craig McGarty, Vincent Y. Yzerbyt, and Russell Spears, "Social, Cultural and Cognitive Factors in Stereotype Formation," in *Stereotypes as Explanations: The Formation of Meaningful Beliefs about Social Groups*, ed. Craig McGarty, Vincent Y. Yzerbyt, and Russell Spears (Cambridge: Cambridge University Press, 2002), 1–15 (2).

[94] Jacques-Philippe Leyens, Vincent Y. Yzerbyt, and Georges Schadron, *Stereotypes and Social Cognition* (London: Sage, 1994), 206.

[95] Monteith, Woodcock, and Gulker, "Automaticity," 87.

characteristics are intended to help the reader of Nahum make "informed judgments" about them.⁹⁶

While it undoubtedly guides the reader, this selectivity also raises difficult questions. Most pointedly, are not Nahum's stereotypes simply the product of prejudice against Assyria and irrational optimism in favor of Judah? Social identity theory, which understands this selection of particular categories in the development of a stereotype as "particularization," helpfully illuminates this aspect of Nahum's depiction of Assyria and Judah.⁹⁷ As we have seen, the book's stereotype of Assyria focuses on the king, elites, and army as those involved in its violent imperialism, and leaves aside the general population. Nahum's critique of Assyria also focuses on the empire's military opposition to YHWH in claiming absolute superiority over Judah, the king's insistent claims to nearly absolute significance, and the empire's violent exploitation of the less powerful. Nahum's particularization of Assyria thus has both *social and moral foci*. As a result, the critique leveled against the "empire" actually targets only *certain groups within it* – the king, elites, diplomats, and army – and, within them, specific actions and dispositions: violence, self-absorption, and disdain for the other. These foci implicitly *exclude* from the stereotype all Assyrians not in those groups or, more precisely, all Assyrians whose actions and dispositions are different from those Nahum condemns.⁹⁸ The inherent limits of the stereotype are also hinted

---

⁹⁶ Charles Stangor and Mark Schaller, "Stereotypes as Individual and Collective Representations," in *Stereotypes and Stereotyping*, ed. C. Neil Macrae, Charles Stangor, and Miles Hewstone (New York: Guilford, 1996), 3–40 (21).
⁹⁷ Perry R. Hinton, *Stereotypes, Cognition and Culture*, Psychology Focus (Hove: Psychology Press, 2000), 132.
⁹⁸ Cf. Michael Billig, "Prejudice, Categorization and Particularization: From a Perceptual to a Rhetorical Approach," *European Journal of Social Psychology* 15 (1985): 79–103.

at in Nahum's glance at Nineveh's *survivors* in 2:7[8], 10[11] over against the focus on the *destruction* of the king and his military and administrative corps in 2:13[14]. In short, the end of "Assyria" consists of the elimination of discrete elements of the empire (the king's defeat, the destruction of the capital city, and the collapse of the empire's ideology) and not of Assyria as a population or ethnic group. What at first glance might appear to be a reductionist, misleading representation of Assyria thus has, as most social representations do, "a certain rationality" and is "not a product of a failure to think 'properly' or a distortion."[99]

Similar limits are present in Nahum's stereotype of Judah, which involves almost no explicit characterization and is essentially the inverted image of Assyria. Judah is stereotyped as submissive to YHWH and recognizing no other deities, its monarch is conspicuously absent from plans for its flourishing, and Judah's relations with other states are not depicted as abusive, deceptive, or violent. By inverting the characteristics used to caricature Assyria, Nahum also inverts the social and moral foci of those particularizations. The Judean king and elites are not mentioned and Judah's moral failings are minimal and limited to the past, while the future is bright with the promise of renewed blessing. Alongside these changes are assumptions that suggest that the stereotype is not applicable to *empirical* Judah. The Judah that the author portrays has accepted YHWH's punishment at Assyria's hands, has not lost confidence in his ability to deliver the nation from Assyria's iron grip, and is amenable to praising him as the one ultimately responsible for her coming deliverance.

Nahum's stereotypes cannot be extended to cover the entire population of either Judah or Assyria, and so they are not

[99] Hinton, *Stereotypes*, 158.

essentialist (i.e., based on supposedly inherent characteristics such as race or ethnicity). What then is their contribution to the book? The stereotypes used in 1:9–3:19 seem designed to develop characterizations of Judah and Assyria that are compatible with the binary characterizations of the two unidentified groups in the opening poem, "positioning" Judah and Assyria in Nahum's discourse so that their characterization and actions, and the consequences that follow upon them, are intelligible in relation to the perspective of 1:2–8.[100] This readily explains why the stereotypes share the opening poem's moral and religious focus and also helps us understand how the contrasting groups relate (i.e., YHWH's enemies and those who trust in him in 1:2–8; stereotyped Judah and Assyria in 1:9–3:19). The collective perspectives employed in 1:9–3:19 inevitably require some sort of qualification in order to be credible. But concrete distinctions within the collectives of Judah and Assyria would obscure or even undo the binary contrast between the two states that is essential to 1:9–3:19. By using stereotypes, the author is able to maintain the collective identities of Judah and Assyria while simultaneously qualifying them. This in turn makes it possible for the cosmic (1:2–8) and geopolitical (1:9–3:19) storylines to interconnect.

This will appear more clearly if we step back and view the two storylines side by side. The absence of stereotypes in 1:2–8 is possible because the theophany it describes involves *individuals* who are identified exclusively and absolutely in terms of their relationship to YHWH, who *directly and exclusively* determines the

---

[100] Hinton, *Stereotypes*, 147; Luk Van Langenhove and Rom Harré, "Cultural Stereotypes and Positioning Theory," *Journal for the Theory of Social Behaviour* 24 (1994): 359–77 (363). Hinton lays out the theoretical bases of approaching Nahum's use of stereotypes cognitively and textually in his work (*Stereotypes*, 128–31).

outcome of this *ultimate, final* intervention. In order to portray YHWH's involvement in a *nonultimate* judgment that involves parties whose identities are *collective* but also *complex*, 1:9–3:19 must either dispense with the collective geopolitical identities in favor of an individual approach or represent YHWH's *involvement as mediated*. The author takes account of this tension by making changes on both fronts. On the one hand, the collective identities are partially undone by the stereotypes' inherent selectivity and limited applicability. On the other hand, YHWH's indirect, limited agency means that the outcome of his confrontation with Assyria is restricted to the geopolitical scene of seventh-century West Asia.

One final point should be made. The book's stereotypical presentations of Judah and Assyria are a two-edged sword. On the one hand, they assuage fears that YHWH would fail to intervene on behalf of his people, for divine intervention is motivated by the injustice that the stereotypes highlight. On the other hand, they undermine the easy assumption that such intervention could never impact negatively an entity other than Assyria, since it is clear that the idealized Judah of Nahum corresponds only very roughly to seventh-century Judean society.[101]

Varied Responses to YHWH's Intervention
The Book of Nahum attempts to convince its readers and hearers of two interrelated truths: YHWH will intervene on Judah's behalf in the context of Neo-Assyrian imperialism, and this intervention

---

[101] So also Edward Ball, "'When the Towers Fall': Interpreting Nahum as Christian Scripture," in *In Search of True Wisdom: Essays in Old Testament Interpretation in Honour of Ronald E. Clements*, ed. Edward Ball, JSOTSup 300 (London: T & T Clark, 1999), 211–30 (226). Hutton, "Southern, Northern, and Transjordanian Perspectives," sketches some of the diversity of Israelite religion.

is organically related to a definitive, ultimate act of judgment and deliverance that will bring an end to Yhwh's enemies and definitively deliver those who trust in him from his vengeance. Given the dire straits in which Judah found itself in the seventh century and later, one might think that a positive reaction to Nahum's message could be taken for granted, and indeed, the book occasionally points in that direction (1:15[2:1]; 3:7, 19). Here we consider in more detail the book's indications of the responses the author wished to see on the part of its audience.

Seek Refuge in Yhwh
The description of Yhwh's wrath and looming judgment in 1:2–5 creates mild suspense by not identifying his enemies (they could be anyone) and by predicting that his wrathful arrival will affect the whole earth, including its inhabitants (1:5). The significance of these undefined categories becomes salient in 1:6, which problematizes human beings' escape from the threat of destruction that this theophany poses: "Who can stand before his indignation? Who can endure his burning anger?" Only after this worrisome intimation that escape will not be easy, and may even be impossible, does the author reveal that escape is in fact possible for those who take refuge in Yhwh, who clearly merits their trust as an all-powerful deliverer (cf. 1:3). The author further encourages trust in God by returning to the contrasting category of his enemies in 1:8: If one does not seek refuge in Yhwh, there is no other possibility of escaping the darkness and annihilation that await his enemies. So, seeking refuge in God is the first intended response.

Celebrate Yhwh as Deliverer
The only explicit commands that indicate how Judah is to respond to Yhwh's deliverance appear in 1:15[2:1]. Since Nahum presents

YHWH as Judah's only deliverer, it is not surprising that her response consists of religious festivals and the payment of vows, both urged on the reader with imperatives: "Celebrate your feasts, Judah! Pay your vows!" "Feast" (*ḥag*) refers to the three pilgrimage festivals (Passover, Feast of Weeks, and Feast of Booths), all of which celebrated God's provision for and deliverance of Israel in the past and present.[102] Among these, both Passover and Booths involved commemoration of aspects of God's preeminent saving act in the Old Testament to this point, the exodus from Egypt and preservation on route to Canaan. The celebration of them that is urged here will inevitably also take account of God's prodigious deliverance of Judah from Assyria. The payment of vows in connection with Judah's deliverance is even more focused on this anticipated event, since their being paid now assumes that the vows were made in the context of Assyrian oppression and relate directly to Judah's deliverance from it. Such robust celebration of YHWH's deliverance is a second intended response.

What of Nahum's Taunts?

A final facet of the anticipated response to Nahum's message, and to Assyria's fall in particular, appears in the taunts that make up much of Chapter 3.[103] While most taunts are uttered for their effect on the other,[104] those in Nahum are for Judahite ears only. Unlike the explicit command to celebrate Assyria's fall in 1:15[2:1], the taunts and sarcastic dirge of Nahum 3 solicit a response less directly by encouraging the reader to resonate with their

---

[102] Miller, *Religion of Israel*, 80–85.
[103] In this section I occasionally draw upon some of the discussion in Timmer, *Nahum*, 158–80.
[104] Robert Desjarlais, *Counterplay: An Anthropologist at the Chessboard* (Berkeley: University of California Press, 2011), 20.

sentiments. These sentiments are anticipatory responses to the full and quite unexpected reversal of Assyria's fortunes, especially the erasure of its military and economic power by its defeat and destruction.[105]

The first taunt begins by pointing out that defensive infrastructure, military might, and foreign alliances were not enough to deliver Thebes from Assyria's attack in 663 BCE. It then predicts that Nineveh will likewise fall in spite of all that makes her appear invincible (3:8–11). The second taunt, in 3:12–15c, undermines the presumption that Assyria's army would be able to defend it against any and all attacks, and announces its defeat alongside the destruction of its fortresses. The prophet sarcastically encourages the empire to prepare for an imminent attack only to interrupt his instructions with the claim that before these preparations are completed, Assyria will have already fallen. The last taunt is directed against Assyria's international economic apparatus (3:15d–17), which, despite its numerous participants, will disappear as swiftly as a swarm of locusts that leaves one place for another. A closing dirge for the Assyrian king follows these taunts in 3:18–19. The general population and its leaders alike are seen as being unable to help the fallen monarch, and no healing is possible for his deadly wound. The attribution of a fatal wound to an enemy is tantamount to announcing his death, and news of his inescapable demise will meet with applause on the part of all who hear it because it spells the end of the "evil" (*rāʿâ*) that he had brought upon them.

Taunts typically assert the inferiority of the other, but explicit comparison does not play a major role in Nahum 3. The first taunt claims that Nineveh is inferior to (or at least not in a better position

---

[105] Berlejung, "Erinnerungen," 340–41.

than) already-fallen Thebes, but predicts only that Nineveh will not survive an unspecified future attack. The next two taunts share this general outlook, asserting that Assyria is inferior to the unidentified forces that will defeat and destroy her. The absence of Judah or any other specific military opponent as a point of comparison, however, coupled with the repeated affirmation elsewhere in the book that Yhwh is Assyria's primary foe, suggest that the basis for these taunts is to be found in the immense disparity between Assyria's power and Yhwh's might rather than of a geopolitical foe. If this is correct, these taunts cast doubt upon Assyria's confidence based on her long-term stability, military might, and economic power, while affirming Yhwh's supremacy regardless of the empire's present power and size. Since the taunts make Yhwh the ultimate point of comparison, they do not involve the self-glorifying element that marks most taunts. They are, rather, well-crafted Yhwhistic challenges to imperial propaganda that dismiss the empire's claims of invincibility before it has in fact fallen.

To summarize, Nahum's multifaceted response to Yhwh's deliverance explicitly or implicitly encourages Yhwh's historic people to interpret their imminent deliverance from Assyrian oppression as organically related to his past saving acts on their behalf (and often against their enemies) and to trust him without reservation. Although the taunts and sarcastic dirge of Chapter 3 are intended to further undermine Assyria's claims that it could not be defeated and would forever dominate the world, their generic tone resists attempts to read them as craven nationalism. The connection between Assyria's fall and Yhwh's final theophanic intervention as described in 1:2–8 would also have encouraged Judean and later readers to interpret that event in theological rather than in nationalistic or ethnocentric terms.

A THEOLOGY OF NAHUM

Having traced key themes through various contexts of Nahum, here we draw them together in a theological synthesis. From the very first lines of the opening hymn, YHWH takes center stage as the only deity worthy of the title, and assumes two contrasting roles. He is, first, the one who will come to judge human beings for their offenses against him and against one another. This retribution, which preserves his holiness and demonstrates his justice, also threatens (at least at first glance) to destroy humanity as a whole. The destructive effects of this divine wrath on the created order that are a sort of prelude to divine destruction of sinful human beings are not simply a reflection of its awe-inspiring scale but also hint that the created order as it currently is has been deeply scarred by human sin. Although the global scale and eschatological significance of the judgment announced in 1:2–8 set it apart from the judgment of Assyria that is in focus in the rest of the book, these two parts of Nahum complement each other because they share the same theme: God's justice and perfection require him to punish those who violate his will, persist in opposition to him, and pursue domination of the people and world around them for their own purposes. In his role as Divine Warrior, YHWH is relentless and unstoppable, and will bring about the total destruction of his enemies (1:8).

This cataclysmic judgment is only one side of this final divine intervention in human affairs, even if it predominates in the opening hymn and in the rest of the book. Alongside judgment, and for very different reasons, YHWH is also the only one who can deliver human beings from the danger that his justice poses to them. The image of finding refuge in him (1:7) expresses the gracious divine commitment to grant protection to those who otherwise would not have it (human beings are clearly unable to save themselves in this scenario). The related deliverance of Judah from Assyria is also gracious, as God decides to end his warranted discipline of Judah although its religious and moral track record remained quite spotty.

In terms of the reasons and ways that divine judgment corresponds to human behavior, the opening hymn shows that at least in its ultimate manifestation, judgment is not determined by the corporate identity that figures largely in the covenant theology of the Old Testament. The descriptions of humanity in 1:2–8 divide humanity into two groups without remainder, and make each person's standing with respect to Yhwh all-important. This binary perspective is significantly more complicated in the rest of the book, but it is nonetheless still present because of the stereotyped and selective ways that Judah and Assyria are presented. This allows Nahum to present a significant judgment against Assyria that, even though it affects the empire as a whole, still focuses on those most responsible for and committed to the empire's ideology, violence, materialism, exploitation, and self-idolatry. The stereotypical presentation of Judah similarly identifies it as made up of those Judeans who accept the validity of God's disciplinary punishment of their nation and recognize that his deliverance of them is due to his grace and his faithfulness to his promises. The complex characterization of Assyria is part of Nahum's argument for the justice of retribution against it despite the imperfect and incomplete nature of the latter, not least because it is brought about at the hands of the Babylonian empire. Similarly, Judah's deliverance comes only after fitting punishment, and brings only limited restoration to a nation that remains deeply divided in its commitment to Yhwh. Judah, too, in other words, is a complex entity. Only the opening hymn describes unqualified destruction and deliverance, and there the correlation between the individual and his or her fate is based exclusively on the nature of one's relationship to Yhwh.

Nahum's rhetoric, imagery, and emphasis on the threat that divine justice poses to all human beings produce a theology that draws the reader into the scenarios its presents. As a first example of this point, the description of Yhwh's theophany in 1:2–8 that focuses on judgment but includes the possibility of deliverance places the reader who has observed God's awesome descent toward the earth for judgment at a crucial juncture, especially following 1:6. How will the reader respond to the assumption that all human beings are in fact imperfect when measured by Yhwh's standards? What will readers do in light of their inability to escape a similar ultimate reckoning by themselves? Nahum leaves only one (surprising) way out of this dilemma: a humble approach to the same God who threatens punishment. Although Nahum offers no explanation of how the "refuge" Yhwh provides deals with the problem of sin that dominates 1:2–8, there is no doubt that this deliverance will be in accord with divine justice.

This leads to a second and complementary dimension of the book's theological engagement with its readers. Judeans delivered from Assyria's imperial clutches no doubt celebrate that deliverance (3:19) but must especially celebrate the God who orchestrated it as part of his ongoing, gracious, and faithful relationship to his covenant people (1:15[2:1]). Judah's celebration of its key feasts connects Judah's deliverance from Assyrian oppression with Yhwh's greatest acts of deliverance from of old: the liberation of Israel from Egypt, his guidance of them to the promised land, and his ongoing provision for them. The open-ended restoration of (especially faithful) Judah connects this response of praise to the ultimate deliverance sketched briefly in 1:7. Nahum's message offers hope in the present to those who trust in Yhwh, and they can celebrate Yhwh's past deliverance in anticipation of their ultimate deliverance as part of his victory over evil.[106]

NAHUM'S CONTRIBUTION TO JEWISH AND CHRISTIAN TRADITIONS

Despite its small size, the Book of Nahum works with a number of important themes and theological traditions. As part of the developing collection of authoritative Hebrew Scriptures, its most significant connections are to other parts of that body of literature and with the related writings of Second Temple Judaism and the New Testament. Because these traditions accorded unequaled authority to Nahum as divine revelation, their use of it is fundamentally different than the reception of Nahum in wider culture that is explored in a later section.

The Old Testament
Nahum and the Book of the Twelve
The existence of the Book of the Twelve (Minor Prophets) as a collection is attested at least as early as the Book of Sirach (ca. 180 BCE).[107] This invites readers to consider Nahum not merely in the context of the Old Testament as a whole but also in relation to the books alongside which it was placed in early

---

[106] See the use of Nahum as a source of comfort for survivors of war trauma in the context of prolonged violent conflict in the Democratic Republic of Congo in Jacob O. Wenyi, *Piles of Slain, Heaps of Corpses: Reading Prophetic Poetry and Violence in African Context*, with a foreword by Ellen F. Davis (Cascade, OR: Cascade Books, 2021).

[107] "May the bones of the Twelve Prophets send forth new life from where they lie, for they comforted the people of Jacob and delivered them with confident hope" (Ben Sira 49:10, NRSV).

biblical collections.¹⁰⁸ Probably for this reason, much investigation has focused on Nahum's relationship to Jonah, which is typically immediately prior to Nahum in the Greek Old Testament, and to Habakkuk, the book that typically follows Nahum in both the Jewish and Christian Bibles.¹⁰⁹ Jonah's claim that Nineveh did indeed repent represents a perspective quite different from that of Nahum. Although the dates of Nahum's various sections complicate some of the arguments for influence or textual dependence, Jonah's historical setting around the middle of the eighth century BCE (see 2 Kgs 14:25) encourages readers to see Nahum as demonstrating that Nineveh's repentance had no lasting effect, but also to see Jonah as evidence that YHWH's mercy extends beyond Israel's borders.¹¹⁰ Indeed, the Book of Jonah makes the point even more

---

¹⁰⁸ Approaches of this sort are examined by Daniel C. Timmer, "Nahum in the Book of the Twelve," in *The Book of the Twelve: Composition, Reception, and Interpretation*, ed. Lena-Sofia Tiemeyer and Jakob Wöhrle, VTSup 184 (Leiden: Brill, 2020), 186–200, and I occasionally draw on that survey here.

¹⁰⁹ The dominant order of the first six Minor Prophets in the Greek tradition is Hosea, Amos, Micah, Joel, Obadiah, Jonah; beginning with Nahum, the Greek and Hebrew orders are generally identical; W. Edward Glenny, "Textual History of the Minor Prophets: Hebrew Manuscripts and Versions," in *The Oxford Handbook of the Minor Prophets*, ed. Julia M. O'Brien (Oxford: Oxford University Press, 2021), 41–55; Russell E. Fuller, "The Book of the Twelve at Qumran," in *The Book of the Twelve: Composition, Reception, and Interpretation*, ed. Lena-Sofia Tiemeyer and Jakob Wöhrle, VTSup 184 (Leiden: Brill, 2020), 271–85. Marvin A. Sweeney, "Twelve, Book of the," in *Dictionary of the Old Testament: Prophets*, ed. Mark J. Boda and J. Gordon McConville (Downers Grove, IL: IVP Academic, 2012), 788–806 (788), considers the potential interpretative significance of the differences between the Hebrew and Greek orders.

¹¹⁰ See Klaas Spronk, "Nahum, and the Book of the Twelve: A Response to Jakob Wöhrle," *JHebS* 9 (2009): article 8; Christopher Seitz, "What Lesson Will History Teach? The Book of the Twelve as History," in *"Behind" the Text: History and Biblical Interpretation*, ed. Craig Bartholomew et al., SHS 4 (Carlisle: Paternoster, 2003), 443–67.

strongly: Not only do the Ninevites lack any existing connection to God's chosen people, but the empire which Nineveh represents was responsible for violence, sometimes egregious, against numerous groups. Yet it is to the Assyrians of Nineveh that YHWH shows himself to be "gracious and merciful, slow to answer and abounding in steadfast love" (Jon 4:2). This description of God, based on his self-description in Exodus 34:6–7, is fundamental to his unique relationship with Israel, yet the same saving goodness is (only here, in these terms) shown to Israel's most formidable enemy – much to Jonah's chagrin!

Habakkuk follows Nahum not only in the order of the Twelve but also in terms of chronology, focusing on the Neo-Babylonian empire that conquered Assyria and gradually took control of Judah near the end of the seventh century BCE, destroying Jerusalem and exiling much of the Judean population shortly thereafter. This proximity in literary order and time lends some plausibility to arguments for Habakkuk's interpretation of Nahum, which include the literary and eschatological *inclusio* that the hymns in Nahum 1 and Habakkuk 3 form around the two books;[111] literary similarities that could suggest the two books were composed or redacted along similar lines;[112] and links between the opening and closing verses of Nahum and the books immediately before and after it that may indicate its intentional incorporation at a specific place within the Twelve.[113] Habakkuk's critique of Babylon

---

[111] Brevard Childs, "The Canonical Shape of the Prophetic Literature," *Int* 32 (1978): 46–55 (51).

[112] Rainer Kessler, "Nahum–Habakuk als Zweiprophetenschrift: Eine Skizze," in *"Wort Jhwhs, das geschah..." (Hos 1,1): Studien zum Zwölfprophetenbuch*, ed. Erich Zenger, HBS 35 (Freiburg: Herder, 2002), 149–58.

[113] James D. Nogalski, *Literary Precursors to the Book of the Twelve*, BZAW 217 (Berlin: de Gruyter, 1993); James D. Nogalski, *Redactional Processes in the Book of the Twelve*, BZAW 218 (Berlin: de Gruyter, 1993); Jakob

as a military empire, its articulation of the hope that YHWH will intervene to punish Babylon and deliver those suffering under its yoke, and its interpretation of this future intervention in terms of YHWH's past saving acts are also quite similar to prominent aspects of Nahum's message.

The Day of YHWH, which in Nahum is prefigured by the fall of Assyria and predicts the destruction of all of God's enemies, has a variety of related meanings within the Twelve and can be referred to by a number of different expressions.[114] In Nahum the "day of distress/trouble" (1:7; similarly Obad 12, 14; Hab 3:16; Zeph 1:15) refers to the final divine judgment of those who refuse to seek refuge in YHWH and persist in autonomy and self-sufficiency, but also includes the divine deliverance of those who seek refuge in God. Within the Twelve, Nahum's inclusion of all humanity in this judgment/salvation event is akin to Joel 4:2; Habakkuk 3:12–15; Zechariah 14:3; and Malachi 4:1–3. Unlike Joel, Amos, and Malachi, Nahum does not explicitly include Israelites of his day in an imminent "Day of YHWH," although this selectivity is likely due to the book's idealized portrayal of Judah and resolute focus on Assyria from Nahum 1:9 onward (similarly Obadiah). As in Habakkuk, the necessity of repentance to survive this ultimate divine judgment is implicit, although Nahum 1:7 connects deliverance directly to

---

Wöhrle, *Die frühen Sammlungen des Zwölfprophetenbuches: Entstehung und Komposition*, BZAW 360 (Berlin: de Gruyter, 2006); Wöhrle, *Der Abschluss des Zwölfprophetenbuches*.

[114] Rolf Rendtorff, "How to Read the Book of the Twelve as a Theological Unity," in *Reading and Hearing the Book of the Twelve*, ed. James D. Nogalski and Marvin A. Sweeney, SBL SymS 15 (Atlanta, GA: Scholars Press, 2000), 75–87. Joel D. Barker, "Day of the LORD," *Dictionary of the Old Testament Prophets*, ed. Mark J. Boda and J. Gordon McConville (Downers Grove, IL: IVP Academic, 2012), 132–43, notes the flexible terminology used to refer to this complex of events but does not include Nahum in his discussion.

YHWH, as does Joel 2:32[3:5]. Overall, Nahum's perspective is arguably closest to Habakkuk and Obadiah, both of which also focus on one nation in the present (Babylon, Edom) and depict its fall as a prologue to the Day of YHWH. Nahum's description of these events as a theophany is most similar to Habakkuk's, and mutual influence is possible even if it remains beyond proof.[115]

Apart from the theme of the Day of YHWH, evidence for Nahum's possible influence on other books of the Twelve (or vice versa) is mostly limited to specific passages. James D. Nogalski, for example, has argued that a network of redactional "catchwords" links Nahum 1:2-8 with Micah 7:18-20, with Micah being the earlier text.[116] This suggestion has been challenged by Gerlinda Baumann, who sees the two passages as bound together by the themes of divine wrath and judgment instead. For her part, Ruth Scoralick has argued that both passages are dependent upon Exodus 34:6-7 (on which see later in this chapter).[117] Others have suggested that the theophanic psalm of Nahum 1:2-8 was added when Nahum was integrated in the developing collection of the Minor Prophets, especially in light of Hosea 4:3, Amos 1:2, and Micah 1:3.[118] Walter Dietrich contends that

---

[115] Kessler, "Nahum-Habakuk als Zweiprophetenschrift," argues that Nah 1:2-8 was composed to connect Nahum to Habakkuk before both books were added to what was to become the Book of the Twelve.

[116] Nogalski, *Literary Precursors*, 170.

[117] Gerlinde Baumann, *Gottes Gewalt im Wandel: Traditionsgeschichtliche und intertextuelle Studien zu Nahum 1,2–8*, WMANT 108 (Neukirchen-Vluyn: Neukirchener, 2005), 186–87; Scoralick, *Gottes Güte und Gottes Zorn: Die Gottesprädikationen in Exodus 34,6f. und ihre intertextuellen Beziehungen zum Zwölfprophetenbuch*, HBS 33 (Freiburg: Herder, 2002), 188–96.

[118] For example, Burkard M. Zapff, "The Perspective of the Nations in the Book of Micah as a 'Systematization' of the Nations' Role in Joel, Jonah and Nahum: Reflections on a Context-Oriented Exegesis," in *Thematic Threads in the Book of the Twelve*, ed. Paul L. Redditt and Aaron Schart, BZAW 325 (Berlin: de Gruyter, 2003), 292–312 (300).

Nahum's psalm was added to the book at the same time that Habakkuk 3:1–19 and Zephaniah 3:9–20 were added to those books, when Jewish religious thought adopted a supranational perspective in which Israel and the nations are diametrically opposed groups in world ruled only by Yhwh.[119] However, the limitation of this perspective to a late period in Israelite religious thought is unlikely. Insofar as these influences or connections depend on verbal or thematic correspondences, it is very difficult to demonstrate dependence.[120]

Nahum Elsewhere in the Old Testament

A number of links also exist between Nahum and other Old Testament books, although disagreement regarding the dating of many of the texts complicates attempts to establish the direction of influence with confidence.[121] The relation between Nahum and Isaiah (the dating of which is still vigorously contested) is a case in point. Some of the material sometimes attributed to First Isaiah of Jerusalem in the late eighth century (e.g., Isa 5:25–30; 10:5–34) draws on Assyrian sources or ideology, as does Nahum, so that the later prophetic book is akin to the older one.[122] Other cases are harder to evaluate. If Isaiah 52:1, 7 is older than Nahum 1:15, the latter text has presumably drawn upon the (Second) Isaiah text, which has a large, eschatological horizon that reaches beyond the return from exile in order to identify the fall of Assyria as "a partial

---

[119] Walter Dietrich, *Nahum, Habakkuk, Zefanja*, IEKAT (Stuttgart: Kohlhammer, 2014), 17.

[120] For a survey of the more plausible cases of influence or dependence between Nahum and other biblical books, see Daniel C. Timmer, "Nahum, Book of," in *Dictionary of the New Testament Use of the Old Testament*, ed. G. K. Beale et al. (Grand Rapids, MI: Baker Academic, 2023), 556–60, on which I occasionally draw in these sections.

[121] This question has been surveyed by Fabry, *Nahum*, 94–104, 113.

[122] So Fabry, *Nahum*, 96.

fulfillment of the Isaianic promise."¹²³ Alternatively, if Isaiah is later and has drawn on Nahum, the citation would depict exiled Judeans' return as much more significant than Judah's deliverance from Assyria in the seventh century. In broader terms, passages in Isaiah and a few in Jeremiah (Jer 30:7–15; 46:2–12) share with Nahum its perspective on the guilty status of non-Israelite nations, on YHWH's prerogative and justice in punishing them, and on YHWH's commitment to deliver Israel/Judah.

Key portions of the Book of Exodus are more commonly accepted to be earlier than Nahum, and share a number of interesting connections with it.¹²⁴ A number of phrases from Exodus 32–34 appear in the opening hymn of Nahum 1, including Exodus 20:5 or 34:14 in Nahum 1:2 ("a jealous and avenging God"), Exodus 34:6 and 32:11 in Nahum 1:3a ("YHWH is patient" and "great in power"), Exodus 34:7 in Nahum 1:3b ("will by no means leave the guilty unpunished"), and Exodus 33:19 in Nahum 1:7 ("YHWH is good"). Nahum draws on this highly significant Exodus passage, which highlights YHWH's justice and grace toward his sinful people, to show that God interacts with the world at large with the same commitment to justice and penchant for mercy.¹²⁵ At the same time, Nahum accentuates

---

¹²³ Timmer, "Nahum, Book of," 557.
¹²⁴ See the brief defense of the J and E sources (to which Exodus 32–34 are often thought to be indebted) as pre-exilic in William H. C. Propp, *Exodus 1–18*, AB 2 (New York: Doubleday, 1999), 48–49. Contrast Thomas B. Dozeman, *Exodus*, ECC (Grand Rapids, MI: Eerdmans, 2009), 48, who dates the texts to the postexilic period.
¹²⁵ Timmer, "Nahum, Book of," 558. A careful reading and interpretation of the passage is offered by Brent A. Strawn, "YHWH's Poesie: The Gnadenformel (Exodus 34:6b–7), the Book of Exodus, and Beyond," in *Biblical Poetry and the Art of Close Reading*, ed. J. Blake Couey and Elaine T. James (Cambridge: Cambridge University Press, 2018), 237–56.

the danger that the global theophany described in 1:2–8 poses to earth's inhabitants by sandwiching the first element linked to the possibility of deliverance (divine patience in 1:3a) between repeated affirmations of divine wrath and justice. This same emphasis delays the mention of the only other feature that raises the hope of surviving divine wrath against sin until 1:7, after a rhetorical question that seems to deny that escape is possible (1:6). Nahum's interpretation of God's justice and mercy toward Israel at Sinai puts divine justice in the foreground, and ends on a very somber note compared to the covenant reestablishment that concludes the narrative interlude in Exodus 32–34. These contrasts emphasize the finality of God's theophanic return to judge the world in Nahum 1:2–8.

Early Judaism

Since Nahum was first composed in Hebrew, its translation as part of the Greek Old Testament (known as the Septuagint or LXX) around the third century BCE reveals the translator's interest in Nahum's continuing relevance. The LXX seems to have followed a Hebrew text quite close to the one preserved by later Hebrew tradition, but in addition to smoothing the Greek text the translator "cautiously actualized" and "eschatologically unpacked" the text, giving an apocalyptic cast to the book's military imagery.[126] For example, Nahum 1:6 LXX speaks of the "melting of the powers," and 1:3 LXX equates God's arrival with the "end."[127] The translator's handling of the book's anthropological and cosmological material leads Fabry to conclude that the translator's background

---

[126] Summarizing Fabry, *Nahum*, 114 (my translation).

[127] Heinz-Josef Fabry, "Naoum/Nahum," in *Introduction to the Septuagint*, ed. Siegfried Kreuzer, trans. D. A. Brenner and P. Altmann (Baylor: Baylor University Press, 2019), 469–73 (471–72).

was that of Hellenistic Judaism.[128] The generally conservative approach to Nahum's translation in the LXX is comparable to how the other Minor Prophets were handled in the LXX, and a scholarly consensus holds that all Twelve were translated by the same individual.[129]

Much more creative interpretation of Nahum can be found in the slightly later Dead Sea Scrolls, first discovered at Qumran in 1946–47 and written (in the case of those writings composed at Qumran) between roughly 150 BCE and 50 CE. This highly varied collection of biblical, interpretative, sectarian, and other works contains partial manuscript evidence of Nahum (4Q82) and an interpretative work known as the *Nahum Pesher* (4QpNah = 4Q169).[130] A *pesher* ("interpretation") characteristically offers explicit identifications for the fulfillments or referents of biblical prophecies. The *Nahum Pesher* does so, for example, by identifying the Seleucid king Demetrius III (d. 88 BCE), who attempted to expand his territory south from Syria, as the lion of Nahum 2:11[12] who entered his den, which is identified as Jerusalem (4QpNah frgs. 3 + 4 i).[131] This practice of identifying a biblical referent with a contemporary one is evident throughout the *Nahum Pesher*. In light of the complex relation of Nahum 1:2–8 to the rest of the book, it is interesting that the author of the *Nahum Pesher* sees the

---

[128] Fabry, *Nahum*, 114.
[129] Jennifer M. Dines, "The Minor Prophets," in *The T&T Clark Companion to the Septuagint*, ed. James K. Aitken (London: Bloomsbury, 2015), 439–55 (439).
[130] Armin Lange, *Biblical Quotations and Allusions in Second Temple Jewish Literature*, JAJS 5 (Göttingen: Vandenhoeck & Ruprecht, 2011), 364, recognize as "uncertain" several quotations of or allusions to Nahum (1:11; 2:12; 3:10) in 1QH^a XIII, XIV, XVI.
[131] Florentino García Martínez, *The Dead Sea Scrolls Translated: The Qumran Texts in English*, 2nd ed. (Leiden and Grand Rapids, MI: Brill and Eerdmans, 1996), 195.

prophet as speaking of both present historical circumstances as well as the distant "final days" (4QpNah frg. 2 ii).

The *Nahum Pesher* is also notable for showing how the Qumran community conceived of its enemies. Here its commitment to moral dualism (good–evil) and determinism, according to which God has predestined the Qumran group and its enemies to contrasting fates, dovetail with its condemnations of "the other."[132] In addition to imitating the literary style of its precursor by means of "allusions" and "explicit historical references," the *pesher* reflects the belief of the Qumran sectarians that their interpretation of the Hebrew Scriptures "was controlled by the presence of the 'Holy Spirit' who dwelled only at Qumran" in the community itself.[133] This gave the *pesher* unsurpassed authority in the eyes of the community.

Another example of Nahum's reception in early Judaism appears in the Book of Tobit, composed sometime around 200 BCE but set in the early seventh century.[134] The story follows Tobit, an Israelite exiled to Assyria who settled in Nineveh and lived a life of exemplary faithfulness to the Torah. At the end of his eventful life, Tobit warns his son Tobiah and daughter-in-law Sarah to leave Nineveh for Media: "I believe the word of God that Nahum spoke

---

[132] Shani L. Berrin, *The Pesher Nahum Scroll from Qumran: An Exegetical Study of 4Q169*, STDJ 53 (Leiden: Brill, 2004), 302–4.

[133] Timothy H. Lim, *Pesharim*, Companion to the Qumran Scrolls (Sheffield: Sheffield Academic, 2002), 79; James H. Charlesworth, "Revelation and Perspicacity in Qumran Hermeneutics?", in *The Dead Sea Scrolls and Contemporary Culture: Proceedings of the International Conference held at the Israel Museum, Jerusalem (July 6–8, 2008)*, ed. Adolfo D. Roitman, Lawrence H. Schiffman, and Shani Tzoref, STDJ 93 (Leiden: Brill, 2011), 161–80 (161).

[134] A comprehensive list of references to Nahum in the Rabbinic corpus can be found in Caleb T. Friedman (ed.), *A Scripture Index to Rabbinic Literature* (Peabody, MA: Hendrickson Academic, 2021), 401.

about Nineveh, that all these things will take place and overtake Assyria and Nineveh" (Tob 14:4). Tobit ties the city's destruction to its "wickedness" and "deceit," accepting Nahum's understanding of Assyria's guilt and of divine justice (cf. Nah 1:11; 3:1, 19).[135]

The New Testament and Early Christianity
While Nahum's contribution to the New Testament is rarely highlighted by direct citation (Nah 1:6 in Rom 6:17; Nah 1:15 in Acts 10:36; Rom 10:15; Eph 6:15), the book is not for that reason unimportant.[136] The Book of Nahum contributes to the New Testament primarily by developing, in parallel with descriptions of Assyria and Babylon in other prophetic books, a representation of Assyria that focuses on it not as a geopolitical entity but as the embodiment of an ideology of opposition to Yhwh that is concretized in its imperial project. The theological and geopolitical dimensions of Assyria so understood are complemented by idolatrous self-aggrandizement. The critique of the Assyrian monarch in Nahum 1:9–10, 14, and especially the taunts against Nineveh in Nahum 3, build an image of Assyria in which its violence, pride, idolatry, divination, and economic power all serve its imperial project.

Biblical and other ancient Near Eastern representations of Assyria/Nineveh and Babylon lend further weight to seeing Nineveh as often represented in Old Testament prophetic books as the beginning of a trope later applied to Babylon, with Nahum as a contributor to this development. The blend of military, theological, and moral critique evident in Nahum is also prominent in Isaiah's descriptions of Assyria (Isa 5:25–30; 10:5–34) and of

---

[135] Carey A. Moore, "Tobit, Book of," *ABD* 6:585–95.
[136] See Steve Moyise, "The Minor Prophets in Paul," in *The Minor Prophets in the New Testament*, ed. Maarten J. J. Menken and Steve Moyise, LNTS 377 (London: Bloomsbury Academic, 2009), 97–114 (110).

Babylon (13:19; 14:3–23; 21:1–10; 46–47). Interestingly, the close relationship of these two cities (whether of parity or of contrast) is also evident in a number of Neo-Assyrian sources.[137] Most notably, Sennacherib's description of the rebuilding of Nineveh presents it "as an antithesis to the destruction of Babylon," with all the religious and ideological baggage that entailed.[138]

In the Book of Revelation, the references to a "prostitute" drinking blood from a cup and characterized by sexual immorality, divination, extravagant wealth, and blasphemy (Rev 17:1–6) are clear echoes of the role of Yhwh's perpetual enemy, previously played by Assyria (especially in Nah 3) and Babylon. Since Babylon had fallen long before the Book of Revelation was composed, its use of "Babylon" is clearly not a simple historical reference. On the contrary, Revelation's "Babylon" remains a danger in the author's day, and he insists that it will continue to wreak havoc far into the future. The divine judgments of Revelation 16–19 that will end world history thus target neither Babylon nor Rome tout court, but "the *systems* – political, economic and religious – which oppose God and his righteousness and are symbolized by the beast, the false prophet, Babylon, and the kings of the earth."[139]

The moral-ideological identity of Assyria in Nahum is also part of its development of the theme of the Day of Yhwh, which in Nahum is prefigured by the fall of Assyria and anticipated in the poem in 1:2–8. Along with most of the other prophetic books,

---

[137] Stephanie Dalley, "Babylon as a Name for Other Cities Including Babylon," in *Proceedings of the 51st Rencontre Assyriologique Internationale*, ed. Robert D. Biggs, Jennie Myers, and Martha T. Roth, SAOC 62 (Chicago: The Oriental Institute of the University of Chicago, 2008), 25–34.
[138] Dalley, "Babylon as a Name," 29.
[139] Richard Bauckham, *The Theology of the Book of Revelation*, NTT (Cambridge: Cambridge University Press, 1993), 102.

Nahum contributes to this theme a strong emphasis on the punitive aspect of this cataclysmic event (cf. Jesus's Olivet discourse, Matt 24–25). This aspect is emphasized to such an extent in Nahum that the element of deliverance appears clearly only once (Nah 1:7), and the corresponding arrival of Yhwh's everlasting kingdom is not developed at all (contrast the fundamental emphasis on the Kingdom of God/Heaven having come with Jesus, in Mark 1:15 and many other contexts).[140] Jesus's teaching in the Gospels holds that this event includes the judgment and restoration of Israel, a rough parallel to the distinction between those who are punished and those who are delivered in Nahum 1:2–8.[141] In the Pauline and Petrine corpora the Day of the Lord is similarly two-sided.

Early Christian authors frequently used Nahum in their homilies and theological works. Theodore of Mopsuestia (south-central Turkey, d. 428) read Jonah and Nahum as earlier and later snapshots of Assyrian history, respectively, with Nineveh's repentance during the time of Jonah being short-lived and the Ninevites returning to their former violence thereafter. While in the Book of Jonah "God gave a demonstration of his characteristic grace in suddenly changing" the Ninevites "for the better," Nahum mentions the retribution that will come upon Assyria "for displaying their arrogance against both the Israelites and Jerusalem" as well as against God.[142] Theodore's exposition of Nahum underlines human moral responsibility and divine justice with respect to the

---

[140] See the thorough discussion in G. R. Beasley-Murray, *Jesus and the Kingdom of God* (Grand Rapids, MI: Eerdmans, 1986).

[141] See Steven M. Bryan, *Jesus and Israel's Traditions of Judgement and Restoration*, SNTSMS 117 (Cambridge: Cambridge University Press, 2002), especially 21–87.

[142] Robert C. Hill, *Theodore of Mopsuestia: Commentary on the Twelve Prophets*, The Fathers of the Church 108 (Washington, DC: Catholic University of America Press, 2004), 247.

Ninevites, who sin "against God and his own," and with respect to Judah, which was guilty of "impiety and sinfulness."[143] It is thus good news indeed that God "is very loving and very practised in bestowing favors on those who look to him and are fearful of his threats."[144]

The interpretation of Nahum offered by Jerome (ca. 347–419; his commentary on Nahum was completed in 391 or 392) understood Nahum on both a literal level, in which its message had reference to Judeans living under Assyrian oppression, and a spiritual level, in which the book threatened judgment against those "who oppose God and reject the safety of the church."[145] Jerome's approach captures Assyria's opposition to Yhwh and Judah, on the one hand, and the global problem of human sin that Yhwh comes to punish, on the other (1:2–8), even as it connects the Christian church with "those who seek refuge" in Yhwh.

PAST AND PRESENT RECEPTION OF NAHUM

Nahum's powerful imagery, strong rhetoric, and passionate response to oppression and injustice can hardly leave the reader unaffected or nonchalant. It is thus not surprising that examples of Nahum's reception (its "use, impact and influence") in Western culture abound.[146] Robert Lowth (1710–87), author of the classic

---

[143] Hill, *Theodore of Mopsuestia*, 247.
[144] Hill, *Theodore of Mopsuestia*, 253.
[145] Edward Ball, "Nahum," in *The SCM Dictionary of Biblical Interpretation*, ed. R. J. Coggins and J. L. Houlden (London: SCM, 1990), 486–88 (487). The date of Jerome's commentary is proposed by R. P. Gordon, *Studies in the Targum to the Twelve Prophets: From Nahum to Malachi*, VTSup 51 (Leiden: Brill, 1994), 25.
[146] For this definition of "reception," see Emma England and William J. Lyons, "Explorations in the Reception of the Bible," in *Reception History and Biblical*

Lectures on the Sacred Poetry of the Hebrews (1753), thought that poetry owes "its essence to the primordial impulse of religion."[147] The beauty that Lowth found in ancient Hebrew poetry and its import for "sublime" religious expression led him to rank Nahum as unparalleled within the Minor Prophets in terms of "boldness, ardour, and sublimity," if not quite the equal of Isaiah, which "abounds in such transcendent excellencies" that it was "the most perfect model of the prophetic poetry."[148]

Depictions of elements of Nahum's message in visual art existed in the early Christian period and appear on the walls of churches as mosaics, and perhaps most frequently as illustrations in Bibles.[149] One such example, in the 1534 Wittenberg Bible, makes Nahum relevant to the sixteenth century by depicting him "preaching in the harbour of a German town to a group of merchants while cargo is unloaded from a nearby ship by crane."[150] The placement of the image just before Nahum's first chapter makes the whole book a warning to "inhabitants of prosperous mercantile communities" such as Nineveh (or a German seaport), who should avoid Nineveh's dishonesty, extortion, injustice, and violence.[151]

Studies: *Theory and Practice*, ed. Emma England and William John Lyons, Scriptural Traces 6 (London: Bloomsbury T & T Clark, 2015), 3–16 (6).

[147] Jordan E. Skornik, "Between the Study of Religion and Literary Analysis: Robert Lowth on the Species of Prophetic Poetry," *JR* 99 (2019): 492–529 (493, 496).

[148] Skornik, "Between the Study of Religion," 508, 515; Robert Lowth, *Lectures on the Sacred Poetry of the Hebrews*, 2 vols., trans. G. Gregory (London: J. Johnson, 1778), 2:99, 2:85. Lowth does refer to Nahum and Isaiah side by side, once each in Lectures 12 and 19.

[149] See the wide variety of representations surveyed by Richard J. Coggins and Jin H. Han, *Six Minor Prophets through the Centuries*, BBC (Chichester: Wiley-Blackwell, 2011), 11–14, where the following example is mentioned.

[150] Bridget Heal, *A Magnificent Faith: Art and Identity in Lutheran Germany* (Oxford: Oxford University Press, 2017), 31.

[151] Heal, *A Magnificent Faith*, 31 (the image appears as plate 3).

Nahum's practical relevance as indicated by its inclusion in lectionaries has slowly declined over time. In the *Book of Common Prayer* (1662) each of its three chapters were a reading, with one (chapter 3) coinciding with a minor feast (Holy Cross Day).[152] The 1969 Roman Catholic lectionary lists only a few passages for one day (2:1–3; 3:1–3, 6–7), and the Revised Common Lectionary (2005) includes only Nahum 1 and 2:1–2.[153] This tendency arguably reflects interpretative trends that increasingly find parts of Nahum's message problematic in some fashion – often unreasonably so. Be that as it may, there is a large body of literature that treats problematic issues such as (divine) violence and gender that has attracted a great deal of attention and that can help address problems raised by modern sensibilities. The following sections deal with objections to, and justifications of, some of these elements in Nahum.

Nahum's Use of Violence as the Object of Moral Critique
There is no doubt that the Book of Nahum both critiques and endorses violence, depending on who exercises violence and how and why it is exercised. Assyria's violence is motivated by an imperial project that glorifies the king and his deities, is excessive in degree and scope, and treats others with disdain or worse. Assyria's violence is therefore thoroughly wrong and merits punishment. On the other hand, as presented by Nahum, Yhwh's violence against Assyria demonstrates his unique deity over against the claims of the empire's deities, delivers victims from the empire's clutches, and vitiates the imperial ideology that validated

---

[152] Coggins and Han, *Six Minor Prophets*, 15.
[153] Coggins and Han, *Six Minor Prophets*, 15; Consultation on Texts, *Revised Common Lectionary: Daily Readings* (Minneapolis, MN: Fortress, 2005), 60, 78.

Assyria's role on the world stage. YHWH's divine violence establishes a moral and religious order that Nahum unquestioningly affirms, although the book does not explicitly evaluate the human violence that achieves it.[154]

The coexistence of these two very different responses to two very different kinds of violence in Nahum poses significant problems for some interpreters. In the eyes of not a few, YHWH is "a god who can only restore justice with violence,"[155] and the conviction that all violence is necessarily wrong entails a critique of such a deity. Maré and Serfontein attempt to resolve the problem of YHWH's violence by dissociating that deity, who on their view is "only a rhetorical-ideological construct of a society whose social tools were violence and bloodshed," from the deity identified as YHWH by much or all of the rest of the Old Testament.[156] While this might solve the theological problem of divine violence in Nahum, such an approach creates another difficulty by running contrary to the book's explicit identification of the deity who takes vengeance as none other than Israel's historic covenant partner (among other things, the echo of Exod 34:6–7 in Nahum stands out as

---

[154] An implicit condemnation of all violence apparently lies behind Tamar Kamionkowski's assertion that "any attempt to condone divine violence in the Hebrew Bible cannot help but become part of the system of violence"; see Tamar Kamionkowski, "The 'Problem' of Violence in Prophetic Literature: Definitions as the Real Problem," in *Religion and Violence: The Biblical Heritage*, ed. David A. Bernat and Jonathan Klawans, Recent Research in Biblical Studies 2 (Sheffield: Sheffield Phoenix, 2007), 38–46 (39). Her assumption that the texts are ideological impositions "of violence on the divine" (40) without referential value essentially denies that these texts have any theological significance.

[155] Leonard Maré and Johan Serfontein, "The Violent, Rhetorical-Ideological God of Nahum," *OTE* 22 (2009): 175–85 (179).

[156] Maré and Serfontein, "God of Nahum," 179. David G. Garber, Jr., "Facing Traumatizing Texts: Reading Nahum's Nationalistic Rage," *RevExp* 105 (2008): 285–94, suggests a similar approach.

particularly important). Beyond pacifism, utilitarian approaches to punishment also assert that punishment understood as deprivation of any kind is inherently bad. Such approaches affirm, however, that moral concerns with violence can be overridden if, and only if, the punishment "prevents even greater suffering, or if it brings about greater good."[157] On such a view, Yhwh's violence against Assyria would be justifiable even if it is not morally good. Justification of God's violence against Nineveh is certainly in line with Nahum's theology, but the transcendent nature of Yhwh the creator and the originally "very good" nature of his creation pose difficulties for a moral critique of divine violence.[158]

Another perspective on Nahum's condemnation of (at least some) human violence while exonerating Yhwh of wrongdoing in the punishment of the guilty focuses on the question of agency. While Nahum insists on Yhwh's involvement in the fall of Assyria, the book does not present Yhwh as directly confronting Assyria on the historical scene. There is also no doubt that the Babylonians considered their conquest of Assyria to be undertaken without compulsion (certainly on the part of Yhwh).[159] These and other considerations argue for an understanding of causation or agency that involves both human and divine aspects.[160] While the

---

[157] C. L. Ten, "Crime and Punishment," in *A Companion to Ethics*, ed. Peter Singer, Blackwell Companions to Philosophy (London: Blackwell, 1993), 366–72 (366).

[158] These and related concerns are helpfully discussed in Daniel Castelo, *Theological Theodicy*, Cascade Companions (Eugene, OR: Cascade Books, 2012).

[159] See the Babylonian Chronicle's report of the battle of Carchemish in 605 in Alan Millard, "The Babylonian Chronicle (1.137)," *COS* 1:467–68.

[160] See Alfred J. Freddoso, "God's General Concurrence with Secondary Causes: Pitfalls and Prospects," *American Catholic Philosophical Quarterly* 67 (1994): 131–56.

Old Testament does not develop a detailed theory of immediate and ultimate causes, it does assert that Yhwh's superintendence of human agents undoes neither Yhwh's sovereign direction of the events nor the agency and responsibility of human actors (Isa 10:5–11; Zech 1:15).[161] If we allow that a historical event can be the result of both divine and human agency and volition, the slippage between the presumably unflawed divine will to use historical circumstances to punish the guilty and the human agent's imperfect exercise of violence can be seen as inevitable for at least two reasons: (1) the involvement of flawed human beings motivated by greed, imperialism, and so on; and (2) the related historical contingencies. It thus does not follow that the end goal of punishment is irreparably and morally wrong.[162]

It is worth noting here that rather than claiming that "nations employed as Yhwh's agent are apparently permitted to do what the nations they punish are not," Nahum nowhere suggests that Babylon would conquer Assyria "without incurring guilt."[163] The book's evaluation of the *result* (deliverance from Assyrian oppression) as good can and should be distinguished from a moral evaluation of the *means* by which the desired result is achieved, not least because Nahum abstains from any such evaluation, whether positive or negative, of human involvement in that event.

---

[161] See the varied interpretations of this relationship in Stephen B. Chapman, "Miqreh and YHWH: Fate, Chance, Simultaneity, and Providence," in *Divine Doppelgängers: YHWH's Ancient Look-Alikes*, ed. Collin Cornell (University Park, PA: Eisenbrauns, 2020), 181–200, who interconnects Yhwh's agency and chance by means of providence.

[162] Terence E. Fretheim, "'I Was Only a Little Angry': Divine Violence in the Prophets," *Int* 58 (2004): 65–75, notes that "the use of divine violence is never an end in itself; it has a twofold purpose: judgment and salvation" (371). His discussion of God's use of human agents is also helpful (368–70).

[163] Crouch, *War and Ethics*, 111.

The motivation of Babylon's conquest of Assyria by factors other than the pursuit of justice on an international level also argues for the plausibility of distinguishing human and divine agency, motive, and intention, even if doing so does not remove the role of faith in accepting divine justice as such.[164]

The question of God's role in human history brings us to the center of Nahum's ethic. The Book of Nahum assumes that YHWH, as the creator of humanity, has by virtue of that role (and relationship) the right and responsibility to punish human wrongs.[165] God's longstanding relationship with Israel/Judah amply illustrates this, and the extension of divine punishment beyond the covenant people demonstrates God's concern for the oppressed, whether Israelite or not. Indeed, Nahum affirms that without divine intervention to punish and deliver at the end of history (the ultimate point of reference in light of 1:2–8), no final resolution to the problem of evil is possible. Moreover, in that eschatological context Nahum foresees God intervening directly, taking back the exercise of power once delegated to human beings and thereby bringing about perfect justice.[166]

---

[164] Roger Scruton, *The Soul of the World* (Princeton: Princeton University Press, 2014), 191.

[165] "Forceful resistance to evil is the prerogative of God," according to J. Gordon McConville, "Human 'Dominion' and Being 'Like God': An Exploration of Peace, Violence and Truth in the Old Testament," in *Encountering Violence in the Bible*, ed. Markus Zehnder and Hallvard Hagelia, The Bible in the Modern World 55 (Sheffield: Sheffield Phoenix, 2013), 194–206 (205–6).

[166] Cf. McConville, "Human 'Dominion,'" 201. Concursus, the parallel and innocuous operation of divine and human activity, seems to preserve both the relative freedom of human beings as agents without "implying that human action and divine action belong in the same genus," as noted by Steven J. Duby, "'For I Am God, Not a Man': Divine Repentance and the Creator–Creature Distinction," *JTI* 12 (2018): 149–69 (156). Contrast the position of Terence Fretheim, "The Repentance of God: A Key to Evaluating Old

While the significant discontinuity between the present and God's eschatological intervention makes any evaluation of the latter inherently premature, the reader of Nahum is left with the question of what to do in the face of evil in the present. Interestingly, Nahum avoids involving Judean arms or commending Israelite imperialism in his proposed solution to Assyrian oppression, most clearly by giving no role whatsoever to the Judean monarchy. In this connection, and as a segue to what follows, it must be observed that some interpreters argue that the biblical mandate for humanity to bear and reflect the image of God can entail "the use of force to resist evil" even if human justice inevitably falls short of "perfect (divine) judgment."[167] This is true not only of retributive punishment but of other forms as well, including those that involve other forms of "censure" that punishment communicates.[168]

Nahum's Use of Violence as the Basis for Moral Critique
Nahum's vivid descriptions of Nineveh's wealth and destruction have captured the attention of a number of Western authors over the last two centuries. This was due especially to the perception of the ancient world as exotic and to resurgent interest in ancient Nineveh following its excavation by A. H. Layard in the 1840s and the flood of previously unknown texts that followed. This newfound knowledge of ancient empires gave new impetus to moral evaluation of their use of power and violence. A notable example is Rudyard Kipling's 1897 "Recessional," composed at the height of the British Empire's power as a "prophetic admonition

---

Testament God-Talk," *HBT* 10 (1988): 47–70, reprinted in his *What Kind of God? Collected Essays of Terence E. Fretheim*, ed. Michael J. Chan and Brent A. Strawn, Siphrut 14 (Winona Lake, IN: Eisenbrauns, 2015), 40–57.
[167] McConville, "Human 'Dominion' and Being 'Like God,'" 206.
[168] Duff, "Punishment," 343.

against nationalistic pomp and pride and self-destructive intoxication with power."[169] Kipling compares the Great Britain of his day with Nineveh and reflects on the possibility that God might do away with the British Empire for the same reasons he had destroyed Nineveh:

> God of our fathers, known of old,
>   Lord of our far-flung battle-line,
> Beneath whose awful Hand we hold
>   Dominion over palm and pine –
> Lord God of Hosts, be with us yet,
> Lest we forget – lest we forget!
>
> The tumult and the shouting dies;
>   The Captains and the Kings depart:
> Still stands Thine ancient sacrifice,
>   An humble and a contrite heart.
> Lord God of Hosts, be with us yet,
> Lest we forget – lest we forget!
>
> Far-called, our navies melt away;
>   On dune and headland sinks the fire:
> Lo, all our pomp of yesterday
>   Is one with Nineveh and Tyre!
> Judge of the Nations, spare us yet,
> Lest we forget – lest we forget!
>
> If, drunk with sight of power, we loose
>   Wild tongues that have not Thee in awe,
> Such boastings as the Gentiles use,
>   Or lesser breeds without the Law –
> Lord God of Hosts, be with us yet,
> Lest we forget – lest we forget!
>
> For heathen heart that puts her trust
>   In reeking tube and iron shard,

---

[169] Coggins and Han, *Six Minor Prophets*, 10.

> All valiant dust that builds on dust,
>   And guarding, calls not Thee to guard,
>   For frantic boast and foolish word –
> Thy mercy on Thy People, Lord![170]

Quite in keeping with Nahum, Kipling is keenly aware of the danger of the empire's pride in its accomplishments. But rather than condemning the imperial enterprise itself, Kipling seems content to call for a humble imperialism that recognizes God as the source of its legitimation. In light of the absence of nationalism from Nahum's opening hymn and Kipling's moralizing tone, it is highly ironic that Kipling identifies the British population as God's people and its colonized populations as the "lesser breeds." The influence of Kipling's quasi-Christian imperial context on his reception of Nahum represents a constriction and conscription of Nahum's message, and is, in the end, implicitly condemned by it.

Moral reflection on the fall of Nineveh was popular on the other side of the Atlantic as well. The circus performance *The Sublime Historic Bible Spectacle, Fall of Nineveh* (1892), produced by A. Forepaugh and directed by J. Rettig, was advertised as including "battles, feasts, processions, festivals, fetes, and every form of ceremonial seen in Nineveh, Earth's first great metropolis, and civilization's first capital."[171] Reviewers interpreted its lavish performance in terms of the biblical "history of Nineveh and its terrible destruction as probably the most striking example of divine vengeance."[172] The production assumed the significance of Nineveh's fall for the

---

[170] Rudyard Kipling, "Recessional," www.poetryfoundation.org/poem/176152.

[171] *The Cortland Standard and Journal*, Friday, August 5, 1892, p. 4, www.nyshistoricnewspapers.org/lccn/sn91066328/1892-08-05/ed-1/seq-4.pdf.

[172] Kevin M. McGoeugh, "Negotiating the Real and the Hyperreal: Nineteenth-Century Experiences of the Bible in the Context of Ancient Near Eastern Discoveries," *Biblical Reception* 1 (2012): 398–423 (409 n. 32), notes the origins of the performance. The quotation is from *The Boston Evening*

American republic, not least by building on the poorly founded understanding of Nineveh's moral degeneracy promulgated by the Greek historian Ctesias.[173] The one-page synopsis of the program twice makes reference to Jonah's preaching and its (supposed) rejection by the populace, and recounts in detail the "bacchanalian revels" of Assyria's final years, including the king's harem and "dining, drinking, [and] feasting," before ending with a description of Nineveh's fall in fulfillment of Jonah's prophecy.[174] At the center of the last scene stands the Assyrian king, whose last words defy history's judgment upon him: "Time shall quench fully many, A people's records, and a hero's acts, … but even then, Shall spare this deed of mine," referring to his self-immolation.[175] The city's collapse and the death of the king and "the voluptuous beauties that had once served his every desire" left little doubt in the audience's mind that its fate was well-deserved.[176]

A more recent moral critique based on Nahum's presentation of Nineveh appears in Julie Woods's argument that the West at the beginning of the twenty-first century resembles the Assyrian capital. Asserting that "maintaining justice" is one of the Bible's fundamental concerns, Woods critiques the West especially for its violence (with reference to the Iraq War that began in 2003)

Transcript, Saturday, June 4, 1892, p. 3, https://news.google.com/newspapers?nid=2249&dat=18920603&id=z28-AAAAIBAJ&sjid=mlkMAAAAIBAJ&pg=6768,5573014&hl=en.

[173] Burke O. Long, "The Circus," in *The Blackwell Companion to Bible and Culture*, ed. John F. A. Sawyer, Wiley-Blackwell Companions to Religion (London: Wiley-Blackwell, 2012), 365–80 (370).

[174] Cited in Long, "The Circus," 370–71.

[175] Adam Forepaugh Shows, *The Sublime Historical Bible Spectacle of Nineveh* (Buffalo: Courier Lithograph Co., 1892), quoting G. G. Byron, *Sardanapalus, a Tragedy; The Two Foscari, a Tragedy; Cain, a Mystery* (London: John Murray, 1821), Act V, scene 1, cited in Long, "The Circus," 371.

[176] Long, "The Circus," 367.

and its oppressive consolidation and misuse of wealth compared to the majority world. Although Woods contends that the West's "oppressive cruelty has reached far more people than Nineveh's ever did,"[177] she ultimately concludes that identifying the West with Nineveh is inaccurate since "it is questionable whether there is any nation that is not indicted by Nahum's message." She consequently broadens her critique beyond the West and contends that in a global context, Nahum provides reasons for the Christian church "to preach Nahum's message to the nations" and to "repent." Appropriate forms of repentance include avoiding participation in unfair economic practices, showing solidarity with the oppressed in meaningful ways, and expressing "empathy and sympathy for the perpetrator under God's judgment" as well as for the victims of violence.[178] Woods's condemnation and call to repentance hinge on the affirmations that "God alone is the avenger" and that divine "[j]udgment [is] a necessary part of the whole order of salvation history."[179]

Ongoing conflict and hardship in the Middle East, Africa, and elsewhere continue to provide egregious examples of human suffering on the part of the weak due to the blunt exercise of power by the strong. Reports of drowned refugees fleeing war, images of children killed when bombs strike their school, and large-scale oppression of religious or ethnic minorities make inescapable the question of "our responsibility and response to the persistence of evil, tyranny, violence, and injustice beyond our own borders."[180]

---

[177] Julie Woods, "The West as Nineveh: How Does Nahum's Message of Judgement Apply to Today?" *Them* 31 (2005): 7–37 (21, 24).
[178] Woods, "The West as Nineveh," 21–27, 29.
[179] Woods, "The West as Nineveh," 27.
[180] D. N. Premnath, "Nahum," in *Dictionary of Scripture and Ethics*, ed. Joel B. Green (Grand Rapids, MI: Baker Academic, 2011), 535.

Nahum challenges its readers to see the world as Yhwh's creation and as responsible to him but terribly flawed and unable to achieve full justice by itself. Yhwh's use of a human agent to bring justice to Assyria suggests that in Nahum as elsewhere in the Old Testament, humanity remains responsible for pursuing justice tempered by mercy as best it can, although for pacifists the option of violence will remain impossible. Human justice will not, of course, bring an end to all injustice with its resultant suffering and destruction, but this hard fact should not make us inert before the problem. Nahum recognizes that human actions (even those not intended to bring justice) can at times – in God's providence – produce good, but Nahum qualifies that recognition by reserving to God alone the full and permanent restoration of moral order.

CHAPTER 3

The Theology of the Book of Habakkuk

It is not difficult to understand why Piotr Krakowczyk entitles his reflections on the Book of Habakkuk, "The World Seems to Be Falling Apart: Violence, Injustice and Ecological Degradation."[1] Regrettably, the concerns expressed in the Book of Habakkuk are also surprisingly relevant in the early twenty-first century. An imposing number of evils and crises plague much of the world at present: a decade-long civil war in Syria, the resurgence of ISIS in Africa, deeply rooted racism and recurrent police violence in numerous countries, mass detention and forced reeducation of Uighur Muslims in China, and a dizzying spectrum of environmental and ecological damage around the globe. These lamentable situations are all the more serious because many of them involve the acquiescence or direct involvement of governments that are ostensibly responsible for protecting their citizens or corporations who satisfy their shareholders at great cost to the environment and ultimately to the public at large.[2]

Habakkuk is no stranger to the worst of these problems, nor does he simply point the finger at others. He recognizes injustice

---

[1] Krakowczyk, in *SEDOS Bulletin* 41 (2009): 125–33.
[2] See, on this latter point, Michael H. Floyd, "The Hope of Habakkuk in the Anthropocene Age," in *Theodicy and Hope in the Book of the Twelve*, ed. George Athas, Beth Stovell, Daniel C. Timmer, and Colin Toffelmire, LHBOTS 705 (London: T&T Clark, 2021), 194–213.

in his own society as well as on the international scene and longs deeply to see justice established, but finds himself (and others) unable to bring about the necessary change. His tracing of the problem's roots to human behaviors and values, and his argument that nowhere is injustice more likely to flourish than in settings where human beings exercise power, convince him that only a transcendent solution involving divine intervention and the human commitment to pursue justice in obedience to God and for the good of one's neighbor will prove viable.

The Book of Habakkuk's exploration of these problems in the context of the last decades of Judah around the year 600 BCE resembles a multi-century itinerary that begins in the radically imperfect world in which the prophet lives, moves through a near-future in which justice can be achieved only imperfectly, and finally reaches an idyllic destination that is entirely free of rebellion against God and human violence and its perpetrators, and where a transformed humanity flourishes under God's rule and blessing.[3] Looking back, such a time traveler would be often deeply troubled by injustice and wrong along the way but would eventually understand that God's plans are often difficult to trace in real time, that he does not always establish justice right away, and that only God can adequately recompense injustice by holding human beings accountable for their actions.[4] Although Habakkuk

---

[3] Gert T. M. Prinsloo, "From Watchtower to Holy Temple: Reading the Book of Habakkuk as a Spatial Journey," in *Constructions of Space IV: Further Developments in Examining Social Space in Ancient Israel*, ed. Mark K. George, LHBOTS 569 (London and New York: Bloomsbury T&T Clark, 2013), 132–54, works out this idea in a roughly parallel way.

[4] Cf. Angelika Berlejung, "Sin and Punishment: The Ethics of Divine Justice and Retribution in Ancient Near Eastern and Old Testament Texts," *Int* 69 (2015): 272–87 (281): "The final divine judgment over all mortals is a theological necessity, because it is the only way to prove the … justice of God."

takes for granted that no one perfectly conforms to God's ethical ideals, it also presents God as amazingly gracious – far more so than nation-states tend to be, since their laws insist on personal punishment even if an offender recognizes guilt and expresses contrition. In a unique way and to an incomparable degree, God extends grace to those who put their trust in his promises and live in faithfulness, ensuring their well-being and creating justice at the same time.

ISSUES IN THE INTERPRETATION OF HABAKKUK

The historical setting for the Book of Habakkuk is not hard to determine. Biblical authors' interest in the rise of Babylon is difficult to explain prior to the Babylonians' victory over Egypt at Carchemish in 605, and equally implausible after 586, when Jerusalem and the rest of Judah fell to Babylon.[5] Within this roughly twenty-year span, it is plausible but not necessary to tie Judean awareness of Babylon's rise to a specific event, such as the siege of Jerusalem and subsequent deportation of many of its skilled workers and military personnel in 598 BCE (2 Kgs 24:10–16). However, although the literary unit introduced by Habakkuk 1:5 refers to the turn of the seventh century, other parts of the book may have been composed somewhat later, in light of further Babylonian aggression.[6] Regardless of the date(s) assigned to the

---

[5] D. J. Wiseman, *Nebuchadnezzar and Babylon: The Schweich Lectures* (Oxford: Oxford University Press, 1985); Lothar Perlitt, *Die Propheten Nahum, Habakuk, Zephanja*, ATD 25.1 (Göttingen: Vandenhoeck & Ruprecht, 2005), 41–42.

[6] This point is made by Francis I. Andersen, *Habakkuk: A New Translation with Introduction and Commentary*, AB 25 (New York: Doubleday, 2001), 27, and others. Richard Whitekettle, "How the Sheep of Judah Became Fish: Habakkuk 1,14 and the Davidic Monarchy," *Bib* 96 (2015): 273–81, wrongly assumes that the language of 1:14 refers to the historical experience of Judah, rather than to

book's formation, the explicit connections between the book and the prophet Habakkuk in 1:1 and 3:1 were essential to its reception as authentic prophecy in ancient Judah.[7]

Unity and Diversity
Questions regarding the date of Habakkuk's composition are often complicated by competing claims regarding the text's ostensible setting – in this case, Babylon's rise – and the dates some scholars assign to the book's different literary forms, theological perspectives, and other traits.[8] One's understanding of the book's composition and literary development is thus inseparable from the evaluation of the book's literary, historical, and theological features. For example, Hiebert proceeds from the conviction that apocalyptic literature developed suddenly in the early post-exilic period and argues on that basis that the apocalyptic nature of chapter 3 in particular requires that it be dated to the late sixth or early fifth century.[9] Gunneweg similarly argues that the liturgical

---

other nations more generally, and so dates that verse and the rest of 1:12–17 after the exile. Contrast William Holladay, "Plausible Circumstances for the Prophecy of Habakkuk," *JBL* 120 (2001): 123–42, who proposes that the book's component parts can be tied to four settings dating between 605 and 594.

[7] John Hilber, "The Culture of Prophecy and Writing in the Ancient Near East," in *Do Historical Matters Matter to Faith? A Critical Appraisal of Modern and Postmodern Approaches to Scripture*, ed. Dennis Magary and James K. Hoffmeier, foreword by John Woodbridge (Wheaton, IL: Crossway, 2012), 219–41; Seth L. Sanders, "Why Prophecy Became a Biblical Genre," *HBAI* 6 (2017): 26–52.

[8] Helpful overviews of these issues and the different responses to them can be found in the extensive survey of Oskar Dangl, "Habakkuk in Recent Research," *CurBR* 9 (2001): 131–68 (135–57) and the briefer surveys of Grace Ko, *Theodicy in Habakkuk*, PBM (Milton Keynes: Paternoster, 2014), 10–29, and Walter Dietrich, *Nahum, Habakuk, Zefanja*, IEKAT (Stuttgart: W. Kohlhammer, 2014), 93–105.

[9] Theodore Hiebert, *God of My Victory: The Ancient Hymn in Habakkuk 3*, HSM 38 (Atlanta, GA: Scholars, 1986), 137.

elements of the book are later than the rest simply because they are liturgical.[10] Otto argues that the anti-Babylonian tone of 1:15–17 and parts of chapter 2 must be dated to the exilic period, presumably because they can only be understood as a reaction against Babylon's final campaign of violence against Jerusalem in 586.[11] Finally, a variety of arguments based on the relationship of passages in Habakkuk to other parts of the Old Testament, including the Psalms, the hymn of Nahum 1 (for Hab 3:3–15), and the Book of Isaiah (for Hab 2:2), have come to varying conclusions as to the dates of particular parts of Habakkuk.[12]

Not all of these arguments are equally convincing. Arguing for a particular date at which apocalyptic literature entered Hebraic or Jewish circles presupposes that this literary genre existed as such (an "essentialist" view) and that it entered these milieu from the outside. However, understanding literary genres as unchanging, pre-existing entities that must be transferred through cultural contact overlooks the reality that there is no single form of apocalyptic literature. Rather, a genre is something constructed by readers who group together different texts that share some (but almost never all) common features.[13] An essentialist approach also fails to account for how these different proto-apocalyptic or apocalyptic

[10] A. H. J. Gunneweg, "Habakuk und das Problem des leidenden צדיק," ZAW 98 (1986): 400–15 (405).
[11] Eckart Otto, "Die Theologie des Buches Habakuk," VT 35 (1985): 274–95 (283).
[12] See Rainer Kessler, "Nahum–Habakuk als Zweiprophetenschrift: Eine Skizze," in "Wort Jhwhs, das geschah..." (Hos 1,1): Studien zum Zwölfprophetenbuch, ed. Erich Zenger, HBS 35 (Freiburg: Herder, 2002), 149–58; and Dominik Markl, "Hab 3 in intertextueller und kontextueller Sicht," Bib 85 (2004): 99–108.
[13] Genre determinations are both socially constructed and based on the characteristics of the texts in question, whether those characteristics be sentence structure, discourse situations, or the apparent purpose of the texts. See Christoph Unger, Genre, Relevance and Global Coherence: The Pragmatics of Discourse Type (New York: Palgrave Macmillan, 2006), 1–10.

compositions arise in their respective settings.¹⁴ Similarly, the more general method of dating attitudes or theological ideas to the period at which one believes they would have been most pertinent is often too dependent upon the individual's historical reconstruction of the era in question[15] and risks confusing plausibility or possibility with near-certainty.[16] The frequently metaphorical nature of prophetic discourse is often a further impediment to historical precision, since metaphorical descriptions of events can be extremely difficult to correlate directly with a particular historical situation.[17] In such cases, it is better to simply recognize that the textual features at issue are plausible in multiple historical scenarios and to avoid using them for purposes of dating the respective literary units.

Behind almost all these questions lie several foundational criteria that guide the interpreter's decisions.[18] Perhaps none is more

---

[14] Cf. Richard J. Clifford, "The Roots of Apocalypticism in Near Eastern Myth," in *The Encyclopedia of Apocalypticism*, ed. John J. Collins, 3 vols. (New York: Continuum, 2000), 1:3–38. Comparative dating of apocalyptic literature in its various forms is complicated by the similarities of proto-apocalyptic and apocalyptic literature, especially their shared used of large-scale dualisms. The studies of Neil Forsyth, *The Old Enemy: Satan and the Combat Myth* (Princeton, NJ: Princeton University Press, 1989); and Florian Forg, *Die Ursprung der alttestamentlichen Apokalyptik*, ABG 45 (Leipzig: Evangelische Verlagsanstalt, 2013), also suggest caution against overly precise periodization of apocalyptic genres and motifs.

[15] Roy Melugin, "Prophetic Books and the Problem of Historical Reconstruction," in *Prophets and Paradigms: Essays in Honor of Gene M. Tucker*, ed. Stephen Breck Reid, JSOTSup 229 (Sheffield: Sheffield Academic, 1996), 63–78 (76).

[16] Benjamin Sommer, "Dating Pentateuchal Texts and the Perils of Pseudo-Historicism," in *The Pentateuch: International Perspectives on Current Research*, ed. Thomas B. Dozeman, Konrad Schmid, and Baruch W. Schwartz, FAT 78 (Tübingen: Mohr Siebeck, 2011), 85–108.

[17] Melugin, "Prophetic Books," 72.

[18] Valuable discussions of criteria involving epistemology and worldview can be found in Roy A. Harrisville, *Pandora's Box Opened: An Examination and Defense of Historical-Critical Method and Its Master Practitioners*

important than the nature of a literary text. How much variety can a text contain and still be a single, coherent text? Can the diverse literary genres that appear in the Book of Habakkuk all contribute harmoniously to its message?[19] How do materials as diverse in subject matter as the book's biographical and autobiographical elements (1:1, 2–4; 1:12–2:1; 2:2; 3:1, 2, 16–19), the descriptions and woes concerning Babylon (2:6–20), and the recollection of YHWH's past theophanic appearances (3:3–15) form a literary whole?

While Habakkuk is surely more diverse than some other biblical and ancient Near Eastern texts, it is not uniquely or unusually so. For example, *Ludlul Bēl Nēmeqi*, a text from Kassite-period Babylon (fourteenth–twelfth century BCE) that explores the question of individual suffering, contains an impressive mix of genres: autobiographical self-description and lament, theological reflection on the attributes of the god Marduk, detailed medical descriptions of the speaker's physical condition, narratives about those who attempted to help the sufferer, and an account of how a diviner facilitated his healing, all of which give rise to a hymn of praise to Marduk at the end of the text. Even so, *Ludlul* is still clearly a unity. While its transmission inevitably includes textual variants and small additions, there is no reason to propose that

---

(Grand Rapids, MI: Eerdmans, 2014); Markus Reiser, *Bibelkritik und Auslegung der Heiligen Schrift: Beiträge zur Geschichte der biblischen Exegese und Hermeneutik*, WUNT 217 (Tübingen: Mohr Siebeck, 2007); and Ulrich Wilckens, *Theologie des Neuen Testaments: Historische Kritik der historisch-kritischen Exegese*, Theologie des Neuen Testaments 3 (Göttingen: Vandenhoeck & Ruprecht, 2016).

[19] For example, Perlitt, *Propheten*, 42–43, thinks that the three sections of the book (1:2–2:5; 2:6–20; 3:1–19) are so distinct that each has its own history of development, genre, and intention, but sees no evidence of a comprehensive redaction that brought them together.

the text was composed by combining previously separate compositions.[20] The mix of literary genres found in Habakkuk is also not without precedent among ancient Near Eastern prophetic texts. In a seventh-century Neo-Assyrian text, the goddess Ishtar replies to a petition from the mother of king Esarhaddon, which she quotes, creating a sort of dialogue like that in Habakkuk 1, and then addresses Esarhaddon himself at the end of the same text.[21] Simo Parpola's opinion that this text and others in the same collection are transcriptions of "freshly received oracles" represents scholarly consensus, and there is no indication that this oracle is a composite of heterogeneous sources.[22] Such examples, which could easily be multiplied, show that literary variety by itself is not a sufficient ground upon which to assert that a text is incoherent, that its parts cannot be adequately related to one another, or that they arose in different settings at different times.

Ultimately, the answer to the question of a text's essential unity can only be developed as one processes a text in its totality. However, readers must be careful not to impose later standards of literary interpretation upon an ancient text.[23] The unity that the

---

[20] See Andrew R. George and F. N. H. Al-Rawi, "Tablets from the Sippar Library VII: Three Wisdom Texts," *Iraq* 60 (1998): 187–206, esp. 187, 192. Takayoshi Oshima, *Babylonian Poems of Pious Sufferers: Ludlul Bel Nemeqi and the Babylonian Theodicy*, ORA 14 (Tübingen: Mohr Siebeck, 2014), 3–9, argues that it is nearly certain that a fourth tablet (after Table III and before Tablet IV) was lost, but considers the text itself to be integral even if only partially attested at present.

[21] Simo Parpola, *Assyrian Prophecies*, SAA 9 (Helsinki: Helsinki University Press, 1997), 9 (text 1.8).

[22] Parpola, *Assyrian Prophecies*, LIII, LXI, LXIX, LXX.

[23] See, for example, John Van Seters, "Editing the Bible: The Romantic Myths about Authors and Editors," *HBAI* 3 (2014): 343–54; and D. Andrew Teeter and William A. Tooman, "Standards of (In)coherence in Ancient Jewish Literature," *HBAI* 9 (2020): 94–129.

reader finds in the text thus grows out of an effort to find that unity for reasons that are inherent in the text's thematic development, statements, and references:

> A text is said to be coherent if, for a certain reader on a certain hearing/reading, he or she is able to fit its different elements into a single overall mental representation. ... A text comes with the presumption of coherence: that is, if a speaker is presenting something as a text, the hearer is entitled to assume that it will yield a coherent interpretation and will direct his or her efforts accordingly. ... A mental representation for a text does not generally come full-blown into the hearer's mind. Rather, it is shaped in successive stages by trial and error ... he or she modifies that representation, updating it as the discourse unfolds, so that each item of information is accommodated in a plausible way.[24]

Of course, in the event that features that undo continuity within or between sections outweigh those that hold the text together, the text (or parts of it) will be found to be incoherent – in other words, not really a (single) text at all. On the other hand, as long as the text's unifying features predominate, it is a genuine unity, even if it is less unified than some other texts.[25] Our exploration of Habakkuk will attempt to put all its pieces on the table, so to speak, leaving the reader to judge the degree to which the whole which they form is in fact a coherent unity.[26]

---

[24] Robert A. Dooley and Stephen H. Levinsohn, *Analyzing Discourse: A Manual of Basic Concepts* (Dallas, TX: SIL International, 2001), 11

[25] Francis Landy, "Three Sides of a Coin," *JHebS* 10 (2010), article 11, page 14, describes this as the case in which "centripetal tendencies overwhelm centrifugal ones."

[26] For a convenient overview of scholarly perspectives on Habakkuk's unity and historical setting, see Carly L. Crouch, "Nahum, Habakkuk, and Zephaniah," in *Enemies and Friends of the State: Ancient Prophecy in Context*, ed. Christopher A. Rollston (University Park, PA: Eisenbrauns, 2018), 359–83 (367–73).

The Present Approach to Habakkuk
In light of this discussion, our point of departure is that the text "comes with the presumption of coherence,"[27] or, to put it in terms of the reader, that the reader inevitably begins reading the text as potentially coherent. Without that assumption, the reader has no criteria or expectations by which breaks, inconsistencies, and other imperfections are identifiable or significant. This approach also commits to taking the whole text into account before deciding whether or not all its parts cohere, not least because texts of many different genres (not only mystery novels) tend to "put the pieces together" near or at the end.[28] Put differently, "the coherence of the whole cannot be determined by the observation of only parts of that whole."[29]

These considerations in favor of accessing Habakkuk as a potentially coherent text and making every reasonable effort to understand the interrelation of its sections and themes in light of the whole are reinforced by a variety of data from the history of the book's transmission and translation in antiquity. The earliest manuscript that preserves much the book's first two chapters in Hebrew, the Habakkuk Pesher (1QpHab) from Qumran that dates to ca. 50 BCE, corresponds very closely to the Hebrew text of the book standardized by the Massoretes in the second half of the first millennium CE, although the Qumran text seems to be closer to the original.[30] A slightly younger textual witness, the

---

[27] Dooley and Levinsohn, *Analyzing Discourse*, 11.
[28] John Barton "Reading Texts Holistically: The Foundation of Biblical Criticism," in *Congress Volume Ljubljana 2007*, ed. André Lemaire, VTSup 133 (Leiden: Brill, 2010), 367–80, correctly qualifies this "anti-atomistic" reading as "critical" (371).
[29] Mignon Jacobs, *The Conceptual Coherence of the Book of Micah*, JSOTSup 322 (Sheffield: Sheffield Academic, 2001), 194.
[30] On the superiority of the Masoretic text of Habakkuk, see Dominique Barthélemy et al., *Critique textuelle de l'Ancien Testament: Tome 3. Ézéchiel,*

Minor Prophets scrolls from Wadi Murabba'at (MurXII/Mur88), preserves almost the entire book in a form that is essentially identical to the standardized Hebrew text transmitted by many later Hebrew manuscripts.[31] The Greek textual tradition – commonly referred to as the Septuagint but reflecting (in the case of Habakkuk 3) no fewer than six different manuscripts – attempts to follow the Hebrew tradition but diverges from it for a number of reasons, some of which we can only speculate upon.[32] Taken together, these data favor the inference that ancient scribes and translators found no insurmountable problems with the coherence of the book as a whole and preserved and transmitted it in a form very much like that which we have now.

No less importantly, the various units of Habakkuk itself show awareness of their immediate literary context.[33] As a first example, Habakkuk's first complaint, in 1:2–4, begins with a question addressed to YHWH: "How long … ?" Following YHWH's response in 1:5–11, the prophet responds in turn in 1:12–2:1, again beginning with a question: "Are you not from everlasting?" God explicitly answers the prophet's second concern in 2:2–5, calling him to wait

---

Daniel et les 12 Prophètes (Fribourg and Göttingen: Éditions Universitaires/Vandenhoeck & Ruprecht, 1992), clv–clvi, who argue that whereas MT deviates from the presumed original largely in terms of vocalization, 1QpHab deviates from the original consonantal text much more often.

[31] Andersen, *Habakkuk*, 23.

[32] Andersen, *Habakkuk*, 23. See the definitive treatment of the relationship between the Hebrew, Greek, and Qumran versions in Barthélemy et al., *Critique textuelle*, cxlv–clvii.

[33] Ernst R. Wendland calls this feature "progression" and explores it in "'The Righteous Live by their Faith' in a Holy God: Complementary Compositional Forces and the Rhetorical Generation of Habakkuk's Dialogue with the LORD," in Ernst R. Wendland, *Prophetic Rhetoric: Case Studies in Text Analysis and Transmission*, with a foreword by L. Zogobo, SIL Publications in Translation and Textlinguistics 7 (Dallas, TX: SIL International, 2014), 423–95, esp. 428–53.

for the realization of a vision. This answer, unlike the first, seems to satisfy the prophet for the time being.³⁴ In literary terms, we can thus argue that 1:2–2:5 is a coherent unit with discernible subunits that document the progression of a conversation. Despite the shift from local to international scenarios and the incomplete resolution of the problems the prophet laments, these subunits present a balanced conversation in which both the prophet and God speak twice, with God answering each of the prophet's questions. The fact that Habakkuk speaks one more time, at the end of chapter 3, is as much a response to the vision of chapter 3 as to the woes of chapter 2, and 2:6–20 and 3:3–15 bring closure to his concerns (3:16–19).

A second example of literary coherence involves the connection between the dialogue in 1:2–2:5 and what follows, beginning with the five woes against Babylon in 2:6–20.³⁵ The "Chaldeans" (another term for the Babylonians; see later in this chapter) are the only group named in the dialogue, and they are the cause of the prophet's deepening chagrin following his initial despair over injustices in Judah. Despite the change in literary genre from dialogue to woe and the absence of explicit references to Babylon in 2:6–20, the woes naturally follow upon the condensed condemnation of Babylon in 2:4–5 and unpack the pride and insatiable appetite highlighted there. Similarly, the author's satisfaction with the reality sketched by the theophanic hymn of chapter 3 connects the end of the book to the Babylonian empire, which dominates most of chapter 1.³⁶

---

[34] Philip Whitehead, "Habakkuk and the Problem of Suffering: Theodicy Deferred," *JTI* 10 (2016): 265–81 (272).
[35] Wendland calls this feature "cohesion" and explores it in "The Righteous," 453–72.
[36] Jakob Wöhrle, *Der Abschluss des Zwölfprophetenbuches: Buchübergreifende Redaktionsprozesse in den späten Sammlungen*, BZAW 389 (Berlin: de Gruyter, 2008), 318.

Shared or equivalent lexemes and consistent structural features than span the book's subunits also favor the conclusion that the book is a unified whole.[37]

Habakkuk and the Reader

A final aspect of engaging the Book of Habakkuk involves the reader. Although literature that does not involve first-person language or second-person addresses to the reader is not for that reason unable to affect the reader, Habakkuk is all the more engaging thanks to the prominence of the prophet's first-person speech. Even more importantly, it encourages the reader to become subjectively involved in the reading of the text by espousing the presumably universal human desire to see justice done and (within the book's monotheistic worldview) by "addressing a common experience of faith, namely, the problem of God's apparent injustice given the lawlessness and oppression present in the world."[38] This is especially clear in the hymn of chapter 3, in which Yhwh's actions in ancient Israel's history are integrated in a vision of the deliverance he will bring about in response to Habakkuk's prayer. By embracing this vision, the prophet moves from a state of agitation and petition in 3:2 to a state of settled, confident expectation at the end of the chapter.[39] The prophet's personal journey from agitation and anguish in chapter 1 through faith and petition

---

[37] For example, Gert T. M. Prinsloo, "Reading Habakkuk as a Literary Unit: Exploring the Possibilities," *OTE* 12 (1999): 515–35.

[38] Whitehead, "Habakkuk," 268.

[39] R. David Moseman, "Habakkuk's Dialogue with Faithful Yahweh: A Transforming Experience," *PRSt* 44 (2017): 261–74, especially 272–74; David S. Vanderhooft, "A Strategy for Overcoming Divine Silence in Psalm 77 and Habakkuk," *Annual of the Japanese Biblical Institute* 44–45 (2018–19): 25–43, especially 41–42.

to a final state of calm and trust invites the reader to view God, suffering, and injustice in the same way so as to experience the same resolution.[40]

Historical Setting

By the time its trajectory crossed that of Judah around the year 600 BCE, Babylon had existed first as a city, then as a southern Mesopotamian city-state, for well over a millennium. First attested as a provincial city of the Ur III dynasty in southern Mesopotamia, Babylon gradually rose to prominence in the nineteenth century BCE, and reached its first zenith under the leadership of the king Hammurabi, who ruled for several decades in the eighteenth century.[41] Hammurabi's reign was marked by his conquest of Ur, Larsa, and Mari, giving him control over much of Mesopotamia.[42] Babylon's substantial cultural contribution began at roughly the same time but is hardly limited to the famous "Code" or law collection of Hammurabi, which was equal parts a collection of legal ideals and a statement of royal propaganda exalting the king as the one whom the gods charged with the task of establishing justice.[43]

---

[40] Suzanne Keen, "A Theory of Narrative Empathy," *Narrative* 14 (2006): 207–36 (213), observes that techniques for "supporting character identification, contributing to empathetic experiences, opening readers' minds to others," and similar effects in literature, have been tied "to a small set of narrative techniques – such as the use of first person narration and the interior representation of characters' consciousness and emotional states." These insights regarding contemporary narrative can be applied, *mutatis mutandis*, to Habakkuk's first-person account.

[41] David S. Vanderhooft, "Babylonia and the Babylonians," in *The World around the Old Testament: The People and Places of the Ancient Near East*, ed. Bill T. Arnold and Brent A. Strawn (Grand Rapids, MI: Baker Academic, 2016), 107–37 (111), adopting the Middle Chronology dates.

[42] Vanderhooft, "Babylonia," 112.

[43] See Raymond Westbrook, "The Character of Ancient Near Eastern Law," in *A History of Ancient Near Eastern Law*, ed. Raymond Westbrook, 2 vols., *HdO*

After Babylon was sacked by the Hittites in the sixteenth century, the Kassites took control of much of its territory, and the Kassite dynasty lasted until Assyrian and Elamite attacks brought about its fall in the middle of the twelfth century.[44]

The rise of Nebuchadnezzar I (1125–1104) contributed to Babylon's renewed ascendancy at the end of the second millennium. Nebuchadnezzar was able to return a captured cult statue of Marduk from Elam, and this event is likely reflected in the composition of *Enuma Elish* about this time.[45] This account of the origins of the cosmos describes the ascent of Marduk amid dissent among the gods. Marduk rises to the head of the pantheon after he agrees to defend the lesser gods against Tiamat, who sought to destroy them. After defeating and dismembering Tiamat, Marduk is feted as king and takes the throne in the Esagila temple that the grateful gods constructed for him.[46] The elevation of Marduk to the head of the Mesopotamian pantheon was a notable development in the religious world of the ancient Near East,[47] and nourished a national and royal ideology in which

---

1/72 (Leiden: Brill, 2003), 1–90 (16–21); and, on the propagandistic function of the code, Jean Bottéro, "The 'Code' of Hammurabi," in *Mesopotamia: Writing, Reasoning and the Gods*, ed. Zainab Balvani and Marc Van De Mieroop (Chicago: University of Chicago Press, 1992), 156–84.

[44] Vanderhooft, "Babylonia," 118.

[45] Jonathon Goldstein, *Peoples of an Almighty God: Competing Religions in the Ancient World*, ABRL (New York: Doubleday, 2002), 28, 31.

[46] See Benjamin R. Foster, "Epic of Creation," *COS* 1.111 (1:390–403).

[47] Beate Pongratz-Leisten, "Divine Agency and Astralization of the Gods in Ancient Mesopotamia," in *Reconsidering the Concept of Revolutionary Monotheism*, ed. B. Pongratz-Leisten (Winona Lake, IN: Eisenbrauns, 2011), 136–87 (142). Note a very similar phenomenon with respect to Ninurta, however, discussed in Barbara N. Porter, "The Anxiety of Multiplicity: Concepts of Divinity as One and Many in Ancient Assyria," in *One God or Many? Concepts of Divinity in the Ancient World*, ed. Barbara N. Porter (Chebeague, ME: Casco Bay Assyriological Institute, 2000), 211–71, esp. 252–55.

Marduk was the supreme deity and Babylon was "at the center of a world empire."[48]

In the first half of the first millennium, Babylon's neighbor Assyria grew stronger, often at the expense of Babylon, which fell increasingly under its control. A "recurring movement in Babylonia to retain national autonomy free of Assyrian rule"[49] was repeatedly curtailed by Assyrian military action, as when the Assyrian king, Shamshi-Adad (823–810), looted Babylon and confiscated some of its cult images.[50] About a century after the restoration of peaceful relations between Assyria and Babylon by the next Assyrian king, Adad-nirari III (809–783), Sennacherib (704–681) destroyed Babylon in a spectacular way (even smashing some of its cult statues) as retribution for handing over his son Ashur-nadin-shumi, then Babylon's interim ruler, to the Elamites.[51] Yet Sennacherib's successor Esarhaddon (680–669) completely rebuilt Babylon with great care, refurbishing the surviving cult statues as part of the process: "I repaired the woeful desecrated state of the gods and goddess who lived in it, who had been displaced by floods and storm, and whose appearances had become dim; I made their dimmed appearance bright, cleaned their dirty garments, (and) had them permanently installed on their daises."[52]

---

[48] Bill T. Arnold, *Who Were the Babylonians?* SBLABS 10 (Atlanta, GA: Society of Biblical Literature, 2004), 83. For far-reaching suggestions concerning the influence of Marduk's supremacy on Middle and Neo-Babylonian literature and thought, see Goldstein, *Peoples of an Almighty God*, 31–61.

[49] Arnold, *Who Were the Babylonians?*, 90.

[50] Hannes D. Galter, "Looking Down the Tigris: The Interrelations between Assyria and Babylon," in *The Babylonian World*, ed. Gwendolyn Leick (London: Routledge, 2007), 527–40 (531, 533).

[51] Galter, "Looking Down the Tigris," 531; the text can be found in Mordechai Cogan (trans.), "Sennacherib: The Capture and Destruction of Babylon (2.119E)," *COS* 2:305.

[52] Erle Leichty, *The Royal Inscriptions of Esarhaddon, King of Assyria (680–669 BC)*, RINAP 4 (Winona Lake: Eisenbrauns, 2011), 198 (BM 78223).

Assyrian attempts to suppress a final Babylonian rebellion lasted from 652 to 648 but weakened the empire enough that by 627, Babylon under Nabopolassar was able to openly pursue independence from Assyria.[53] Shortly thereafter, Babylon overcame Egyptian control of the Levant and became Judah's new overlord for a time (the Judean king Josiah had already been killed in what was presumably a failed attempt to prevent Egypt from helping Babylon topple Assyria; 2 Kgs 23:29). Josiah's son and successor, Jehoahaz, refused to remain Egypt's vassal, so Pharaoh Neco replaced him with another son of Josiah, Eliakim (also known as Jehoiachim). When Babylonian forces again reached the Levant, Eliakim became Babylon's vassal for a time, but later rebelled. His death in 598 meant that Babylon's punishment fell on Judah during the reign of his son Jehoiachin (598–597), and Babylon took a good deal of wealth as well as military and administrative personnel from Judah (2 Kgs 24:10–17). The consequences of a final Judean rebellion against Babylon under the king Zedekiah (587–586) were catastrophic: Babylon destroyed Jerusalem and its temple, executed the king's sons, and ended Judah's existence as a state.[54] The author of the Book of Kings attributes the fall of Judah to its failure to remain faithful to the covenant YHWH made with

---

[53] Joan Oates, "The Fall of Assyria (635–609 B.C.)," in *The Assyrian and Babylonian Empires and Other States of the Near East, from the Eighth to the Sixth Centuries B.C.*, ed. John Broadman et al., vol. 3/2 of Cambridge Ancient History, 2nd ed. (Cambridge: Cambridge University Press, 1991), 162–93 (173).

[54] Nebuchadnezzar's account of this event can be found in Bill T. Arnold, "Chronicle 5," in *The Ancient Near East: Historical Sources in Translation*, ed. Mark W. Chavalas, BSAH (Oxford: Blackwell, 2006), 417: "Seventh year. In the month of Kislev, the king of Akkad … encamped against the city of Yahuda. On the second day of the month of Adar, he captured the city and defeated its king. He appointed a king of his own choosing over it. He to[ok away] its heavy tribute and brought it into Babylon."

the nation, and literary and archaeological testimony bear witness to the presence of non-Yhwhistic or syncretistic worship at sites in Judah at that time.⁵⁵

This brings us to the early sixth century, the historical setting for the Book of Habakkuk. The task of developing the Babylonian imperialism project fell to Nebuchadnezzar II (605-562), who defeated Egypt at Carchemish in 605 and went on to establish his control westward in the years following, even subjugating the island-city of Tyre after a thirteen-year siege. Since Babylonian imperialism reached its zenith in the same period in which the Book of Habakkuk is set, a closer look at this phenomenon will shed significant light on Habakkuk's critique of the empire.

The importance of the city of Babylon is evident from its massive size, which at roughly 900 hectares made it "the largest city of the ancient Mediterranean until imperial Rome."⁵⁶ The moats that surrounded the city's walls and the symbolic significance of water as the primordial matrix from which the gods emerged would likely have created the visual message that Babylon was "the primordial mound that had risen out of the water at the beginning of creation itself, the geographical and temporal point from which all else was made."⁵⁷

---

⁵⁵ See Jeremy M. Hutton, "Southern, Northern, and Transjordanian Perspectives," in *Religious Diversity in Ancient Israel and Judah*, ed. Francesca Stavrakopoulou and John Barton (London: T & T Clark, 2010), 149-74; Patrick D. Miller, *The Religion of Ancient Israel*, LAI (Louisville: Westminster John Knox, 2000), esp. 46-105; Richard S. Hess, *Israelite Religions: An Archaeological and Biblical Survey* (Grand Rapids, MI: Baker Academic, 2007), 269-90, 297-332.

⁵⁶ Marc Van De Mieroop, "Reading Babylon," *AJA* 107 (2003): 257-75 (260). For an extensive survey of its excavation and the interpretation of Babylon as an archaeological site, see Mario Liverani, *Imagining Babylon: The Modern Story of an Ancient City*, SANER 11 (Berlin: de Gruyter, 2016).

⁵⁷ Mieroop, "Reading Babylon," 262.

Similarly, Marduk's temple "was an entire universe on its own, housing all the gods, representing universal order."[58] Marduk's prominence in the Babylonian pantheon and his consequent political significance are evident from the height of the ziggurat in the Marduk temple complex (estimated at 84 meters or 276 feet), the location of this complex at the center of the inner city, and the orientation of major streets in relation to the complex.[59] It is even reflected in the design of cult sites themselves: Marduk was "the main object of attention" in a chapel of the Esagila temple dedicated to Ninurta and probably even in Ninurta's own temple.[60]

City, temple, and gods (Marduk above all) were connected to the Babylonian king by a royal ideology in which the gods equipped and enabled the king to rule and fight on their behalf, and the king reciprocated by restoring, maintaining, and providing for the gods' cults and temples.[61] In one of his inscriptions, Nabopolassar, Nebuchadnezzar's father, asserts that Marduk "called me to the lordship over the country and the people. ... He let (me) succeed in everything I undertook. He caused Nergal, the strongest

---

[58] Mieroop, "Reading Babylon," 273.
[59] Vanderhooft, "Babylonia and the Babylonians," 131; Mieroop, "Reading Babylon," 260.
[60] A. R. George, "Marduk and the Cult of the Gods of Nippur at Babylon," *Or* 66 (1997): 65–70 (66–67). Because Babylon suffered significant destruction as late as 689, and because the site was repeatedly picked over in later antiquity, it is usually assumed that the extant remains bear witness especially to Babylon of Nebuchadnezzar II (see, e.g., Mieroop, "Reading Babylon," 260).
[61] On this last point, see especially Caroline Waerzeggers, "The Pious King: Royal Patronage of Temples," in *The Oxford Handbook of Cuneiform Culture*, ed. Karen Radner and Eleanor Robson (Oxford: Oxford University Press, 2011), 725–51. On Neo-Babylonian imperial ideology in general, see Leo G. Perdue and Warren Carter, *Israel and Empire: A Postcolonial History of Israel and Early Judaism*, ed. Coleman A. Baker (London: Bloomsbury T & T Clark, 2015), 72–76.

among the gods, to march at my side; he slew my foes, felled my enemies."[62] He also lauds Babylon and its wall, which he intended to restore, as "the solid border as ancient as time immemorial, the lofty mountain peak which rivals heavens, the mighty shield which locks the entrance to the hostile lands ... the fortification of the great gods whose foundations the Igigi and the Anunnaki had (originally) established in the jubilation of their hearts."[63]

Against the backdrop of the city's primordial and cultic importance, he describes how he mustered a workforce and oversaw the removal of the "accumulated debris, surveyed and examined its old foundations, and laid its brickwork in the original location" before ending the text with an exhortation to royal piety:

> Any king ... who will succeed me, (and) whose name Marduk will call to rulership of the country, do not be concerned with feats of might and power. Seek the sanctuaries of Nabû and Marduk and let them slay your enemies. The lord Marduk examines utterances and scrutinizes the heart. He who is loyal to Bēl, his foundations will endure. He who is loyal to the son of Bēl will last for eternity.[64]

The commitment of Nabopolassar's son, Nebuchadnezzar, to expanding Marduk's ziggurat and temple complex in Babylon further illustrates the importance of the relationship between king, temple, and deity.[65] A text inscribed on a prism found in Nebuchadnezzar's palace and dated to his seventh year (598) details his scrupulous commitment to cults even outside Babylon:

---

[62] Paul-Alain Beaulieu, "Nabopolassar's Restoration of Imgur-Enlil, the Inner Defensive Wall of Babylon (2.121)," *COS* 2:307–8 (307).
[63] Beaulieu, "Nabopolassar's Restoration," 307.
[64] Beaulieu, "Nabopolassar's Restoration," 308.
[65] Paul-Alain Beaulieu, "Mesopotamia," in *Religions of the Ancient World*, ed. Sarah I. Johnston (Cambridge, MA: Belknap Press of Harvard University Press, 2004), 165–72 (171).

> As for the Ezida, I adorned its form. As for Nabu and Nanaya, in joy and celebration, I made them dwell within it. Daily, [I offered] one fattened sacrificial bull, a blemishless bull, (and) 16 choice sacrificial lambs, for (the statues) of the gods of Borsippa; an allocation of fish, fowl ... the finest from the marshland, honey, butter, milk without fat, beer, and pure wine....[66]

This piety led the king to undertake military action with confidence. During the coronation of Nabopolassar as king, the king replied (probably to Bel), "With the standard I shall constantly conquer [your] enemies, I shall place [your] throne in Babylon." Later in the same ceremony the officials in attendance pronounced the following wish: "O lord, O king, may you live forever! [May you conquer] the land of [your] enemies! May the king of the gods, Marduk, rejoice in you!"[67] The concept of worldwide dominion as a task entrusted to the king by the gods reached its zenith under Nebuchadnezzar, and this idea is "ubiquitous ... in the royal inscriptions" he authored.[68] Like his father, Nebuchadnezzar too was confident that "Marduk ... entrusted me with the rule of the totality of peoples, Nabu ... placed in my hands a just scepter to lead all populated regions aright and to make humanity thrive."[69]

As Nebuchadnezzar's words reveal, Babylon's imperial ideology held that its rule was exercised for the good of those it controlled. On such a view, "the conquest ... of non-Babylonian populations is not to

---

[66] Benjamin Studevent-Hickman (trans.), "The Court and State Document of Nebuchadnezzar II," in *The Ancient Near East: Historical Sources in Translation*, ed. Mark W. Chavalas, BSAH (Oxford: Blackwell, 2006), 387. Similarly, descriptions of temple restorations outside Babylon can be found in Paul-Alain Beaulieu (trans.), "Nebuchadnezzar II (2.122)," *COS* 2:308–10.

[67] A. K. Grayson, *Babylonian Historical-Literary Texts*, Toronto Semitic Texts and Studies 3 (Toronto: University of Toronto Press, 1975), 85.

[68] David J. Vanderhooft, "'Nebuchadnezzar, King of Babylon, My Servant': Contrasting Prophetic Images of the Great King," *HBAI* 7 (2018): 93–111 (95).

[69] David J. Vanderhooft, *The Neo-Babylonian Empire and Babylon in the Latter Prophets*, HSM 59 (Atlanta: Scholars, 1999), 35 (VAB 4 112).

their detriment, since the Babylonian elite views the 'eternal shadow of Babylon' as a restorative one."⁷⁰ The enslavement and taxation of conquered peoples by the empire leave ample room for doubting this rosy claim, however. Nebuchadnezzar describes the construction of the Etemenanki ziggurat in Babylon in unabashedly imperial terms:

> (All the widespread peoples), the governance of whom I exercise at the command of Marduk, my lord, and who carried mighty cedars from the mountain of Lebanon to Babylon, my city – all the peoples of the wide inhabited regions whom Marduk, my lord, bestowed upon me, I subjected them to corvée to build Etemenanki and I imposed the *tupšikku* [work basket] upon them.⁷¹

The labor and skills of conquered peoples were essential to maintaining Babylon's status and strength, and Judah was no exception. In Nebuchadnezzar's first years, he records that "all the kings of Hattu," including Jehoiakim, came before him and he "received their heavy tribute."⁷² It is thus ironic that the ultimate goal of the Babylonian king's piety, building projects, and military action was symbolized by images of the Babylonian monarchs at rest. Their "sense of quiet repose" as depicted on imperial monuments suggests "an empire held firm by its position at the heart of the cultic universe and its consequent alignment and unity with the sacred realm,"⁷³ but this tranquility and ease were the result of the conquest, oppression, and arduous work of Judeans and many other formerly free populations.

---

⁷⁰ Vanderhooft, *The Neo-Babylonian Empire*, 43.
⁷¹ From the Nebuchadnezzar Cylinder IV, 1, translated in Vanderhooft, "Nebuchadnezzar, King of Babylon," 95.
⁷² Wiseman, *Nebuchadnezzar and Babylon*, 23.
⁷³ Erica Ehrenberg, "Dieu et Mon Droit: Kingship in Late Babylonian and Early Persian Times," in *Religion and Power: Divine Kingship in the Ancient World and Beyond*, ed. Nicole Brisch, OIS 4 (Chicago: Oriental Institute of the University of Chicago, 2008), 103–32 (106). See further Deryck Sheriffs, "'A Tale of Two Cities': Nationalism in Zion and Babylon," *TynB* 39 (1988): 19–57; and more generally Rocío Da Riva, *The Neo-Babylonian Royal Inscriptions: An Introduction*, GMTR 4 (Münster: Ugarit-Verlag, 2008).

A THEOLOGICAL EXPLORATION OF HABAKKUK

Because much of Habakkuk is a dialogue, our exploration of its theology will follow in sequence the series of protests and responses that constitute the first two chapters. That sequence, completed by the final perspective that appears in the prayer of Habakkuk 3, will help us track the expanding range of injustice that troubles the prophet while emphasizing the climactic significance of chapter 3 as the definitive response to the problems the book explores.

Habakkuk's First Problem: Local Injustice in Judah Is Incompatible with Divine Justice (1:2–4)
The opening words of the prophetic message in 1:2 ("How long ... ?") draw the reader into the middle of an ongoing crisis. This crisis deeply affected Habakkuk, who assumed that regardless of the human agent involved, Yhwh was also responsible, albeit in an unclear way, for what was happening. He therefore addresses his complaint directly to Yhwh. Furthermore, "How long ... ?" shows that, in the prophet's opinion, God should have responded long ago but had remained inactive even after hearing Habakkuk's cry for help. Not one to mince words, Habakkuk even identifies God as the one who "makes me see" or himself "looks idly upon" these wrongs (1:3) rather than saving the prophet and other victims from them. This means that *two* crises exist simultaneously in the prophet's experience: (1) Wrong and injustice are dominant within Judean society, and (2) this crisis draws into question Yhwh's justice, which Habakkuk assumes exists but finds lacking in this situation.

We can begin developing an answer to the contested question of who caused this crisis in Judah by examining the language used to describe it. The first description of the moral chaos in Judah affirms that it consists of, or includes, *ḥāmās* ("violence," 1:2, 3; also used of Babylon in 1:9; 2:8, 17).[74] Numerous other terms follow in 1:3 and sketch a fuller picture of rampant injustice in Judah: *'awen*, "sin, injustice," and *'āmāl*, "harm," similarly refer to harm involving moral wrong, as do the "violent acts" (Hab 1:3b) that capture the interpersonal nature of these wrongs perpetrated by the strong against the weak. The resulting "contention" and "strife" underline the discord and animus that these actions produced in Judean society at large.

The collective force of these complaints points to nothing less than the "disintegration of society," with a focus on the moral failings and abuses of power that caused it.[75] God's own moral guidance has been neutralized or rendered powerless as a source of justice (1:4). The prominence of the pair *tôrâ* and *mišpaṭ* in the Book of Deuteronomy, which gained renewed standing following Josiah's reforms, makes that book a likely referent of Habakkuk's remark here, and its focus on the way that Israelites should treat one another corresponds to the prophet's focus on the social-ethical issues around him.[76]

The Judeans responsible for the unraveling of Judah's social fabric are bluntly referred to as "the wicked" in 1:4 (also used of

---

[74] Cf. Kevin J. Cathcart, "'Law Is Paralysed' (Habakkuk 1:4): Habakkuk's Dialogue with God and the Language of Legal Disputation," in *Prophecy and Prophets in Ancient Israel*, ed. John Day, LHBOTS 531 (New York: T & T Clark, 2010), 339–53 (342).

[75] The phrase is used by Gert T. M. Prinsloo, "Inner-Biblical Allusion in Habakkuk's משא (1:1–2:20) and Utterances Concerning Babylon in Isaiah 13–23 (Isa 13:1–14:23; 21:1–10)," *OTE* 31 (2018): 663–91 (665).

[76] Since the nations are never held to account on the basis of Israel's *tôrâ*, and since there is no evidence that Babylonian interference in or control of Judah's affairs impacted the exercise of the religion, it is unlikely that Babylon would be connected to the "paralysis" of Israel's law.

Babylon in 1:13). At first glance this word may seem overly harsh or even unsuitable as a description of other Judeans. However, Habakkuk's statement finds many parallels in the Book of Psalms, where the authors use the same term to describe their fellow citizens, not necessarily foreign opponents or insurgents (see Ps 1:1, 4; 10:2–3; 26:5; 37:12, 14, etc.). In these psalms and Habakkuk alike, "the wicked" flouted the moral guidelines and ideals elaborated in Deuteronomy and other authoritative scriptures in pursuit of something they considered more important and valuable. No further details are given here, but the fact that Habakkuk invokes God's intervention implies that the prophet and those like him (the "righteous") were ultimately powerless to remedy this lamentable situation themselves. Indeed, the statement that the wicked "surround" the righteous (1:4) implies that they are more numerous (if literal) or simply more powerful (if metaphorical). In short, an unknown fraction of the powerful in Judah were acting in violent ways, using their power to protect their interests or advance their agendas (see the similar accusations in Isaiah 1; Amos 2:13–16; 3:10–11; 4:1–4; 6:1–7; Mic 2–3; Zeph 3:1–5).[77]

The root issue, as far as the human actors are concerned, is not that some have more social, political, or religious power than others, but that some of those who have such power use it in ways that advance their interests while flouting God's covenantal claim upon them and their responsibility to care for their fellow citizens as much as for themselves. Whether these actions involved unjust appropriation of another's land, exploitation of the poor by arranging rapacious loans, or political and judicial stratagems

---

[77] For arguments in favor of seeing the "wicked" in 1:4 as Babylon, see Michael H. Floyd, "Prophetic Complaints about the Fulfillment of Oracles in Habakkuk 1:2–17 and Jeremiah 15:10–18," *JBL* 110 (1991): 397–418 (403).

that put the abuser above the law, these activities all involve making oneself and the power, fame, or wealth that one craves *more important than the other*. Regardless of the degree to which Josiah's reforms and the renewed prominence of Deuteronomy strengthened Habakkuk's revulsion at these social and moral wrongs, this enacted inequality at the level of anthropology ("I am inherently more important than you") is incompatible with the ethic that Deuteronomy in particular promotes. Deuteronomy uses the term "brother" to refer to one's fellow Israelites almost fifty times, and even the king is "one of your brothers" (Deut 17:15). Since one is a "brother" of one's fellow Israelites "regardless of social status or tribal divisions," the term has "a levelling function in Israel" that makes the nation's unity inseparable from this fundamental equality.[78] Habakkuk was certain that without this foundation, Judean society could not endure.

As problematic as mistreatment of others is, it is not the only dimension of the issue. Not only did the ones who misused power in Judah mistreat those who are less powerful, they simultaneously dismissed Yhwh's commands as irrelevant or simply impractical: "what I want is more important than what Yhwh wants." While this pattern of behavior had given these people the upper hand in Judah for the moment, one cannot contravene God's will with impunity for long. This was guaranteed, so to speak, by Israel's covenant with Yhwh, which asserted that he will bless and prosper those who follow his will (Deut 28:1–14) but will discipline and eventually punish those who persist in disobedience (Deut 28:15–69).

But it is exactly this apparent guarantee that gave rise to the problem that Habakkuk now faces and decries. The prophet

---

[78] J. Gordon McConville, *Law and Theology in Deuteronomy*, JSOTSup 33 (Sheffield: JSOT, 1984), 19.

finds unacceptable the delay between the flouting of the covenant's guidelines and the consequences that the same covenant announces against those who disobey it. Not only were some Judeans running roughshod over their fellow citizens and YHWH's law, but YHWH himself was not imposing the promised punishments upon them or delivering the oppressed when they called to him for help. This, in short, is the problem of theodicy – if God is just, which Habakkuk thought to be the case (at least until now), why is he not actively maintaining and exercising justice? Recognizing the validity of the prophet's question, God immediately offers an answer to this problem of *uncorrected* inner-Judean injustice.

YHWH's Solution to the First Problem: YHWH Will Punish Judah by Means of Babylon (1:5–11)
The introduction to YHWH's response, which is equivalent to "you're not going to believe what I am about to do," suggests that the coming divine intervention will not be simple and tidy (1:5). And indeed, the ongoing dialogue between the prophet and his God shows that YHWH's plan for punishing flagrant sinners in Judah troubles the prophet deeply. The root of the problem, from Habakkuk's point of view, has to do with *the means that YHWH will use* to punish Judah, which is here identified as the "Chaldeans" – that is, the Babylonians – more specifically that empire's "military forces."[79]

[79] David J. Vanderhooft, "Depictions of כשדים 'Chaldeans' in Judean Prophecy and Historiography," in *"Now It Happened in Those Days": Studies in Biblical, Assyrian, and Other Ancient Near Eastern History Presented to Mordechai Cogan on His 75th Birthday*, ed. Amitai Baruchi-Unna, Tova l. Forti, Shmuel Ahituv, Israel Eph'al, and Jeffrey H. Tigay, 2 vols. (Winona Lake, IN: Eisenbrauns, 2017), 1:171–82 (181).

Interestingly, the way that YHWH presents Babylon seems calculated to encourage one to question in what way their military action against Judah might resolve the initial problem raised by Habakkuk. The majority of the first divine response to Habakkuk details Babylon's military might and prowess using Mesopotamian "tropes for depicting raging conquerors"[80] and a number of negative moral and theological evaluations of Babylon-as-empire. Babylon is described in very unflattering terms:

- "takes what it does not own" by force (1:6; theft);
- is the source of its own "justice" and self-exaltation[81] (1:7; autonomy and pride);
- is focused on illegitimate violence (1:9, with ḥāmās, as in 1:2, 3); and
- incurs "guilt" by attributing its strength to its "god" (1:11; worship of false gods).

In practical terms, Babylon's army was almost unstoppable at this point in history, and Babylon was therefore more than able to inflict serious if not fatal damage upon Judah – a definitive (albeit apparently excessive) response to Habakkuk's first problem. Recent events left no doubt on this point. After taking the key Assyrian city of Ashur in 614, the Babylonian king Nabopolassar pursued the Assyrian king to Takritain, where he "inflicted a major defeat upon Assyria."[82] Similarly, Nebuchadnezzar's decisive

---

[80] Vanderhooft, "Nebuchadnezzar, King of Babylon," 109, with reference to Peter Machinist, "Assyria and Its Image in First Isaiah," *JAOS* 103 (1983): 719–37.

[81] This rare term (שׂאת) is evocative of Babylon's self-attributed exaltation (cf. Isa 14:13–14; 47:8) and is used elsewhere of humans only (1) in YHWHistic blessings (Gen 49:3), (2) of those whom YHWH blesses (Ps 62:5), or (3) of YHWH's own pre-eminence (Job 13:11; 31:23). There is one use with respect to Leviathan in Job 41:17.

[82] Grayson, *Assyrian and Babylonian Chronicles*, 92 (Chronicle 3).

victory over Egypt in 605 was the result of his decision to "cut the Egyptians off from their direct line of retreat and force them out to battle,"[83] after which he "finished them off completely," as his royal chronicle puts it.[84]

By including a subtle undercurrent of condemnation (theft, pride, violence, and worship of false gods, per 1:6–11), Yahweh's description of Babylon's military ability provides fodder for the prophet's second speech to God, and suggests that this solution is self-evidently imperfect and incomplete. As noted earlier, Babylonian imperial ideology held that the empire's gods, and pre-eminently Marduk, authorized and enabled the king to subdue his enemies as part of Marduk's supposedly beneficent rule over "the totality of peoples" and "all populated regions" so as to "make humanity thrive."[85] The contrast between YHWH's and the Babylonians' interpretation of Babylon's imperialism reveals sharply contrasting worldviews in which different deities with different characters and priorities act in space and time to establish their rule over the world. What YHWH calls theft Marduk calls appropriation; YHWH's condemnation of Babylonian pride presupposes that it is much less important and much more fragile than it believes;[86] Babylon's calculated use of violence was at best excessive (if not completely unjustified) in YHWH's (and

---

[83] D. J. Wiseman, "Babylonia 605–539 B.C.," in *The Assyrian and Babylonian Empires and Other States of the Near East, from the Eighth to the Sixth Centuries B.C.*, ed. John Broadman et al., vol. 3/2 of Cambridge Ancient History, 2nd ed. (Cambridge: Cambridge University Press, 1991), 229–51 (230).

[84] Grayson, *Assyrian and Babylonian Chronicles*, 99 (Chronicle 5).

[85] Vanderhooft, *The Neo-Babylonian Empire*, 35 (VAB 4 112).

[86] Cf. Mark G. Brett, *Decolonizing God: The Bible in the Tides of Empire* (Sheffield: Sheffield Phoenix, 2009), 109, "Even in those cases where the empires of Assyrian or Babylon have been deployed in judgment against Israel, they have no justification for their arrogance."

its victim's) eyes; and Babylon's recognition and exaltation of Marduk were incompatible with YHWH's even more radical claim to exclusive deity.[87] Most pointedly, what Babylon would describe as the triumph of its gods over other gods turns out to be, instead, something quite different: God's exercise of his worldwide control, whereby he used Babylon to punish his own people.[88]

One more dimension of this description of Babylon-as-empire must be noted: its overlap with the description of Judah in 1:2–4. This similarity may initially strike one as highly implausible: Babylon regularly misused or misunderstood its massive military might, while Judah had none to speak of; Babylon had brought violence against a number of other peoples and cultures, while Judah in the seventh century did nothing of the sort; and Babylon was unreservedly committed to a polytheistic, iconic religion that differs markedly from the aniconic monotheism that Judah was to practice per the Torah. Some of these contrasts probably lie behind Habakkuk's second complaint, but without denying clear differences between Babylon and Judah, the text still encourages the reader to recognize fundamental *similarities* between the two states. The most evident parallel is the presence of "violence" (*ḥāmās*) in both polities (1:2, 9). Similarly, the overlapping semantic fields of "wicked" (1:4, Judah) and "guilty" (1:11, Babylon) and the repetition of "wicked" in 1:13 (of Babylon) highlight the comparable statuses of some within Judah and Babylon

---

[87] I follow here Jean Bottéro's claim that "true monotheism" was "completely unknown in Mesopotamia" – Jean Bottéro, *Religion in Ancient Mesopotamia*, trans. T. L. Fagan (Chicago: University of Chicago Press, 2001), 42 – nuanced by an awareness of a spectrum of divinity in the ancient Near East as outlined in the essays in Beate Pongratz-Leisten (ed.), *Reconsidering the Concept of Revolutionary Monotheism* (Winona Lake, IN: Eisenbrauns, 2011).

[88] This point is made by Dietrich, *Nahum, Habakuk, Zefanja*, 120.

with respect to Yhwh's character and standards.⁸⁹ Thus, despite their very different geopolitical profiles, some portion of the two states' populations shared a commitment to self-advancement that produced various forms of violence against a less powerful victim. In the case of Babylon this involved a complete disregard for moral norms that protect the well-being of the other, while some Judeans gave no heed to the more specific moral guidance found in Yhwh's *tôrâ*.

Habakkuk's Response (the Second Problem): Using Babylon to Punish Judah Is Incompatible with Divine Justice (1:12–2:1)
Despite Yhwh's claim that some Judeans and some Babylonians were guilty of the same kind of sins and so are similarly culpable, the actions and attitudes alleged of Babylon in 1:5–11 make it impossible for Habakkuk to accept Babylonian violence as a comprehensive, morally impeccable solution to the problem of injustice in Judean society. In the prophet's opinion, Babylon (more specifically, its military) did what the wicked Judeans did but on a radically larger scale. God's response to his initial complaint therefore makes the question of theodicy *more* pressing, not less.

Habakkuk's second complaint begins with a rhetorical question, and despite his doubts, the prophet still believes Yhwh is the only possible source of justice in this situation. "Are you not from long ago?" echoes earlier Old Testament texts in which Yhwh's rule over his creation from the beginning is stressed, sometimes under the image of suppressing primitive chaos (e.g., Ps 74:12; Isa 51:9) and sometimes under the more general images of king

---

[89] Daniel C. Timmer, *The Non-Israelite Nations in the Book of the Twelve: Thematic Coherence and the Diachronic-Synchronic Relationship in the Minor Prophets*, BibInt 135 (Leiden: Brill, 2015), 140, 146.

or creator (Ps 44:1[Heb 2]; 77:12; 143:5; Isa 45:12).⁹⁰ Alongside his doubts, Habakkuk affirms God's "eternity and power" as the foundation of his uninterrupted rule, and even believes that "we shall not die!"⁹¹ The adjective "holy" that makes up the title the prophet gives to Yhwh, "my Holy One," further emphasizes his distinction from all other beings as well as his moral impeccability.⁹² These beliefs all support Habakkuk's interpretation of Babylon's predicted aggression against Judah as "judgment/justice" (1:12, as in 1:4, 7) and "reproof/adjudication." This facet of Babylon's role, isolated from the moral failings of the empire, is intelligible to the prophet in light of the connection between widespread sin and national punishment established by Israel's covenant with Yhwh.

Habakkuk's primary concern remains, however: How can Yhwh, *if he is as described in 1:12*, use Babylon to punish Judah? To make the point as forcefully as possible, the prophet introduces new descriptions of God's intolerance of "evil" and "wrong" in 1:13, and contrasts them with God's apparent toleration of "treacherous persons" (a reference to Babylon's military-political corps) and the destruction of the less wicked by the more wicked. This

---

⁹⁰ I owe this point to Cathcart, "Law," 344. On the relevance of Canaanite mythology for these allusions in the Old Testament, compare the classic study of John Day, *God's Conflict with the Dragon and the Sea: Echoes of a Canaanite Myth in the Old Testament*, UCOP 35 (Cambridge: Cambridge University Press, 1985) with Richard E. Averbeck, "Ancient Near Eastern Mythography as It Relates to Historiography in the Hebrew Bible: Genesis 3 and the Cosmic Battle," in *The Future of Biblical Archaeology: Reassessing Methodologies and Assumptions*, ed. James K. Hoffmeier and Alan R. Millard (Grand Rapids, MI: Baker, 2004), 328–56.

⁹¹ As noted by Perlitt, *Propheten*, 58, the inclusion of this phrase in the later rabbinic list of pious scribal corrections, with the original text presumably reading "you [Yhwh] will not die," is undermined by the fact that our oldest texts preserve "we will not die" (e.g., MT, 1QpHab, and the Old Greek tradition).

⁹² Jackie A. Naudé, "קדש," *NIDOTTE* 3:877–87 (879, 882–83).

last element is crucially important for understanding the prophet's theodicy at this point. The problem at this point in his argument is not the punishment of sin per se, even by an imperfect agent; nor is it the involvement of the whole population in a punishment that focuses primarily on a subset of it. Rather, Habakkuk question's God's choice to use an instrument (Babylon) that Habakkuk considers *less righteous* than the Judah it is sent to punish. This leads to the prophet's blunt accusation that YHWH makes the "human beings" who fall victim to Babylon like fish or invertebrates that have no ruler (1:14). In other words, by letting Babylon do what it does, YHWH is failing to exercise the rule that is properly his and ignoring the inherent and unique value of those who are made in his image (Gen 1:26–28).

Habakkuk's critique of Babylonian imperialism under the metaphor of Babylon as a fisherman and the rest of humanity as fish is worth lingering over. The metaphor trenchantly dehumanizes the empire's human victims by likening them to fish; only Babylon retains a human identity. The prophet presents Babylon's multifaceted military and strategic skills by means of various fishing techniques: a hook and line, a (small) net, and a (larger) dragnet (1:15).[93] While a hook and line can be effective, nets are a superior and more effective instrument – and Babylon has all these means at its disposal.[94] Finally, the Babylonian fisherman "is glad and

---

[93] These methods of fishing are well attested across the ancient Near East. See Piotr Bienkowski, "Fishing," *Dictionary of the Ancient Near East*, ed. Piotr Bienkowski and Alan Millard (Philadelphia: University of Pennsylvania Press, 2000), 117–18.

[94] J. J. M. Roberts, *Nahum, Habakkuk, Zephaniah: A Commentary*, OTL (Louisville, KY: Westminster/John Knox, 1991), 104, notes that Marduk used a net to capture Tiamat in *Enuma Elish*. Othmar Keel, *The Symbolism of the Biblical World: Ancient Near Eastern Iconography and the Book of Psalms*, trans. T. J. Hallett (London: SPCK, 1978), 89, includes an image of human

rejoices" over his catch, while the catch feels otherwise as it draws its final breath in utter terror. The metaphor thus represents the pathos experienced by the populations captured by the empire, whether they were destroyed outright or conscripted into the empire's workforce and military. Babylon's appropriation of the victim's material goods by force makes this scenario even worse.

The metaphor of the fisherman prepares the way for two further critiques of Babylonian imperialism. The first (1:16a) focuses on its idolatrous nature, in which the gods responsible for the fisherman's success are honored with sacrifices and offerings. This is highly objectionable because it gives worship to entities other than Yhwh, but also because such worship is inseparable from the violence and injustice of the imperial project.[95] The association of the metaphor of fishing with illicit worship is probably strengthened by the longstanding prominence of fish as divine offerings, a practice that Nebuchadnezzar renewed during his reign.[96]

The second critique (1:16b) focuses on the significant economic benefit created by Babylonian imperialism. Babylon's acquisition of material wealth through military conflict is attested even before the beginning of the Neo-Babylonian period proper, during the reign of Nergal-ushezib (694–693), who is said to have "captured Nipp[ur], plundered and sacked (it)."[97] According to the Babylonian Chronicle, some cities capitulated and paid tribute

---

beings trapped in a net from the Stele of the Vultures. The accompanying text from Eannatum reads: "Over the people of Umma, I, Eannatum, threw the net of the god Enlil." Keel also presents a relief from the Edfu temple in Egypt in which the Pharaoh has captured in a net "everything that lives on earth" (ibid.).

[95] Michael C. Legaspi, "Opposition to Idolatry in the Book of Habakkuk," *VT* 67 (2017): 458–69, helpfully explores this point.

[96] Vanderhooft, *Neo-Babylonian Empire*, 156.

[97] Grayson, *Assyrian and Babylonian Chronicles*, 78 (Babylonian Chronicle 1).

during Nabopolassar's tenth year (616) rather than risk destruction, but the Chronicle more often records instances in which cities were taken, "plundered," and "sacked extensively."[98] The same theme appears in the chronicles dedicated to the reign of Nebuchadnezzar, whose army collected "vast tribute" (years 1, 7, 10), plundered and sacked cities (year 1), and "plundered extensively the possessions, animals, and gods of the numerous Arabs" (year 3).[99]

The close interrelation of these critiques of Babylonian imperialism as idolatrous and violently avaricious is evident from the fact that a significant portion of the wealth that Babylon gained by conquest flowed into various temples: "Gold, silver, exceedingly valuable gemstones, thick cedars, heavy tribute, expensive presents, the produce of all countries, goods from all inhabited regions, before Marduk the great lord, the god who created me, and Nabû his lofty heir who loves my kingship, I transported and brought into Esagil and Ezida."[100] With this multifaceted critique of Babylon in view, Habakkuk's struggle with God's seeming (in)justice reaches its peak. The prophet asks in exasperation (1:17): "Will he then keep on emptying his net and continuously slaughtering nations without sparing any?" The prophet's assumption that only YHWH can remedy this situation makes it likely that the question is rhetorical. But his is a posture of agitated expectation rather than of calm repose, and there is significant tension between Habakkuk's urgent tone and

---

[98] See, for example, Chronicle 3, Grayson, *Assyrian and Babylonian Chronicles*, 91, 92, 94 ("plunder and exiles"), 95 ("vast booty of the city and the temple").

[99] Vanderhooft, *Neo-Babylonian Empire*, 45. Grayson, *Assyrian and Babylonian Chronicles*, 100–2, concludes that "[t]he supply of precious and manufactured items, raw materials, and workmen for Babylon and for the other principal cities of Babylonia is often emphasized in Nebuchadnezzar's inscriptions."

[100] CT 37 pl. 6–7, cited in Vanderhooft, *Neo-Babylonian Empire*, 46.

his decision to take up his prophetic post and watch for God's response to his "argument." This tension expresses Habakkuk's dissatisfaction with Yhwh's plan to use Babylon to punish Judah, but it also recognizes (and accepts) that there would be a delay between this rhetorical question and Yhwh's response. The prophet is reasonably confident that some sort of explanation is forthcoming, but his attitude is not one of patient waiting. To return to the fishing metaphor, every passing moment sees more fish caught in the net. Something must be done! The prophet also anticipates that he will eventually continue the dialogue by responding to what Yhwh says or does ("what I will answer concerning my complaint," 2:1), so he evidently does not assume that the divine reply will be fully satisfactory. This unresolved tension indicates the direction of the plot that unfolds in the rest of the book: Yhwh "answers" Habakkuk in 2:2–20, and the prophet responds in his prayer of chapter 3.[101]

Yhwh's Promised Solution to the Second Problem: Babylon's Wrongs Will Not Go Unpunished (2:2–20)
Habakkuk's urgent desire to receive an answer to his second complaint is met with the divine promise of a vision that is "for an appointed time." Although it is yet to come, its timely realization is sure, such that there will be no delay from Yhwh's point of view (2:3) – he has precisely determined the timing of his intervention.[102]

---

[101] I understand 2:2–20 as a multipart speech by Yhwh. Little changes if Habakkuk reports Yhwh's response in 2:2–4 and explains it in 2:5–20, as Marvin Sweeney suggests, "Structure, Genre, and Intent in the Book of Habakkuk," *VT* 41 (1991): 63–83 (71).

[102] This is all the more clear if the Hebrew word normally translated "if" (*'im*) that begins the second half of the verse is understood as introducing an oath, as it often does elsewhere. See James W. Haring, "'He Will Certainly Not Hesitate, Wait for Him!': Evidence for an Unrecognized Oath in Habakkuk

The vision itself is to be written on tablets and "made clear" or "confirmed,"[103] so that "the one who reads it may run," a phrase expressing either the legibility of the tablet or the speedy dissemination of the message. In either case, the sense of this command remains the same: "Write the message so that it may be delivered," with Habakkuk in the role of Yhwh's emissary.[104] The content of the vision is most likely the immediately following series of woes against Babylon, which is a direct response to Habakkuk's second complaint.[105] However, it is of little import whether one limits the vision to 3:3–15,[106] so that the woes of chapter 2 lead up to it, or whether Habakkuk's prayer in chapter 3 is a response to a vision that consists of 2:6–20, or whether both the woes and the prayer together constitute the vision. Habakkuk's patience in awaiting the vision's realization, expressed in 3:16–19, clearly shows that what he heard or saw provided a solid foundation for his faith.

 2,3b, and Its Implications for Interpreting Habakkuk 2,2–4," *ZAW* 126 (2014): 372–82. This possibility aligns well with the translation of 2:2b as "a truthful witness for a time to come" (so NJPS), in favor of which see Dennis Pardee, "YPḤ 'Witness' in Hebrew and Ugaritic," *VT* 28 (1978): 204–13, and Cathcart, "Law," 348–49.

[103] For arguments in favor of understanding the verb in question as "confirm" (i.e., establish the veracity of the vision), see David T. Tsumura, "Hab 2:2 in the Light of Akkadian Legal Practice," *ZAW* 94 (1982): 294–95, and the literature cited by Haring, "He Will Certainly Not Hesitate," 375.

[104] So Ko, *Theodicy*, 68; Andersen, *Habakkuk*, 203–5.

[105] Dietrich's suggestion, *Nahum, Habakuk, Zefanja*, 143, that the vision refers to 1:5–10 fails to explain the relevance of the vision to Habakkuk's second protest in 1:12–2:1.

[106] For example, Roberts, *Nahum, Habakkuk, Zephaniah*, 116. James W. Watts, "Psalmody in Prophecy: Habakkuk 3 in Context," in *Forming Prophetic Literature: Essays on Isaiah and the Twelve in Honor of John D. W. Watts*, ed. James W. Watts and Paul R. House, JSOTSup 235 (Sheffield: Sheffield Academic, 1996), 209–23 (217), observes that "[u]sing the introspective perspective of psalmody, the hymn comes as close as any Hebrew text to portraying the interior experience of prophetic vision."

The importance of how one responds to this eminently trustworthy vision is underlined by 2:4, which explores contrasting responses to God and his promises. The hearer either remains impudent and self-reliant,[107] or believes the vision and "lives" in and by faithfulness (*'ĕmûnâ*) to Yhwh. In terms of the groups mentioned in Habakkuk 1, this makes the righteous person the opposite of the one who practices violence and place himself and his desires above all else, including Yhwh's torah. To that partial sketch is added the defining characteristic of trusting God and his word of promise, for which humility is a prerequisite.[108] Conversely, the one who is impudent or proud is inevitably not "upright," since his or her life is not guided by God's word (cf. the "twisted" justice that runs counter to Yhwh's law in 1:4). The connection that the rest of the book makes between the responses of proud unbelief and death and destruction suggests that the "life" here cannot be limited to a lifestyle of faithfulness, although that is presupposed. Faith in God's promise to set all things to rights also includes the prophet's dependence on God for deliverance from divine punishment to which even he was exposed (3:2).

Beginning in 2:5, the focus of the conversation between Yhwh and Habakkuk shifts from individuals, especially the "impudent" who refuse to walk in faithfulness to Yhwh, to Babylon, which "gathers to itself all the nations, and collects for itself all

---

[107] Roberts, *Nahum, Habakkuk, Zephaniah*, 111, translates 2:4a as "Now the fainthearted, his soul will not walk in it," but the textual evidence favors retaining the verb √*'-p-l*, which probably means "be impudent" (*HALOT* 860); cf. Anthony Gelston, *The Twelve Minor Prophets*, BHQ 13 (Stuttgart: Deutsche Bibelgesellschaft, 2010), 95, 118*.

[108] J. Gerald Janzen, "Habakkuk 2:2–4 in Light of Recent Philological Advances," *HTR* 73 (1980): 53–78, argues that 2:4 refers to "the *relation* of the soul or self, by way of attitude, feeling or desire, or action, toward something *other* than itself."

the peoples." If instead of "wine" (so the Hebrew text) we read "wealth" with the Habakkuk Pesher from Qumran (so NJB, NJPS),[109] this verse explores the causes and consequences of not recognizing God and following his will: "wealth deceives." The juxtaposition of the proud person's insatiable desire for more and the fact that wealth deceives is particularly ironic, and anticipates the judgments announced in the woes that follow. No less incisive is the comparison of Babylon with death and Sheol, domains that in the Old Testament are under Yhwh's exclusive control, but which the empire arrogates to itself.[110]

The association of Babylon with death and the text's references to individuals as well as groups suggest that "Babylon" in Habakkuk is not a precise, socio-political label designating all those living in the territories it controls (recall the similar significance of "Assyria" in Chapter 2 on Nahum). Rather, Habakkuk's use of "Babylon" refers first of all to those who espouse the empire's ideology and participate in, support, or promote its realization by social, political, and military means. "Babylon" in the Book of Habakkuk thus overlaps, but is not identical to, the Babylonian empire defined in geographic or demographic terms.[111] This point can be illustrated by contrasting Habakkuk's destructive, rapacious "Babylon" with the more conventional, evidently rather tame Babylonian state in which many Judean exiles found themselves after 586. Far from being swallowed alive (cf. 2:5), the deportees were not deprived of the rights of free persons.

---

[109] As suggested by Perlitt, *Die Propheten*, 67, and others. For arguments to the contrary, see Prinsloo, "Inner-Biblical Allusion."

[110] See Legaspi, "Opposition to Idolatry," 468–69, on the link between Babylon and "Death personified."

[111] This distinction parallels that within Judah between the "righteous/just" and the "wicked."

They lived a family life, had property (land, slaves, silver), were creditors and debtors, had the right to engage in litigation and in commerce and business transactions, and had the right to witness contracts and suits and to maintain their ancestral relations.[112]

It is of course true, as Jean-Philippe Delorme has argued, that forced deportations "radically disturb the collective consciousness of displaced populations," exposing "their culture and identity to foreign influences."[113] But these realities map on to others in complex ways, as shown by his recognition that the Judean deportees "were in fact able to live a quiet and undisturbed life in southern Babylonia, while Judean identity thrived and prospered."[114] To note an overtly religious dimension of this experience, the theological significance of the worship of Marduk and other Babylonian deities contrasts with the experience of Judean deportees living in Babylonia, who often bore names linked to YHWH.[115] In the same vein, there is "no information that the exiles in Assyria and

---

[112] Bustaney Oded, *Mass Deportations and Deportees in the Neo-Assyrian Empire* (Wiesbaden: Ludwig Richter Verlag, 1979), 87. Oded's more recent work, such as "Observations on the Israelite/Judean Exiles in Mesopotamia during the Eighth-Sixth Centuries BCE," in *Immigration and Emigration within the Ancient Near East*, ed. K. Van Lerberghe and A. Schoors, OLA 65 (Leuven: Peeters, 1995), 205–212 (208), recognizes that immediately after 586 some Judeans may have been compelled to labor for the state for a short time.

[113] Jean-Philippe Delorme, "The Āl-Yāḫūdu Texts (ca. 572–477 BCE): A New Window into the Life of the Judean Exilic Community of Babylonia," in *Next Year in Jerusalem: Exile and Return in Jewish History*, ed. Leonard J. Greenspoon, SJC 30 (West Lafayette, IN: Perdue University Press, 2019), 71–98 (71).

[114] Delorme, "The Āl-Yāḫūdu Texts," 72.

[115] Paul-Alain Beaulieu, "Yahwistic Names in Light of Late Babylonian Onomastics," in *Judah and the Judeans in the Achaemenid Period: Negotiating Identity in an International Context*, ed. Oded Lipschits, Gary N. Knoppers, and Manfred Oeming (Winona Lake, IN: Eisenbrauns, 2011), 245–66 (258–59).

Babylonia ... were subject to religious coercion by the rulers of the Assyrian and Babylonian empires."[116] These points underline the distinction between rapacious "Babylon" as cipher and Babylon the real-world diverse social entity into which the Judean exiles moved. This distinction is essential to understanding the significance of the announcements of woe in 2:6–20 and their relation to the global horizon presented in chapter 3.

Habakkuk 2:6–20 consists of five pronouncements of woe against Babylon that critique various dimensions of its imperialism, with idolatry emphatically concluding the series. "These" refers to "all nations" and "all peoples" that Babylon takes as its prey, and connects this section to the previous one (2:5–6). These woes allege several new offenses of Babylon, the most important of which is elicits the explicit affirmation that Yhwh *will punish* Babylon for these sins.[117] Indeed, punishment is inherent in woe oracles, which typically consist of: (1) the announcement of woe and a descriptions of the actions of the guilty party; (2) "a description of the negative consequences" that will follow upon that behavior; and (3) "a conclusion describing the final outcome of these negative consequences."[118] Within the Book of Habakkuk, this literary form is notable for its contribution to the theme of theodicy: Yhwh *will* punish Babylon's imperialism, and in doing so will uphold justice *despite* the delay that intervenes between crime and punishment. The masculine singular grammar used throughout the woes most naturally refers to the Babylonian king, the consummate representative of the empire. Although the rhetorical audience of these woes is the Babylonian monarch and the

---

[116] Oded, "Observations," 209.
[117] Brian Peckham, "The Vision of Habakkuk," *CBQ* 48 (1986): 617–36 (625–26), offers a full list of the attitudes and activities that the book condemns.
[118] Floyd, *Minor Prophets*, 135.

empire that he represents, they are announced for the benefit of Judah, the real audience. This underlines further the point made in the woes themselves that Babylon is unaware of the destruction that looms over it.

The first woe (2:6–8) condemns Babylon and especially its king for taking "what is not his." This accusation of theft is specified as plundering later in the oracle, where it is connected to bloodshed and violence (recurrent themes in the Babylonian royal annals surveyed earlier). This series of woes asserts that the inevitable (if not immediate) consequence of such action is retribution, which ironically sees the empire plundered by its former victims. The participation of "all the remnant of the peoples" (2:8) in this punishment and the restoration of stolen wealth hints that the reestablishment of justice will be widespread (cf. 2:14, 20).

The second woe, in 2:9–11, focuses on the contribution of the empire's ill-gotten gain to its imperial project, described first as a house, then as a nest that is placed so high as to be beyond the reach of its enemies. The theme of construction may have in view Nebuchadnezzar's many building projects in Babylon and elsewhere,[119] and the metaphor of a house elegantly includes the "peoples" that Babylon hews down as raw material for its construct. The ironic reality that wealth deceives (2:5) is modified here by connecting it to the practice of excessive violence, in which Babylon unwittingly "sins against its own life" (2:10).[120] The imperial project thus inevitably sows the seeds of its own destruction, above all because it is pursued without regard to Yhwh, whom it ignores, and without regard to the inherent value and significance

---

[119] Roberts, *Nahum, Habakkuk, Zephaniah*, 120.
[120] Some contemporary examples of this same irony are explored by Charles King, "How a Great Power Falls Apart: Decline Is Invisible from the Inside," *Foreign Affairs* (30 June 2020).

of the human beings that it abuses, exploits, and destroys. The chorus of voices that arises in response reveals that such a "house" is inherently unstable. This chorus is evidently heard by Yhwh, who guarantees the end of the empire.

Like the first two woes, the third (2:12–14) condemns the violence and moral wrongs that accompanied Babylon's rise. To this it adds the idea that the empire turned the labor of its conquered subjects to evil ends, and ultimately to "fire" and "nothing."[121] As the rhetorical question that begins 2:13 suggests, this is the bitter fruit of Babylon's imperialism *and* of God's action in history. The nations' involuntary contribution to the Babylonian imperial project will come to nothing precisely because Babylon has taken it by violence and uses it for corrupt purposes. The last verse of the oracle contrasts this "nothing" with the establishment of Yhwh's rule, summarized by the recognition of his unique divine "glory" by individuals across the globe. This perspective reaches beyond the fall of Babylon to an ideal reality like that presented in Habakkuk 3, and foresees the replacement of the violence and injustice of Babylon by divinely established peace and justice.

The fourth woe (2:15–17) focuses first on a component of imperial strategy that, like the fishing metaphor in chapter 1, involves the dehumanizing of Babylon's victims by creating trust and a lack of vigilance in the potential victims that expose it to exploitation. In the metaphor used here, an individual provides his "neighbor" with alcohol not to celebrate peacefully with him (as is

---

[121] Dietrich, *Nahum, Habakuk, Zefanja*, 151, thinks that "nations" and "peoples" refer to Babylon. Brian Tidiman, *Nahoum, Habaquq, Sophonie*, CEB (Vaux-sur-Seine: Edifac, 2009), 191, suggests that Babylon's destructive military tactics are in view. Roberts, *Nahum, Habakkuk, Zephaniah*, 123, seems most correct when he argues that this futility is the result of Babylon's appropriation of the goods and wealth of the conquered; cf. Jer 51:58.

often the case in the Old Testament, cf. Deut 12:15–18; Ps 104:15), but in order to inebriate him and then strip him naked so as to satisfy his own lust. Although sexual violence likely accompanied some military campaigns in the ancient Near East,[122] the metaphor focuses on the way that political conquest, "after rendering the conquered peoples helpless, systematically strips away their dignity and honor for the conqueror's own selfish, shameful, and insatiable gratification."[123] This exploitation will be punished by YHWH, who will make Babylon drink the cup of divine wrath. The empire will also be stripped of its glory and shamed for its onerous acts, suffering a fate like that which it brought upon its victims (Nahum 3 affirms the same against Assyria). This punishment is both appropriate (the punishment fits the crime) and effective, since it manifests the empire's weakness and fragility to those it had dominated.[124]

The focus then shifts slightly to the now-familiar theme of generic violence against the inhabitants of the states and territories Babylon has conquered, but adds violence against Lebanon and the wildlife found there. This ecological condemnation of "humanity's abuse of its authority over the rest of creation"[125] probably refers to hunting for sport and to Nebuchadnezzar's use of lumber from Lebanon for construction projects in Babylon. A royal inscription that he authored begins with the king's assertion that: "I have made ... the city of Babylon to the foremost

---

[122] Philippe Clancier, "Hommes guerriers et femmes invisibles, le choix des scribes dans le Proche-Orient ancien," *Clio* 39 (2014): 19–36, reviews some rather ambiguous Neo-Assyrian evidence of this phenomenon.

[123] Roberts, *Nahum, Habakkuk, Zephaniah*, 124.

[124] Cf. R. Antony Duff, "Punishment," in *The Oxford Handbook of Practical Ethics*, ed. Hugh LaFollette (Oxford: Oxford University Press, 2003), 331–57 (343).

[125] So Roberts, *Nahum, Habakkuk, Zephaniah*, 125.

among all the countries and every human habitation; its name I have [made/elevated] to the (most worthy of) praise among the sacred cities."[126]

Nebuchadnezzar goes on to recount that Lebanon, "the luxurious forest of Marduk, the smell of which is sweet," has cedars that no other god had desired and no other king had felled, but which "Marduk [had desired] as a fitting adornment for the palace of the *ruler* of heaven and earth."[127] Ironically, as background to his account of his use of Lebanon's forests, the king states that he liberated Lebanon from "a foreign enemy [that was] ruling and robbing (it of) its riches." Then follows his most impressive exploit:

> What no former king had done (I achieved): I cut through steep mountains, I split rocks, opened passages and (thus) I constructed a straight road for the (transport of the) cedars. I made the Arahtu flo[at] (down) and carry to Marduk, my king, mighty cedars, high and strong, of precious beauty and of excellent dark quality, the abundant yield of Lebanon, as (if they be) reed stalks (carried by) the river. ... I ere[cted there] a stela (showing) me (as) everlasting king (of this region).[128]

Several features of the YHWHistic worldview that Habakkuk reflects establish the culpable nature of the Babylonian king's appropriation of Lebanon's resources. First, Lebanon, like the rest of the world, belongs to YHWH its creator (cf. Ps 104:16), so the use of its trees without acknowledging him as ultimate owner is illicit. This offense is made worse because the lumber will be used in a temple for another god. Further, the wild animals that lived in Lebanon also belong to YHWH, and their needless killing (whether for sport or as the result of the reckless destruction of their habitat)

---

[126] A. Leo Oppenheim, "Historical Documents: Nebuchadnezzar II," *ANET*, 307.
[127] Oppenheim, "Historical Documents," 307 (italics original).
[128] Oppenheim, "Historical Documents," 307.

is morally wrong (cf. Ps 104:17–18).[129] Finally, the "violence" mentioned in 2:17 is not be limited to flora and fauna in light of the fact that Nebuchadnezzar destroyed those who were taking Lebanon's resources before his arrival; their spilled blood, and that of victims in "cities," brings the woe oracle to a close.

The fifth and final woe (2:18–20) is the only one to focus on Babylon's idolatry. It first asserts that iconic worship is futile because the gods connected to the images do not in fact exist.[130] In contrast to such pseudo-deities, YHWH alone can act freely in history, and the closing warning for "all the earth to be silent before him" expands the scope of the woe to include the world as a whole. This emphasis on YHWH's awesome and unparalleled majesty and authority is the theological foundation for all the woes against Babylon in this section, and points "to the root cause of the oppressor's atrocities: its failure to recognize YHWH as sovereign."[131] In slightly different terms, "the prophet understands the cultic activities of the Babylonians within the context of their characterization as insatiable, death-dealing overlords. …

---

[129] See, for arguments in this vein, Daniel Miller, *Animal Ethics and Theology: The Lens of the Good Samaritan* (London: Routledge, 2012). In contrast to the treatment of animals in Nebuchadnezzar's text, Philip M. Sherman, "Animals," in *The Oxford Encyclopedia of the Bible and Law*, ed. Brent A. Strawn (Oxford: Oxford University Press, 2015), 24–32, draws attention to Scripture's contrasting ideal of "a future when the relationship between humans and animals will be healed." Saul M. Olyan, "Are There Legal Texts in the Hebrew Bible That Evince a Concern for Animal Rights?" *BI* 27 (2019): 321–39, argues that texts like Exod 23:10–12 grant "rights" defined as "entitlements guaranteed by law that are not contingent upon the needs or demands of others" to a variety of animals, both wild and domesticated (327, 329). Beth A. Berkowitz, "Animal Studies and Ancient Judaism," *CurBR* 18 (2019): 80–111, surveys Jewish perspectives on the question.

[130] The Hebrew term used for these deities, ʾĕlîlîm, has the meaning of "non-existent things," cf. Andersen, *Habakkuk*, 254.

[131] Sweeney, "Structure," 73.

They [Babylonian cultic activities] are merely a screen, a means by which the Babylonians conceal a deeper allegiance to their actual god: Death."[132]

This final woe thus sets God over against – and above – the agents of empire whose ultimate fate all five woe oracles detail. In response to Habakkuk's second complaint, YHWH is coming to inflict definitive punishment on Babylon and, ultimately, to establish his rule on earth.[133] In bringing down Babylon, God brings life to those it has dominated and used for its own purposes. The related consummation of God's purposes globally will bring life in all its fullness to those who know him and flourish in his kingdom (2:14).

Habakkuk's Faithful Prayer: YHWH Will Ultimately Bring about Full Justice and Full Deliverance (3:1–19)

The prayer that concludes the five-part dialogue between Habakkuk and YHWH includes a vision of what YHWH has done and will do in response to the prophet's earlier complaints. Considering the sharp tone and urgency of Habakkuk's argument in 1:12–2:1, it is remarkable that he trusts God's word enough to wait for him to bring about what he promises, especially since that means witnessing "the day of trouble" that will bring destruction and chaos upon the prophet and his fellow Judeans.

Habakkuk's petition at the beginning of the prayer identifies its subject matter as YHWH and his "work." Interestingly, the prophet both "fears" this activity and asks YHWH to revive and make it

---

[132] Legaspi, "Opposition to Idolatry," 469.
[133] Perlitt, *Propheten*, 80, thinks the Jerusalem temple is in view, since YHWH's presence was manifest there, while Tidiman, *Nahoum, Habaquq, Sophonie*, 198, implies that the theophanies summarized in chapter 3 make Jerusalem his destination rather than his point of departure.

known, with the parallel request that mercy would limit this manifestation of divine wrath and justice (3:2).[134] While this petition has reference primarily to Judah, the homeland of the prophet that will soon be invaded (3:16), the significant destruction caused by Babylon's destruction of Jerusalem and the deportation of many Judeans seem to stand in tension with this request. Yet the rest of the prayer never mentions Judah, and the absence of Babylon is equally striking. In the vision and the prophet's subsequent reflection upon it (3:3–15), we find instead the generic categories of the "nations" and "the wicked" as God's enemies and "your people" and "your anointed one," as those on God's side. Alongside the references to a wide variety of geographical and temporal settings, these features create a global stage on which the smaller Judah-Babylon scenario plays out as only part of a much larger drama. In the same way, God's role and deeds as Divine Warrior relativize the actions of the Babylonian monarch and his armies described in earlier chapters.[135] In other words, chapter 3 assumes the reliability of the divine promises to punish Babylon in the series of woes in chapter 2, but widens the field of view so that the punishment of Babylon is seen as part of a "work" that will ultimately eliminate *all* evil and fully establish Yhwh's kingdom in fulfillment of 2:14, 20.

The prayer consists of two sections: a vision of Yhwh's theophanic appearances (3:3–7) referring to Yhwh in the third person and reflection upon those events addressed to Yhwh in the second person (3:8–15). One of the more difficult questions regarding

---

[134] While some contemporary translations emend the Hebrew verb "fear" (NAU) or "be in awe" (NJPS) in favor of "see" (e.g., Luther Bibel 2017), textual and other considerations favor retaining "fear"; see Jamie A. Banister, "'I Feared' or 'I Saw' in Habakkuk 3:2?," *Bib* 97 (2016): 527–36.

[135] Watts, "Psalmody in Prophecy," 215.

the interpretation of this hymn is whether these theophanic snapshots are in the past, the present, or the future. The variety of verbal forms used throughout the passage makes it impossible to resolve the chronological question apart from more complicated interpretative issues (see later in this chapter).[136] Similarly, although 3:3–7 echoes a number of theophanies described elsewhere in the Old Testament, including "the exodus (3:5; cf. Exod 9:3), the crossing of the Reed Sea (Hab 3:10; cf. Exod 14:22), the Sinai theophany (Hab 3:4; cf. Exod 19:16–18), and the divinely enabled entry of Canaan (Hab 3:11; cf. Josh 10:12–14),"[137] it is not clear that Habakkuk is seeing a sort of highlight reel from the past.[138] Indeed, the very first verb, in 3:3, arguably sets what follows in the *present* or *future*: "God comes from Teman." This suggests that the psalm extrapolates from biblical accounts of past theophanies and sketches a composite, present–future theophany in which God fully triumphs over his enemies. As Watts explains:

> Habakkuk 3 employs simultaneously both a climactic victory hymn and an expression of trust *prior to deliverance*, a combination never found in Hebrew narrative. Neither does the book

---

[136] Contra Crouch, "Nahum, Habakkuk, and Zephaniah," 372, the use of (not only) the imperfect/prefix conjugation to describe "YHWH's actions against the chaotic waters" does not settle the question. John A. Cook, *Time and the Biblical Hebrew Verb: The Expression of Tense, Aspect, and Modality in Biblical Hebrew*, LSAWS 7 (Winona Lake, IN: Eisenbrauns, 2016), offers careful arguments for a tense, aspect, and modality understanding that does not tie temporal succession solely to verbal forms.

[137] Timmer, *Nations*, 145. For additional intertextual connections, see Gert T. M. Prinsloo, "Yahweh the Warrior: An Intertextual Reading of Habakkuk 3," *OTE* 14 (2001): 475–93 (478–82).

[138] Shmuel Aḥituv, "The Sinai Theophany in the Psalm of Habakkuk," in *Birkat Shalom: Studies in the Bible, Ancient Near Eastern Literature, and Postbiblical Judaism Presented to Shalom M. Paul on the Occasion of His Seventieth Birthday*, ed. Chaim Cohen et al. (Winona Lake, IN: Eisenbrauns, 2008), 225–32 (232), even suggests that "the psalm … is devoid of any historical allusions."

reflect the actual events of deliverance as stories surrounding psalms always do, either prior to victory hymns or after thanksgivings. Habakkuk replaces narrative closure with prophetic *anticipation*, with the result that the tension between oppressive reality (chs. 1–2) and salvific hope (3.2–15) remains taut to the end (cf. 3.16–17 with 3.18–19).[139]

Understood in this way, the hymn presents Yhwh as the only true (divine) warrior, whose glory, weapons, and strength are unequaled. His anger is directed against "the nations" (3:6, 12) and "the wicked" (3:13), while he brings "salvation" and "deliverance" (3:8, 13) to "his people" and "his anointed" (3:13). The frequent references to various parts of creation, including the heavens and the earth, the "eternal mountains" and the "everlasting hills," the rivers and the sea, the mountains, the raging waters, the deep, and the sun and the moon make clear the cosmic extent and significance of God's intervention and simultaneously relativize the claims of other ancient Near Eastern deities by depicting these domains as parts of the world over which Yhwh exercises control.[140] The outcome of Yhwh's intervention is binary and definitive: the wicked lie fallen before him, while his people and anointed are fully delivered. The theophany Habakkuk foresees does more

---

[139] Watts, "Psalmody in Prophecy," 213–14, emphasis added.
[140] For example, Marduk smashes the skull of the already dead Tiamat as he prepares to take his place at the head of the Babylonian pantheon; see Benjamin R. Foster, "Epic of Creation," *COS* 1:390–402 (398) (tablet 4, line 130). Similarly, the power to establish order is attributed to several ancient Near Eastern deities by depicting their victory over the sea or rivers (see, e.g., Keel, *Symbolism*, 47–49, figs. 42–43). Koert van Bekkum, "'Is Your Rage against the Rivers, Your Wrath against the Sea?' Storm-God Imagery in Habakkuk 3," in *Playing with Leviathan: Interpretation and Reception of Monsters from the Biblical World*, ed. Koert van Bekkum et al., Themes in Biblical Narrative (Leiden: Brill, 2017), 55–76 argues that Yhwh "wears the garment of the storm-god," as it were, while retaining his unique identity as Eloah and the Holy One (72).

than resolve his doubts about divine justice and the problem of Babylon's unchecked imperialism in the Levant and surrounding areas: It presents a "comprehensive response to human sin and injustice."[141] This divine intervention encompasses not only the end of Babylon-as-empire but the end of evil and injustice on a cosmic scale.

The book's closing verses (3:16–19) describe the prophet's reaction and response to the vision.[142] Notably, the resolution of the theodicy problem is not yet a historical fact at the end of the book, so the prophet remains expectant (3:16–17). On the other hand, his trust in YHWH's justice, grace, and wisdom are so determinative for his attitude and outlook that he can "rejoice in YHWH" and "take joy in the God of my salvation" *before this deliverance appears* (3:18).[143] The triumph of his faith, inseparable from God's promised triumph over all sin and injustice, "makes his experience paradigmatic for all the faithful who wait for Yahweh's deliverance."[144]

A THEOLOGY OF HABAKKUK

Presented as it is in the form of an animated dialogue between Habakkuk and YHWH, the Book of Habakkuk makes for engaging reading. This is all the more true in light of its focus on grave

---

[141] Timmer, *Nations*, 145.
[142] For reasons stated earlier, I am treating the chapter as a whole, without reference to its possible history of formation; for suggestions regarding the latter, see Anderson, "Awaiting." Note also Peckham's claim, "Vision," 617–18, that the "pervasive unity of the book is evident from close literary analysis, and an appeal to alternate theories of editing or redaction eliminates its complexity without explaining its composition."
[143] Van Bekkum, "Is Your Rage against the Rivers," 72, observes that YHWH's "grace" makes possible his "support" of the prophet just as his "compassionate deeds" delivered Israel in the past.
[144] Watts, "Psalmody in Prophecy," 216.

injustices in Habakkuk's homeland and on the international scene. The addition of theodicy, in which God's justice with respect to Judah and Babylon alike is initially called into question, makes the book's theology all the more robust. Since God's justice (even when questioned) is the book's central theme, Habakkuk's progressive understanding of and response to God's actions in the past and future weaves these threads together into a whole that resolves his concerns without oversimplification or obfuscation.

The initial problem of interpersonal injustice in Judah highlights the first major theme that the book develops: the *moral significance of human attitudes and actions.* Human beings are uniquely important as volitional beings accountable to God, who gives them life and volition. Despite some differences created by Yhwh's greater proximity to Judah by election and covenant, Babylon is no less accountable to him. The human actions, attitudes, and values that the book considers culpable are evident in Judah and Babylon alike, although there is an important difference of scale due to the latter's imperial size and might. The behavior the book criticizes in both nations is condemned on the level of person-to-person relationships as well as the relations between persons or groups and Yhwh.

The relation of wrong behavior to Yhwh is tied to a second major theme, that of *yhwh's commitment to maintain and ultimately to perfect justice.* Despite Habakkuk's temporary doubts about divine justice, the prophet appeals to Yhwh, whose justice appears to be in doubt, for the resolution of that very problem. These two themes are thus interconnected. The prophet's protests take for granted that God has established certain norms for human behavior *and* that he as creator should hold human beings accountable for their actions. The book's response to this tension involves the qualification that God does not always impose the consequences of one's actions immediately. Delay is possible, and this delay may indeed raise doubts concerning divine justice. God asserts all the same that he is fully aware of the wrongs that the various parties have committed, and that he will respond appropriately to them in due time.

This very real but temporary tension adequately explains the world as Habakkuk sees it while providing a solid basis for his belief that it will not always be so. On the one hand, the volitional nature of human beings and their penchant for self-advancement make injustice, wrong, and violence not only possible but inevitable. On the other hand, YHWH's unlimited power and perfect justice mean that wrong will not prevail or go unpunished, and his provision of atonement allows him to forgive their guilt while maintaining his justice. The final stage of human history will see God overcome and remove sin and injustice from the cosmos and fully establish his rule. In that context, the remnant of humanity will experience life in its fullness, free from the threat of exploitation, without the danger of self-deception and self-destruction, and in harmony with God, one another, and the world.

The book's message recognizes that one's initial response to injustice may implicate God. If God is all-powerful and all-just, how can injustice go unpunished? The exchanges between Habakkuk and YHWH show that YHWH is aware of the delay between human sin and divine punishment of it, but he does not consider that delay to be unjustified. Indeed, the delay between sin and punishment allows for repentance by which the guilty can escape punishment (cf. Zeph 2:1–3).[145] Another of Habakkuk's

---

[145] For a careful explanation of the delay of the Parousia (cf. 2 Pet 3:9), see Christopher M. Hays (ed.), *When the Son of Man Didn't Come: A*

responses also receives a mild correction. While it may seem unjust for God to use an apparently more guilty Babylon to punish Judah, either: (1) the prophet is wrong to assume that Judah's sins committed against the Torah put it on par with Babylon, or (2) the limited scope and imperfection of punishment enacted by human agents mean that such incongruities are inevitable. The latter option is preferable: Given the consistent inability of human beings to conform to God's will, the justice accomplished by human action simply cannot accord with divine justice in every respect.[146] In summary, Habakkuk presents a theology in which God and his justice are transcendent, based on standards that are not limited to personal whims, social conventions, or human decision. This transcendent understanding of divine justice aligns with other elements of Habakkuk's theology, notably its anthropology, in order to press readers toward trust in Yhwh and a commitment to live by and promote that justice as they await Yhwh's full and complete deliverance of those who do just that.[147]

    Constructive Proposal on the Delay of the Parousia (Minneapolis, MN: Fortress, 2016), especially 261–64.

[146] Eleonore Stump, "The Problem of Evil and the History of Peoples: Think of Amalek," in *Divine Evil? The Moral Character of the God of Abraham*, ed. Michael Bergmann, Michael J. Murray, and Michael C. Rea (Oxford: Oxford University Press, 2010), 179–97, draws attention to the similar case of human punishment of sin within ancient Israel's legal system (187–89). M. Daniel Carroll R. distinguishes between God's moral judgments and their historical realization by humans in "'I Will Send Fire': Reflections on the Violence of God in Amos," in *Wrestling with the Violence of God: Soundings in the Old Testament*, ed. M. Daniel Carroll R. and J. Blair Wilgus, BBRSup 10 (Winona Lake, IN: Eisenbrauns, 2015), 113–32.

[147] Van Bekkum, "Is Your Rage against the Rivers," 76, observes that Habakkuk's prayer uses Yhwh's transcendent justice and supremacy over creation "in order to transcend the horrific political-religious reality of the presen[t] and to create eschatological hope."

HABAKKUK'S CONTRIBUTION TO JEWISH AND CHRISTIAN TRADITIONS

The Old Testament and Related Literature

The preceding discussion of Habakkuk's theology has made passing reference to Old Testament texts that may have some genetic relationship with Habakkuk, including Isaiah 11 (for Hab 2:14),[148] Isaiah 13–23 (for Habakkuk 1–2),[149] and some passages in Jeremiah.[150] The dates of composition of the books of Jeremiah and Habakkuk are so close that mutual influence is a distinct possibility, but there is no consensus as to the direction or significance of their literary relationship. The direction of influence from Isaiah to Habakkuk is more likely insofar as the relevant parts of the Book of Isaiah predate Habakkuk. The relationship between Nahum and Habakkuk, too, may involve either the sequential or simultaneous composition of Habakkuk with respect to the probably earlier Book of Nahum.[151] The allusions in Habakkuk's vision to Israel's liberation from Egypt and its experience of YHWH's theophany at Sinai found in Exodus (cf. Hab 3:4 with Exod 19:16–18; Hab 3:5 with Exod 9:3; and Hab 3:10 with Exod 14:22; note also Hab 3:11) are somewhat easier to establish as the prophet's theological interpretation of earlier Scripture in light of the turn toward an earlier dating of much of the Pentateuch in some recent scholarship.[152]

---

[148] See the brief discussion in Roberts, *Nahum, Habakkuk, Zephaniah*, 123–24.
[149] Prinsloo, "Inner-Biblical Allusion."
[150] See Vanderhooft, "Nebuchadnezzar, King of Babylon," esp. 108–11.
[151] Kessler, "Nahum-Habakuk als Zweiprophetenschrift."
[152] Matthias Armgardt, Benjamin Kilchör, and Markus Zehnder (eds.), *Paradigm Change in Pentateuchal Research*, BZABR 22 (Wiesbaden: Harrassowitz, 2019); and L. S. Barker, Jr., Kenneth Bergland, Felipe A. Masotti, and Rahel Wells (eds.), *Exploring the Composition of the Pentateuch*, BBRSup 27 (University Park, PA: Eisenbrauns, 2020).

The contribution of these Pentateuchal echoes and allusions to Habakkuk 3 is multifaceted (see earlier discussion), and mirrors later Scripture's use of Habakkuk's message.

Michael Fishbane notes the fulfillment of Habakkuk 2:3 in Daniel 11:27, where Daniel's vision (see Dan 9:21) adds "consolation and assurance" by promising that the lies of the enemies of God and of his people will be of no avail, "for an end remains for the appointed time."[153] Habakkuk 2:3 is thus part of a group of prophetic texts that emphasize that the "fulfillment of the oracle was temporarily delayed or soon to be realized."[154] Habakkuk also contributed to later prophets' negative depictions of Babylon, and Zechariah 2:6–9[Heb 10–13] probably echoes both the verb "spoil" in Habakkuk 2:8 as well as the larger theme of "the expected reversal of Babylonian fortunes" that runs throughout Habakkuk 2.[155] With respect to the corresponding Assyrian empire that dominates the horizon in Nahum and is also mentioned in Zephaniah, Mark Boda and others suggest that the Book of the Twelve "amalgamates Assyria and Babylon into a single entity," a plausible conclusion in light of their ideological and moral resemblance in these books.[156] Finally, Yhwh's statement in Zechariah 1:15 that he is angry with the nations that he used to punish Judah, with Babylon being foremost among them, picks up the discussion of theodicy where the Book of Habakkuk left off.[157] The Zechariah

---

[153] Michael Fishbane, *Biblical Interpretation in Ancient Israel* (Oxford: Clarendon, 1985), 492.
[154] Fishbane, *Biblical Interpretation*, 509.
[155] Mark J. Boda, *The Book of Zechariah*, NICOT (Grand Rapids, MI: Eerdmans, 2016), 201, 205.
[156] Mark J. Boda, "Babylon in the Book of the Twelve," *HBAI* 3 (2014): 225–48 (245).
[157] This point is made by Julia M. O'Brien, "Nahum – Habakkuk – Zephaniah: Reading the 'Former Prophets' in the Persian Period," *Int* 61 (2007): 168–83 (177).

text shows that the unnamed foe who "will invade us" (Hab 3:16) will not escape divine judgment. As a result, Habakkuk's acceptance of God's promise to settle accounts with Babylon is shown to have been well grounded.

Early Judaism

Habakkuk's translation into Greek as part of what is commonly called the Septuagint has received some scholarly attention, but the complexities of translation make it difficult to determine if the translator lent a specific perspective to his work.[158] With those caveats in mind, recent study suggests that the translator of Habakkuk was an expert scribe who ably preserved the poetic character of the Hebrew text, neither bowing to literalism nor embracing unbounded freedom from the source text. The resulting translation transmitted the theology of the Hebrew text within "a Jewish Hellenistic (Greek) interpretative tradition" that was organically related to the rest of the Hebrew Bible and its developing Greek translation.[159] Even so, several significant differences between LXX Habakkuk and its Hebrew base are evident: The original emphasis on Babylon's destructive power in 1:5–11 becomes instead "a positive promise in a situation of oppression" and the addition of "in me" after "will live by faith" in Habakkuk 2:3 focuses the faith of the just person directly on God; translating the Hebrew *ḥāmās* as ἀσέβεια, "godlessness," in 2:17 may reflect negatively on the Syrian Seleucid rulers of Judea at the time of the translation; and some LXX manuscripts read the plural "anointed ones" rather than the

---

[158] James A. E. Mulroney, *The Translation Style of Old Greek Habakkuk: Methodological Advancement in Interpretative Studies of the Septuagint*, FAT 2.86 (Tübingen: Mohr Siebeck, 2016).

[159] Summarizing Mulroney, *Translation Style*, 199–202.

singular "anointed one" of the Hebrew text in 3:13.[160] Since the Septuagint preserves the Book of Habakkuk as a whole, it is a clear and very early witness to the literary unity of the book (the slightly later transmission of Habakkuk in the Dead Sea Scrolls preserves only chapters 1–2).[161]

The prophet Habakkuk makes a brief appearance in the Greek additions to the Book of Daniel, composed in the last few centuries before the Common Era.[162] After Daniel is thrown into a den of lions in Babylon as his conflict with the priests of Bel intensifies, an angel appears to "the prophet Habakkuk," who was living in Judah and had providentially prepared a stew for some agricultural workers there. The heavenly messenger commands Habakkuk to "[t]ake the food that you have to Babylon, to Daniel, in the lions' den" (Bel 14:33–34, NRSV). When the prophet protests that he does not know the way, the angel takes him by the hair and transports him to the very edge of the den (Bel 14:35–36). This miraculously delivered food sustains Daniel until he is released, and the angel returns Habakkuk to his homeland (Bel 14:37–42). Habakkuk's role in frustrating Babylonian efforts to do away with Daniel in this text may have been conceived in light of the book's strident tone against Babylonian idolatry, with Daniel

---

[160] These are noted by Heinz-Josef Fabry, "Naoum/Nahum," in *Introduction to the Septuagint*, ed. Siegfried Kreuzer, trans. D. A. Brenner and P. Altmann (Baylor, TX: Baylor University Press, 2019), 475–82 (477–78).

[161] Heinz-Josef Fabry, "The Reception of Nahum and Habakkuk in the Septuagint and Qumran," in *Emanuel: Studies in Hebrew Bible, Septuagint, and Dead Sea Scrolls in Honor of Emanuel Tov*, ed. Shalom Paul et al., VTSup 94 (Leiden: Brill, 2002), 241–56 (243–44). Eugene Ulrich, *The Biblical Qumran Scrolls: Transcriptions and Textual Variants*, VTSup 134 (Leiden: Brill, 2010), 617, concludes that fragments 100 and 101 of 4QXII^g preserve small portions of Nah 3:1–3 and 3:17, respectively.

[162] John J. Collins, "Daniel, Book of," *ABD* 2:36.

having a hand in the destruction of the priests and cult statue of Bel, the dragon, and the Babylonians who conspired (unsuccessfully) to have Daniel fed to the lions.

Finally, Habakkuk receives relatively extensive attention in *The Lives of the Prophets*, a Jewish work composed around the turn of the era.[163] This account presents a very compressed account of Habakkuk's voyage to Babylon and Daniel's conflict with idolatry there, focusing instead on his prophecy of the Temple's destruction by "a western nation" (presumably Rome) and of the Jewish cult's "eschatological renewal ... on Mount Sinai," an idea that appears "multiple times" in *The Lives*.[164]

The Dead Sea Scrolls

The Habakkuk Pesher (1QpHab) from Qumran has proven extremely significant for research on the Dead Sea Scrolls and the community at Qumran that transmitted, modified, or created the texts found there.[165] This is due especially to its mention of the "wicked priest" in viii 8; ix 9; xi 4; xii 2, 8, and the "Teacher of Righteousness," both of whom are crucial to understanding the

---

[163] Anna Maria Schwemer, "The Lives of the Prophets and the Book of the Twelve," in *The Book of the Twelve: Composition, Reception, and Interpretation*, ed. Lena-Sofia Tiemeyer and Jakob Wöhrle, VTSup 184 (Leiden: Brill, 2020), 415–40 (415).

[164] Schwemer, "The Lives of the Prophets," 429. It is possible that the geographic locations near Sinai in Hab 3:3–7 and the absence of any mention of Jerusalem or the Jerusalem temple encouraged the presentation of the cult's relocation in the Habakkuk *vita*.

[165] See Timothy H. Lim, *The Earliest Commentary on the Prophecy of Habakkuk*, Oxford Commentary on the Dead Sea Scrolls (Oxford: Oxford University Press, 2020). Armin Lange, *Biblical Quotations and Allusions in Second Temple Jewish Literature*, JAJS 5 (Göttingen: Vandenhoeck & Ruprecht, 2011), 364, recognizes as "uncertain" quotations of or allusions to Hag 1:12 in 1QH^a XIII 10–11, to Hab 2:1 in CD A 4.11–12, and to Hab 2:15 in 1QH^a XII 12–13.

history of the group.¹⁶⁶ We leave these issues aside in order to reflect on how the author of this text appropriated the Book of Habakkuk, to which he unambiguously accorded the status of authoritative Scripture by referring to it as an "[o]racle received by the prophet Habakkuk in a vision" (i 1.) At the same time, the very classification of this document as a *pesher*, a document whose author sought "to uncover new divine messages in ancient biblical prophecies" by reinterpreting them in accord with the sect's beliefs, distinguishes it from other biblical manuscripts that simply transmit, rather than interpret, the biblical text.¹⁶⁷

The sectarian interpretation of Habakkuk begins with the identification of the "wicked" and "righteous" in Habakkuk 1:4 as the Wicked Priest and the group's leader, the Teacher of Righteousness, respectively (col. i).¹⁶⁸ The "traitors of the last days" are defined as those Jews who do not keep the law as the Qumran sect did and who "will not believe" what the Teacher of Righteousness says (col. ii). The Babylonians in Habakkuk 1:6 are identified as "the Kittim," non-Israelite enemies of the Jews who

---

[166] James C. VanderKam, "The Wicked Priest Revisited," in *The "Other" in Second Temple Judaism: Essays in Honor of John J. Collins*, ed. Daniel C. Harlow, Karina Martin Hogan, Matthew Goff, and Joel S. Kaminsky (Grand Rapids, MI: Eerdmans, 2011), 350–67, surveys briefly the decades-long discussion.

[167] See Bilhah Nitzan, "The Continuity of Biblical Interpretation in the Qumran Scrolls and Rabbinic Literature," in *The Oxford Handbook of the Dead Sea Scrolls*, ed. Timothy H. Lim and John J. Collins (Oxford: Oxford University Press, 2010), 337–50 (338). Whether or not the author of the *pesher* modified the text of Habakkuk with which he worked is much harder to determine. See Timothy H. Lim, "Eschatological Orientation and the Alteration of Scripture in the Habakkuk Pesher," *JNES* 49 (1990): 185–94, who argues that the document is essentially a commentary that cites, largely unchanged, the Habakkuk text upon which it is based.

[168] Quotations are from Florentino G. Martínez, *The Dead Sea Scrolls Translated: The Qumran Texts in English*, 2nd ed. (Grand Rapids, MI: Eerdmans; Leiden: Brill, 1996), 198.

are "swift and powerful in battle" (ii 12–13) but who will ultimately not be able to destroy God's people. Rather, in the end, "by means of his chosen ones God will judge all the nations" and "all the evildoers of his people will be pronounced guilty" (v 4–5).

The *pesher* manifests an eschatological focus and validates its new insights regarding the meaning of Habakkuk by stating that "God told Habakkuk to write what was going to happen to the last generation, but he did not let him know the end of the age" (vii 1–2). These eschatological events, the author argues, are inseparable from the Qumran sect's formation under the leadership of the Teacher of Righteousness, who is the only one "to whom God has disclosed all the mysteries of the words of his servants, the prophets" (vii 4–5). God will "free from punishment" the members of the sect "on account of their deeds and of their loyalty to the Teacher of Righteousness" (viii 1–3, commenting on Hab 2:4). The woes against Babylon in Habakkuk 2 are then reapplied to the Wicked Priest and others in Jerusalem whom the author believes are unfaithful and disobedient to God (cols. viii–xii). Since the *pesher* does not include commentary on Habakkuk 3, it concludes by interpreting Habakkuk 2:20 as a worldwide judgment against "all the worshippers of idols, and all the wicked," whom God will "obliterate … from the earth" (xiii 3–4).[169] In summary, the *pesher*'s adept use of Habakkuk demonstrates that its eschatological significance was not lost on some readers even in the late Second Temple period.

The New Testament and Early Christianity

Despite its small size, Habakkuk is cited or interpreted at several points in the New Testament, including Acts 13:41 (Hab 1:5–11)

---

[169] See Fabry, "The Reception of Nahum and Habakkuk," 252–55, for more discussion.

and Hebrews 10:37–38 (Hab 2:3–4).[170] Paul's uses of Habakkuk 2:4 in Romans 1:17 and Galatians 3:11 are well known due to the importance of these passages for the Christian doctrine of justification by faith. In Romans 1, Paul quotes from the Septuagint translation of Habakkuk to argue that God's righteousness as revealed in the gospel can be obtained by "faith" (Greek *pistis*, one of several possible translations of the Hebrew 'ĕmûnâ). "Faith" and "faithfulness" are hardly incompatible, since in the context of Habakkuk 2:4 one must have faith in God's promised deliverance if one is to life faithfully.[171] That being said, the immediately preceding context of Habakkuk 2:4 and the prophet's reactions to God's word here and the vision of chapter 3 begin with his acceptance of God's message of deliverance and then move toward a life of fidelity to Yhwh on that basis. It is probably for this reason, among others, that Paul places the same stress on belief in Romans 1.[172] No less significant is Paul's connection of the righteousness that God will bring with the death and resurrection of Jesus Christ, and indeed with the righteousness of God himself. This event and its significance exceed all but the most far-reaching elements of Habakkuk's message (cf. 2:14, 20; 3:3–15) and establish justice at the highest possible level, giving a robust eschatological dimension to "life" in Romans 1. Galatians 3:11 serves a more focused purpose by denying, on the presupposition of humanity's generally sinful nature, that righteousness

---

[170] See Huub van de Sandt, "The Minor Prophets in Luke-Acts," in *The Minor Prophets in the New Testament*, ed. Maarten J. J. Menken and Steve Moyise, LNTS 377 (London: T & T Clark, 2009), 57–77 (70–73).

[171] Steve Moyise, "The Minor Prophets in Paul," in *The Minor Prophets in the New Testament*, ed. Maarten J. J. Menken and Steve Moyise, LNTS 377 (London: T & T Clark, 2009), 97–114 (99–100).

[172] These points are made by E. Ray Clendenen, "Salvation by Faith or by Faithfulness in the Book of Habakkuk?" *BBR* 24 (2014): 505–13 (511–13).

can be attained through obedience to the law, and insisting on the contrary that it can be had only by faith.

Although Babylon is mentioned in many books of the Old Testament, Habakkuk is among those that most clearly give it a definitively negative portrayal, and Babylon as negative symbol is thus part of the book's theological legacy. As a case in point, Habakkuk's portrayal of Babylon as a combination of imperial, theological, and ideological features that make it God's enemy and guarantee its destruction contributes to the use of "Babylon" in the Book of Revelation. Revelation presents Rome as another instance of "Babylon," defined as a world-city committed to the worship of fallen gods, divination, violence, and the amassing of wealth by exploiting and dominating less powerful states. All of this is articulated already in Habakkuk. Babylon as presented in Habakkuk thus lies at the beginning of a trajectory that passes through Rome and ends in a larger eschatological collective opposition to Jesus Christ as God's resurrected and exalted Messiah (Rev 17:2).[173]

Later Christian tradition gave attention to these and other facets of Habakkuk's message. Martin of Brage (modern-day Portugal, 520–580 CE) warned against the pride exemplified by Babylon, noting that it tempts people to imagine "that they are great, that they need nothing, that whatever they do, think or say is all due to their wisdom and prudence ... they seize the glory of God and offer themselves to be admired in his likeness."[174] In the same vein,

---

[173] See Klaus Wengst, "Babylon the Great and the New Jerusalem: The Visionary View of Political Reality in the Revelation of John," in *Politics and Theopolitics in the Bible and Postbiblical Literature*, ed. Henning Graf Reventlow, Yair Hoffman, and Benjamin Uffenheimer, JSOTSup 171 (Sheffield: JSOT Press, 1994), 189–202; Richard Bauckham, "Babylon IV: New Testament," *EBR* 3:269–73; Ulrike Sals, "Babylon II," *EBR* 3:259–65.

[174] Martin of Brage, "On Pride 8," cited in Alberto Ferreiro, ed., *The Twelve Prophets*, ACCS 14 (Downers Grove, IL: InterVarsity, 2003), 189.

Augustine (North Africa, 354–430 CE) observed in a letter on the nature of grace that pride is contrary to the justice of God "because it puts its trust in its own works."[175] He goes on to cite Romans 1:17 or Habakkuk 2:4: "This justice is the grace of the New Testament, by which the faithful are just, while they live by faith, until … the perfection of salvation."[176] Ambrose of Milan (ca. 340–397 CE) cites Habakkuk 2:6 in exhorting the bishop Constantius to warn his people of the dangers of amassing wealth and encouraged its proper use in these words:

> Let your people not desire many things, for the reason that a few things are many to them. … Let no one spurn a widow, or cheat an orphan, or defraud his neighbor. Woe to him who has a fortune amassed by deceit, and builds in blood a city, in other words, his soul. … Wealth is redemption if one uses it well; so too it is a snare if one does not know how to use it. For what is a man's money if not provision for the journey?[177]

Rabbinic Judaism and Beyond

The prophet Habakkuk occasionally appears, or his book is quoted, in the Babylonian Talmud (completed ca. 600 CE).[178]

---

[175] Augustine, Letter 140.30, cited in Ferreiro, *The Twelve Prophets*, 192.

[176] Augustine, Letter 140.30, in Sister Wilfrid Parsons, *Saint Augustine: Letters, Volume III (131–164)*, The Fathers of the Church 20 (Washington, DC: Catholic University of America Press, 1953), 122.

[177] Ambrose, Letter 15, in Mary Melchior Bevanka, *Saint Ambrose: Letters 1–91*, The Fathers of the Church 26 (Washington, DC: Catholic University of America Press, 1954), 80–81.

[178] The date at which the Babylonian Talmud was completed is uncertain; see Richard Kalmin, "The Formation and Character of the Babylonian Talmud," in *The Late Roman-Rabbinic Period*, ed. Steven T. Katz, CHJ 4 (Cambridge: Cambridge University Press, 2006), 840–76 (842). On the use of prophetic texts in early Jewish literature, see Jacob Neusner, *Habakkuk, Jonah, Nahum and Obadiah in Talmud and Midrash: A Source Book*, Studies in Judaism (Lanham, MD: University Press of America, 2007). A comprehensive list

There he is an example of patient waiting until God responds to one's prayer (b. Taʿan. 23a), expressed in the words of Habakkuk 2:1. In a detailed discussion of the chronology of the end of the world in b. Sanh.n, the quotation of Habakkuk 2:3 is attributed to Rabbi Nathan and interpreted as a warning to those "who calculate the end time" – may they "puff [their last] breath!"[179] Perhaps most strikingly, b. Mak. of the Babylonian Talmud ends its discussion of the condensation of the 613 commandments of the Torah "to one, as it is said, 'The righteous lives by his faith.'"[180]

In the Jewish calendar of Scripture readings for synagogue worship, Habakkuk 3 is read on the second day of the Feast of Weeks (Shavuot), and the book's mention of agriculture alongside the vision of the theophany matches perfectly the Feast's dual focus on "the wheat harvest along with the lawgiving on Mount Sinai."[181] The venerable tradition of "arguing with God" within Judaism looks back to Abraham's intercession for the city of Sodom (Gen 18:22–32) as well as to Habakkuk's protests against apparent divine injustice, but it maintains "deepest reverence and

---

of references to Habakkuk in the rabbinic corpus can be found in Caleb T. Friedman (ed.), *A Scripture Index to Rabbinic Literature* (Peabody, MA: Hendrickson Academic, 2021), 402–3.

[179] Norman Solomon (trans.), *The Talmud: A Selection*, Penguin Classics (London: Penguin, 2009), 515–16.

[180] Solomon (trans.), *Talmud*, 527. For a perceptive analysis of the reception of Hab 2:4 in this tractate, see Devora Steinmetz, "Justification by Deed: The Conclusion of Sanhedrin-Makkot and Paul's Rejection of Law," *HUCA* 76 (2005): 133–87. Shimon Bakon, "Habakkuk: From Perplexity to Faith," *JBQ* 39 (2011): 25–30, ties the interpretative differences on this text to the translation (and interpretation) of *ʾĕmûnâ* (28).

[181] See Richard J. Coggins and Jin H. Han, *Six Minor Prophets through the Centuries*, BBC (Chichester: Wiley-Blackwell, 2011), 48.

full acceptance of the Father's will."[182] Wrestling with God's (in) justice is particularly evident in Elie Wiesel's struggle with God after the Holocaust.[183] Wiesel's approach borders on paradox but never abandons God: "Only the Jew knows that he may oppose God as long as he does so in defense of His creation."[184]

PAST AND PRESENT RECEPTION OF HABAKKUK

Over the centuries, a number of elements of the Book of Habakkuk have been taken up in various media and different cultures. In literature, Victorian poetry made frequent use of the powerful image of dangerous foes as "evening wolves" (1:8; Authorized Version).[185] In art, the representation of the prophet by the Italian Dontaello (ca. 1386–1466 CE) presents him "prophesying with oratorical expressiveness," which is quite fitting for a prophet who expressed his complaints to YHWH without reserve and inveighed forcefully against the Babylonian empire.[186] Numerous musical compositions, both secular and sacred, have also drawn on themes and motifs found in Habakkuk.[187]

Much subsequent reception of Babylon in Western culture takes up the negative evaluation of Babylon evident in Habakkuk and the New Testament but applies it to different settings.[188] William

---

[182] Leo Trepp, *Judaism: Development and Life*, 4th ed. (Belmont, CA: Wadsworth, 2000), 279.
[183] See Anson Laytner, *Arguing with God: A Jewish Tradition* (Lanham, MD: Rowman & Littlefield, 2004), 214–15.
[184] Wiesel attributes this dictum to his "Master" in Elie Wiesel, *A Jew Today*, trans. M. Wiesel (New York: Vintage, 1978), 7.
[185] Coggins and Han, *Six Minor Prophets*, 41.
[186] Coggins and Han, *Six Minor Prophets*, 44.
[187] See the discussion in Coggins and Han, *Six Minor Prophets*, 48–50.
[188] See Anthony Swindell, "Babylon VII: Literature," *EBR* 3:277–78, who briefly mentions Cowper's *The Task*.

Cowper's *The Task* (1784) compares the London of his day with Babylon, and recognizes both the glory and the injustice of the city and the empire it represents. The power and knowledge that Great Britain exhibits and deploys over much of the globe are evident to all:

> In London. Where her implements exact,
> With which she calculates, computes, and scans
> All distance, motion, magnitude, and now
> Measures an atom, and now girds a world?" (lines 715–18)[189]

London is

> ...opulent, enlarged, and still
> Increasing London? Babylon of old
> Not more glory of the earth than she.... (lines 721–23)[190]

Yet London "so fair / May yet be foul; so witty, yet not wise" (lines 727–28).[191] Cowper develops this condemnation partly by reference to the impunity accorded to its imperial endeavors:

> ...thieves at home must hang, but he that puts
> Into his overgorged and bloated purse
> The wealth of Indian provinces, escapes. (lines 736–38)[192]

Similarly, in the novel *Remembering Babylon* (1993), David Malouf "makes Babylon ... a warning about the consequences of the activities of 19th-century settlers in Australia."[193] Other representations of Babylon, particularly in film, "celebrate the West's putative ascendancy over the East."[194]

---

[189] Citations are from Book 1 of *The Task*, "The Sofa," in C. P. Mason, *Cowper's Task, Book I, With Notes on the Analysis and Parsing* (London: Walton and Maberly, 1859), 22.
[190] Mason, *Cowper's Task*, 22.
[191] Mason, *Cowper's Task*, 22.
[192] Mason, *Cowper's Task*, 23.
[193] Swindell, "Babylon," 278.
[194] Erin Runions and Steven D. Mears, "Babylon X: Film," *EBR* 3:282–84 (283).

The mixed reception of Babylon in the two and a half millennia since Habakkuk's composition witnesses to "the way in which biblical interpretation has operated at different and potentially confusing levels."[195] Especially evident is the diversity of moral and ethical standpoints according to which some readers promote solidarity and the collective good over the advancement of individuals or subgroups while others favor the inverse.[196] These characteristically modern concerns are not unlike Habakkuk's concerns about human autonomy and abuse of power. But Habakkuk's solution is not primarily political or even achievable by human agents. The Book of Habakkuk cautions against the temptation to see oneself as entirely or even mainly self-determined and autonomous. Instead, it invites its readers to see the world as created by God and suitable for human flourishing when God's supremacy, justice, and mercy are recognized in tandem with the inherent and equal value of every human being as made in his image to resemble and reflect him, live in fellowship with him, and rule as his vice-regent.[197] When these basic values and paradigms are flouted, the pride and pursuit of self-determinism that follow ironically make human well-being an increasingly dim prospect

---

[195] R. J. Coggins, "Babylon," in *The SCM Dictionary of Biblical Interpretation*, ed. R. J. Coggins and J. L. Houlden (London: SCM, 1990), 74–75 (74).

[196] A convenient overview of some of the challenges involved in establishing suitable political and power relations in society is offered by William Rehg, "Solidarity and the Common Good: An Analytic Framework," *Journal of Social Philosophy* 38 (2007): 7–21.

[197] For these relational, functional, and ontological dimensions of the *imago Dei*, see, respectively, Richard Lints, *Identity and Idolatry: The Image of God and Its Inversion*, NSBT 36 (Downers Grove, IL: Intervarsity, 2015); Michael Horton, "Image and Office: Human Personhood and the Covenant," in *Personal Identity in Theological Perspective*, ed. Richard Lints, Michael S. Horton, and Mark R. Talbot (Grand Rapids, MI: Eerdmans, 2006), 178–203; Colin Gunton, "In the Image and Likeness of God," in Colin Gunton, *Christ and Creation* (Eugene, OR: Wipf & Stock, 2005), 99–116.

by creating injustice and fostering violence. A number of recent authors see in contemporary Western culture the essence of the violent, self-serving imperialism that Habakkuk critiques.[198] The widespread visibility of these wrongs means that they are evident both in individuals' behaviors and in collectives such as corporations and political entities whose "massive technical power" and "spiritual surrender" form a volatile mix.[199]

The prophet Habakkuk, facing a similar specter of a world upside-down, was fully convinced that evil will not triumph. The book that bears his name promises deliverance to those who condemn self-focused individualism, who practice grace and compassion in conjunction with justice, and who ultimately trust not in themselves but in a creator whose commitment to justice is unshakable and whose offer of the righteousness they lack provides hope in the darkest of times.[200] Regardless of whether or not one can accept some or all of the elements that underlie Habakkuk's message, the book's articulation of the perennially complicated relationship between power, human flourishing, and things transcendent continues to press its readers to reckon with the magnitude of these problems as part of finding suitable solutions to them.

---

[198] See Philip Rieff, *My Life among the Deathworks: Illustrations of the Aesthetics of Authority*, with an introduction by Jamies Davison Hunter (Charlottesville: University of Virginia Press, 2006).

[199] René Girard, *Things Hidden since the Foundation of the World*, trans. S. Bann and M. Metteer (Stanford, CA: Stanford University Press, 1987), 261. I owe this reference to Samuel Kimbriel, "Habits for Ideological Times," *Comment* 38 (2020): 10–22.

[200] See Philip Rieff's reflections on the importance of grace and humility for preserving culture in his *Charisma: The Gift of Grace, and How It Has Been Taken Away from Us* (New York: Pantheon, 2007).

CHAPTER 4

The Theology of the Book of Zephaniah

Despite its almost identical historical setting, Zephaniah is quite different from Nahum and Habakkuk. There is no empire that dominates the book's horizon and attracts the majority of the its critique, and non-Israelite nations in general have a secondary role in the book. This inevitably makes Judah the primary figure in the book, and Judah's prominence is amplified by the many allegations that the author brings against it. This same focus on Judah is also present in the contrasting theme of deliverance, and the Judean remnant that survives judgment takes on very clear contours in connection with concrete, personal responses to YHWH such as confession of sin and repentance. The renewal of Judah brings with it, finally, the renewal and blessing of non-Israelites, and what happens to the nations in Zephaniah can be explained only in terms of their relationship to Judah and YHWH. Thus even if the Book of Zephaniah is like the inverted image of Nahum or Habakkuk in terms of the attention those books give to a particular non-Israelite nation, the relationship between Judah and the nations remains connected to Zephaniah's major themes.

Another feature of Zephaniah should be noted at the outset: Despite the significant attention it gives to condemnation, Zephaniah's focus on Judah is neither hopeless nor detached but confrontational, passionate, and ultimately optimistic. The book addresses its readers repeatedly, urging them to recognize their failings toward Yhwh and each other, and to respond in concrete and profoundly personal ways. Although Zephaniah gives some attention to bad behavior on the part of elites, its analysis of the human condition makes its critiques and warnings applicable to all Judeans and indeed to all readers. The drama the book sketches is a matter of life and death, of right and wrong, of good and evil on a cosmic scale.

If there is one meta-theme that includes all the others in the Book of Zephaniah, it is that of a divine kingdom begun at the creation of the world, then resisted and contested in human history but now becoming fully present when God intervenes at the end of history to right all wrongs and bring the world to its intended goal. The progressive unfolding of the Day of Yhwh will see Yhwh's kingdom, first in a nascent form in Judah and then in the world, expand and move rapidly toward its consummation. This full realization of God's rule will bring good in the fullest and most absolute sense to those who live in fidelity to him as members of his kingdom. Conversely, the last chapter of world history will bring woe to those who pursue autonomy and refuse God's royal claims upon them. The twin movements of purification and perfection lead to a world in which all has been set right and God's people enjoy his peace and presence in a renewed cosmos.

ISSUES IN THE INTERPRETATION OF ZEPHANIAH

Unity and Diversity
As was the case with the Books of Nahum and Habakkuk, much interpretation of Zephaniah has problematized a straightforward

relationship of the book's various parts to one another. In what follows, I summarize and critically evaluate various approaches to Zephaniah that separate its constituent parts into historically and literarily distinct units, and typically conclude that the "book" that these parts form retains serious tensions and is better seen as an intermingling of disparate parts.

As a first example, Christoph Levin's theory of the formation of Zephaniah 1:1–2:3 analyzes the different genres and content of these units and subunits. Although Levin thinks prophetic books generally developed in three phases – collecting, editing, and commenting – he nonetheless proposes seven (!) "main layers" for the development of Zephaniah 1:1–2:3.[1] In short, an original "cultic proclamation" scattered across what is now 1:7, 14–16 was gradually elaborated upon, reused, and developed to produce what is now 1:1–2:3.[2] In more detail, the original "liturgy for the celebration of the theophany on the Day of YHWH-festival" (layer 1) was interpreted in light of Amos 5:18, 20 (layer 2) and then used to explain the fall of Jerusalem as a punishment (layer 3) that later focused on worship of other gods (layer 4) before being connected to the future Day of YHWH (layer 5) that would leave no survivors (layer 6) except for the pious (layer 7). The complexity of Levin's proposal significantly reduces its plausibility, let alone its probability, which diminishes with each additional hypothesis. The overall probability of seven distinct hypotheses, if each has a very healthy 75 percent probability individually, is 0.75^7 or 13 percent. Furthermore, Levin's reconstruction depends upon the

---

[1] Christoph Levin, "Zephaniah: How This Book Became Prophecy," in *Constructs of Prophecy in the Former and Latter Prophets and Other Texts*, ed. Lester L. Grabbe and Martti Nissinen, ANEM 4 (Atlanta, GA: Society of Biblical Literature, 2011), 117–39 (118).
[2] Levin, "Zephaniah," 120–22.

assumption that each author or redactor contributed only one literary element to the growing text, which is simply conjecture. In any case, some parts of this work such as the "prophecy of doom" would be quite awkward without later parts such as the "reason for the announced punishment,"[3] and it is thus more likely that they did not exist independent of one another.

In another extreme example of redaction criticism, Tchavdar Hadjiev proceeds from the assumption that oracles of salvation are inevitably later than oracles of judgment, and separates those sections literarily and historically. Observing that 1:2–3:8 "has its own independent integrity, structure, and theme,"[4] Hadjiev breaks that section into distinct parts on the basis of "thematic and structural tensions" that he believes are not possible within a unified literary unit.[5] The result is that the history of the book's formation is based in part on Judah's historical experience and in part on Hadjiev's convictions regarding the points in time at which different literary genres such as eschatology emerged.[6] As already noted in Chapters 2 and 3, however, it is very difficult to assign clear dates to literary genres, and equally risky to tie a particular idea such as the deliverance of the nations to one (and only one) point in Judah's history. The wide variety of conclusions that readers and interpreters reach, despite holding largely compatible views of Israel's religious history and the ways that Israelite prophetic texts were composed, suggests that there are simply too many unknowns in such approaches and that tighter methodological controls for textual and historical reconstructions are

---

[3] Levin, "Zephaniah," 138.
[4] Tchavdar S. Hadjiev, "The Theological Transformations of Zephaniah's Proclamation of Doom," ZAW 126 (2014): 506–20 (509).
[5] Hadjiev, "Transformations," 511, 515, etc.
[6] Hadjiev, "Transformations," 516–19.

required if such approaches are to be convincing to anyone other than the author who penned them.⁷

Nevertheless, Hadjiev's work highlights a feature of Zephaniah that has led many readers to doubt its coherence or homogeneity – namely, its juxtaposition of judgment against some nations and deliverance of others. This is most evident in 2:11, which is surrounded by oracles of doom against several near or far neighbors of Judah but which also foresees an unspecified group of non-Israelites bowing down to Yнwн and thus either escaping or surviving that judgment. This sharp juxtaposition leads Daniel Ryou to conclude that this verse "presents a striking tension within its context in that it envisages a wider horizon than Moab and Ammon." Ryou therefore attributes this sentence to the latest redactor that worked on the passage.⁸

In evaluating this kind of juxtaposition, readers must determine whether, and to what degree, the pairing of judgment and deliverance makes sense within the immediate literary context. Since the states and nations mentioned in the larger context (Philistia in 2:4–7, Moab and Ammon in 2:8–9, Cush in 2:12, and Assyria in 2:13–15) are not a complete list of Judah's present potential enemies,⁹ one could infer that they merely represent a larger global horizon that more or less overlaps with that of 2:11 (they lie to the west, east, south, and north of Judah, respectively). In this case, the religious transformation of *some* non-Israelites

---

⁷ For similar examples, see Heinz-Dieter Neef, "Vom Gottesgericht zum universalen Heil: Komposition und Redaktion des Zefanjabuches," *ZAW* 111 (1999): 530–46; Nicholas R. Werse, "Realigning the Cosmos: The Intertextual Image of Judgment and Restoration in Zephaniah," *JSOT* 45 (2020): 111–27.

⁸ Daniel H. Ryou, *Zephaniah's Oracles against the Nations: A Synchronic and Diachronic Study of Zephaniah 2:1–3:8*, BibInt 13 (Leiden: Brill, 1995), 301, 302.

⁹ Ehud Ben Zvi, *A Historical-Critical Study of the Book of Zephaniah*, BZAW 198 (Berlin: de Gruyter, 1991), 299, notes that Edom and Egypt are absent.

in 2:11 can quite easily be understood as one side of a complex reality that also includes the judgment of *other* non-Israelites.[10] Alternatively, one could understand the "islands" or "coasts" in 2:11 as referring to those entities that witness the judgment of Moab and Ammon.[11] If these or similar explanations do not facilitate a coherent understanding of the book's content, modern readers may understand the tension as diachronic: resulting from later additions that do not fit the earlier texts to which they were added.

The Present Approach to Zephaniah
The problems purportedly besetting the process of reading Zephaniah as a unified whole tend to focus on individual words and relatively simple concepts, such as: Can some non-Israelites be judged while others survive? In what follows, I consider the structure of the book as a whole and observe how its structure, themes, and other features hold it together.

Zephaniah as a Dialogue
Larger-scale literary features of the Book of Zephaniah invite readers to make sense of it as a unified whole. Somewhat like the Book of Habakkuk, but in a more fine-grained way, the alternation between God's first-person speech and Zephaniah's responses to the same create a dialogical nature for the book,

---

[10] So Daniel C. Timmer, *The Non-Israelite Nations in the Book of the Twelve: Thematic Coherence and the Diachronic–Synchronic Relationship in the Minor Prophets*, BibInt 135 (Leiden: Brill, 2015), 250–54.

[11] So Adele Berlin, "Zephaniah's Oracle against the Nations and an Israelite Cultural Myth," in *Fortunate the Eyes that See: Essays in Honor of David Noel Freedman in Celebration of His Seventieth Birthday*, ed. Astrid B. Beck, Andrew H. Bartelt, Chris A. Franke, and Paul R. Raabe (Grand Rapids, MI: Eerdmans, 1995), 175–84 (179).

TABLE 4.1 Alternation between Yʜᴡʜ and Zephaniah as speaker in chapter 1

Yʜᴡʜ	2–6	8–10	12–13	17	
Zephaniah		7	11	14–16	18

TABLE 4.2 Alternation between Zephaniah and Yʜᴡʜ as speaker in chapter 2

Zephaniah	1–5b	6–7		10–11	13–15
Yʜᴡʜ		5c	8–9	12	

TABLE 4.3 Alternation between Zephaniah and Yʜᴡʜ as speaker in chapter 3

Zephaniah	1–5		7c		14–17	
Yʜᴡʜ		6b–7b		8–13		18–20

with each statement closely tied to those around it.[12] God speaks in 1:2–6, 8–10, 12–13, 17; 2:5c, 8–9, 12; 3:6b–7b, 8–13, 18–20; Zephaniah either responds to the divine speech or begins a new speech in 1:7, 11, 14–16, 18; 2:1–5b, 6–7, 10–11, 13–15; 3:1–5, 7c, 14–17 (see Tables 4.1–4.3).

This dialogical structure (among other things) leads Ernst Wendland to see a "masterful arrangement of the book as a whole, in which the form of the text makes a significant contribution to its ultimate 'meaning.'"[13]

---

[12] Ernst R. Wendland, "The Drama of Zephaniah: A Literary-Rhetorical Analysis of a Proclamatory Prophetic Text," in Ernst R. Wendland, *Prophetic Rhetoric: Case Studies in Text Analysis and Translation*, 2nd ed. (Dallas, TX: SIL International, 2014), 497–530 (501).

[13] Wendland, "Drama," 499.

Zephaniah's Structure

A composition's overall literary structure, if it can be confidently identified, can also offer support for reading it as whole. Since "[t]he deletion or rearrangement of any part destroys the existing pattern,"[14] a clearly structured book favors the conclusion that no parts have been added or deleted, at least not without attention to the structural integrity of the final product. Of course, a self-evident structure does not exclude the possibility that the text may have developed over time through the work of various authors, but it does favor the conclusion that any additions or modifications were carefully integrated into the whole with purpose and design. It has been suggested, for example, that Zephaniah 2:1–7 and the book as a whole reflect a structure in which various themes are interconnected: a "warning of the fast approaching Day of YHWH" (2:1–3; 1:2–18), followed by "oracles against the nations" (2:4; 2:8–18), and, lastly, announcements of "salvation for the remnant as a result of a woe oracle" (2:5–7; 3:1–20).[15] The fact that Zephaniah 2:1–7 and the book as a whole share this same structure favors the inference that both this passage and the book have at least literary integrity, not only in terms of structure but also in terms of message: "the message of the book of Zephaniah in its entirety is not punishment which is often taken as the final word of YHWH. Rather, the punishment is merely the means by which the remnant of Israel will receive restoration and salvation."[16]

---

[14] Ivan J. Ball, Jr., "The Rhetorical Shape of Zephaniah," in *Perspectives on Language and Text: Essays and Poems in Honor of Francis I. Andersen's Sixtieth Birthday, July 28, 1985*, ed. Edgar W. Conrad and Edward G. Newing (Winona Lake, IN: Eisenbrauns, 1987), 155–65 (165).

[15] Ball, "Rhetorical Shape," 163, who supports his arguments with lexical, structural, and thematic arguments.

[16] Ball, "Rhetorical Shape," 165 (to which one should add the salvation of some of the nations per 2:11; 3:9).

Similarly, Nicholas Werse has argued that Zephaniah 2:1–3 and 3:6–8, which exhort or warn the audience, frame the oracles against the nations (including Judah) in 2:4–3:5 and are connected to the rest of the book by 1:18 and 3:8.[17] The joining of these sections, which depends less on literary sequence than does the previous argument, "binds the nations and Judah into a shared paradigm of divine judgment and restoration that secures a lasting peace and security for Jerusalem."[18] This argument integrates a proposal for the diachronic literary development of the text – including the addition of part of 1:18 and all of 3:8, verses that "reconceive the nations as the objects of divine wrath rather than warnings for the audience"[19] – with a coherent understanding of the book as a whole. The exploration of Zephaniah's theology that follows later in this chapter explores the book along these and similar lines.

Historical Setting

The opening of the Book of Zephaniah identifies the prophet to whom the work is attributed as well as the historical period in which he lived: the reign of the Judean king Josiah (639–609).[20] Nothing is known of this prophet apart from what is stated in 1:1, which likely identifies him as a descendant of the earlier Judean king Hezekiah (727–698).[21] A connection between Zephaniah and Hezekiah would suggest a critique "from within," something quite

---

[17] Nicholas R. Werse, "Reconsidering the Problematic Tripartite Structure of Zephaniah," *ZAW* 130 (2018): 571–85 (573).
[18] Werse, "Tripartite," 573.
[19] Werse, "Tripartite," 580. One can imagine that both functions (wrath and warning) might exist simultaneously.
[20] Iain Provan, V. Philips Long, and Tremper Longman III, *A Biblical History of Ancient Israel*, 2nd ed. (Louisville, KY: Westminster John Knox, 2015), 328.
[21] Provan, Long, and Longman, *History*, 328.

plausible given Zephaniah's familiarity with the habits of the royal family and Jerusalem elites.[22]

As argued in Chapters 2 and 3 on Nahum and Habakkuk, the importance in many ancient Near Eastern cultures of linking a prophetic text to the prophet whose messages it transmits favors maintaining the link between the prophet Zephaniah and the book that bears his name.[23] More to the point, there is likewise little reason to doubt the late seventh-century setting of Zephaniah. The absence of Babylon from these oracles is an important (if implicit) argument for a date prior to 605 or thereabouts, since Babylon did not intervene in Judean affairs before the very end of the seventh century. The mention of Assyria in 2:13–15 presumes its fall has not yet begun and so allows a relatively early date in Josiah's reign. The other material dealing with foreign nations in 2:4–10, 12 is compatible with the same period. Since Ashkelon fell to Babylon in 604, its mention presumably predates that event, and Moabite and Ammonite incursions into Judean territory fit well Assyria's waning power in the Levant in the last half of the seventh century.[24] The fall

---

[22] Carly L. Crouch, "Nahum, Habakkuk, and Zephaniah," in *Enemies and Friends of the State: Ancient Prophecy in Context*, ed. Christopher A. Rollston (University Park, PA: Eisenbrauns, 2018), 359–83 (377).

[23] John Hilber, "The Culture of Prophecy and Writing in the Ancient Near East," in *Do Historical Matters Matter to Faith? A Critical Appraisal of Modern and Postmodern Approaches to Scripture*, ed. Dennis Magary and James K. Hoffmeier, foreword by John Woodbridge (Wheaton, IL: Crossway, 2012), 219–41; Seth L. Sanders, "Why Prophecy Became a Biblical Genre," *HBAI* 6 (2017): 26–52. For less positive evaluations of the superscription, see Levin, "Zephaniah."

[24] For these two points, see Dan'el Kahn, "The Historical Setting of Zephaniah's Oracles against the Nations (Zeph 2:4–15)," in *Homeland and Exile: Biblical and Ancient Near Eastern Studies in Honour of Bustaney Oded*, ed. Gershon Galil, Mark Geller, and Alan Millard, VTSup 130 (Leiden: Brill, 2009), 439–53 (441, 444–45).

of Cush may refer to the collapse of Cushite control of Egypt in 663[25] or to Judean participation in an Egyptian offensive against Cush during Josiah's reign (see discussion later in this chapter).[26] Although it is very likely that Zephaniah 1:2–3 echoes the first creation account in the Book of Genesis, traditionally attributed to a Priestly author and so dated to after the exile, this is not a convincing reason to date the entire Book of Zephaniah (or even that section) to the same period. This reticence is encouraged by recent Pentateuchal research that has begun to question any exclusively late date of Priestly texts and the significant uncertainty regarding how long the so-called Priestly creation story had circulated in Israel before it was integrated into Genesis 1.[27]

In the immediate context of the Book of the Twelve, a date for Zephaniah in the second half of the seventh century means that the order Nahum–Habakkuk–Zephaniah is not strictly chronological (the same is most likely true of Joel, Obadiah, and perhaps other books in the collection). The current order almost certainly places Habakkuk after Nahum because Babylon came to power as the Assyrian empire disintegrated, and Zephaniah may follow both

---

[25] Nicolas Grimal, *A History of Ancient Egypt*, trans. I. Shaw (Oxford: Blackwell, 1992), 352.

[26] See Dan'el Kahn, "Judean Auxiliaries in Egypt's Wars against Kush," *JAOS* 127 (2008): 507–16.

[27] On the first point, see Susan Niditch, *Oral World and Written Word: Ancient Israelite Literature*, LAI (Louisville, KY: Westminster John Knox, 1996), 134; on the second, see Noam Mizrahi, "The Numeral 11 and the Linguistic Dating of P," in *The Formation of the Pentateuch: Bridging the Academic Cultures of Europe, Israel, and North America*, ed. Jan C. Gertz, Bernard M. Levinson, Dalit Rom-Shiloni, and Konrad Schmid, FAT 111 (Tübingen: Mohr Siebeck, 2016), 371–89, and in more detail Matthias Armgardt, Benjamin Kilchör, and Markus Zehnder (eds.), *Paradigm Change in Pentateuchal Research*, BZABR 22 (Wiesbaden: Harrassowitz, 2019).

those books due to its focus on the still later fall of Jerusalem.[28] But as Ivan Ball has observed, not all of Zephaniah's parts need to be explained against the same historical background. Ball proposes that Zephaniah 2:1–7 is the oldest section, followed by the Deuteronomistic chapter 1, with Zephaniah 2:8–15 reflecting the time when Assyria's fall was imminent and Judah's restoration was a real possibility. Zephaniah 3 was completed last in Ball's opinion, late in Josiah's reign when his reform had failed to bring about the changes Zephaniah hoped for.[29]

Chapter 2 of the present work, on Nahum, has already sketched the political and religious situation in seventh-century Judah, and so it may be quickly summarized here. The primary dynamic during this time was the political influence of the Assyrian empire on Judah. This reached a zenith during the reign of Manasseh (698–642), whose troops occasionally served under Assyria's flag.[30] Rainer Albertz argues that Judean religious practice during this time "came under the strong influence of the Syro-Babylonian religions" (those attested in Mesopotamia and the Levant), something that Zephaniah refers to more than once (1:4–5, 8).[31] This period of Assyrian influence was followed by Assyria's rapid

---

[28] So Thomas Renz, "Habakkuk and Its Co-Texts," in *The Book of the Twelve: An Anthology of Prophetic Books or the Result of Complex Redactional Processes?*, ed. Heiko Wenzel, OSJCB 4 (Göttingen: Vandenhoeck & Ruprecht, 2017), 13–36 (17).

[29] Ivan J. Ball, Jr., *Zephaniah: A Rhetorical Study* (Berkeley: BIBAL, 1988), as summarized by Marvin A. Sweeney, "Zephaniah: A Paradigm for the Study of the Prophetic Books," *CurBR* 7 (1999): 119–45 (131).

[30] *ANET*, 291, 294; Lester Grabbe, "The Kingdom of Judah from Sennacherib's Invasion to the Fall of Jerusalem: If We Had Only the Bible…," in *Good Kings and Bad Kings: The Kingdom of Judah in the Seventh Century BCE*, ed. Lester Grabbe (London: T & T Clark, 2007), 78–122 (103).

[31] Rainer Albertz, "Personal Piety," in *Religious Diversity in Ancient Israel and Judah*, ed. Francesca Stavrakopoulou and John Barton (London: T & T Clark, 2010), 135–46 (143).

decline in the second half of the seventh century, when it was preoccupied with internal conflicts and a final Babylonian revolt that eventually led to Babylon's independence and Assyria's collapse.[32] Assyrian and other Mesopotamian and Levantine influences upon various religious practices in Judah seem to have endured all the same, because Josiah's reforms seem to have focused in part on eliminating such foreign elements (2 Kgs 23:1–20).[33]

For Zephaniah, these religious practices are significant primarily because they are incompatible with the reforms of Josiah and the Book of Deuteronomy on which they were based.[34] According to biblical accounts, Josiah's reform was initiated by the rediscovery of the scroll of Deuteronomy and the renewal of the covenant that Deuteronomy presents (2 Kgs 23:3).[35] This covenant entailed, among other things, the removal and destruction of articles associated with foreign cults that were in the temple and the dismissal

---

[32] H. W. F. Saggs, *The Might that Was Assyria*, Sidgwick & Jackson Great Civilizations Series (London: Sidgwick & Jackson, 1984), 117–21; Mordechai Cogan and Hayim Tadmor, *II Kings: A New Translation with Introduction and Commentary*, AB 11 (New York: Doubleday, 1988), 291–93.

[33] Norbert Lohfink, "The Cult Reforms of Josiah of Judah: 2 Kings 22–23 as a Source for the History of Israelite Religion," in *Ancient Israelite Religion: Essays in Honor of Frank Moore Cross*, ed. Patrick D. Miller et al. (Minneapolis, MN: Fortress, 1987), 459–75 (467–68); cf. 2 Kgs 16:18.

[34] For different evaluations of the historicity of the biblical accounts of Josiah's reform, see Lester L. Grabbe, *Ancient Israel: What Do We Know and How Do We Know It?*, rev. ed. (London: Bloomsbury T & T Clark, 2017), 247–50; and Provan, Long, and Longman, *History*, 374–76.

[35] For representative discussions of Deuteronomy's origin, see Joel S. Baden, *The Composition of the Pentateuch: Renewing the Documentary Hypothesis* (New Haven, CT: Yale University Press, 2012); Georg Fischer, Dominik Markl, and Simone Paganini (eds.), *Deuteronomium: Tora für eine neue Generation*, BZABR 17 (Wiesbaden: Harrassowitz, 2011); Peter Vogt, "Deuteronomy: A History of Interpretation and Evangelical Responses," in *Sepher Torath Mosheh: Studies in the Composition and Interpretation of Deuteronomy*, ed. Daniel I. Block and Richard L. Schultz (Peabody, MA: Hendrickson, 2017), 7–29.

of priests anywhere in Judah who practiced foreign cults (2 Kgs 23:6). According to the Book of Kings, these reforms reached as far as what had been the northern kingdom of Israel but was now the Assyrian province of Samarina (2 Kgs 23:15–20), something possible only if Assyrian control over the area had weakened.

A THEOLOGICAL EXPLORATION OF ZEPHANIAH

Zephaniah's focus on Judah's population as largely disobedient and therefore in danger of being judged and even destroyed by YHWH lends the book a dramatic tone. This tone is sharpened by the assertion that non-Israelites stand exposed to the same danger for the same reason. While the detailed condemnations of various groups provide very clear characterizations of those who will be affected by God's judgment, this negative plotline is eventually joined by a second that reveals that some will not only escape judgment but will also flourish as never before in a radically renewed relationship with God and one another.

Zephaniah's macrostructure is quite similar to texts from across the ancient Near East that grapple with societal decline in real time. Beginning with the realization that the current situation is far removed from an earlier ideal, these texts connect the unfavorable behavior of those responsible to negative consequences but also anticipate or describe the undoing or resolution of the current lamentable situation.[36] This past, present, and future continuum also drives the plot of the Book of Zephaniah. Beginning against the backdrop of a primordial and pristine world in which

---

[36] Alan Millard, "From Woe to Weal: Completing a Pattern in the Bible and the Ancient Near East," in *Let Us Go Up to Zion: Essays in Honour of H. G. M. Williamson on the Occasion of His Sixty-Fifth Birthday*, ed. Iain Provan and Mark Boda, VTSup 153 (Leiden: Brill, 2012), 193–201.

Yhwh's rule is not contested and justice and peace are ubiquitous, Zephaniah announces judgments that will destroy a sizable fraction of humanity and affect the entire world. These judgments are a necessary divine response to uncorrected human disobedience; by the same token, if Zephaniah's audience remains indifferent it will not escape. Second, Zephaniah subtly introduces – initially in subplots, and then dramatically in the final section – a second theme, that of deliverance, which attains its high point in a sinless world in which humanity's relationships with God and with one another are permanently restored. This perfect world is inhabited by those who repent of their sins, live righteously, and "seek" Yhwh.

Taking a cue from Zephaniah's dramatic features and message, the present theological examination will explore the book through the lens of drama, giving attention to the stage it sets, the divine and human actors upon that stage, and the plot development toward its two-part conclusion.[37] I will also attend to the nuances that each successive section of Zephaniah, taken as an act in the book's drama that is rather like Yhwh's "script" for world history, contributes to the themes it develops.[38]

---

[37] I use "drama" in a non-technical sense here and throughout what follows to highlight the distinct chronological aspects integrated in the events Zephaniah recounts and predicts as well as their interrelated movements. For discussion of relatively recent understandings of drama, see Kirsten Dickhaut, "History – Drama – Mythology," in *History and Drama: The Pan-European Tradition*, ed. Joachim Küpper, Jan Mosch, and Elena Penskaya (Berlin: de Gruyter, 2019), 96–100. For its application to Zephaniah in a more focused way, see Paul R. House, *Zephaniah: A Prophetic Drama*, Bible and Literature 16, JSOTSup 69 (Sheffield: Almond, 1988), who argues that conflict and resolution are largely determinative of the "shape and effectiveness" of the plot (61–62) and draws attention to "rising action" and "falling action" (62).

[38] Walter Brueggemann, *Theology of the Old Testament: Testimony, Dispute, Advocacy* (Minneapolis, MN: Fortress, 1997), 552, stresses the importance of capturing a text's "dramatic movement[s]" by focusing on themes as they develop across a work.

Setting the Stage: YHWH's Initially Good World Corrupted

Zephaniah sets the stage by presenting the first plot element (judgment) in terms that evoke the biblical deluge. As described in Genesis 6–8, the flood was a punishment for the worsening "evil" of the human race (Gen 6:5). Zephaniah announces a similar cataclysm in which God will "totally remove ... everything from the face of the earth" (Zeph 1:2; echoing Gen 6:7; 7:4, 23), which should be understood as the consequence of a similarly holistic departure from God's will and a deformation of the originally "very good" world (Gen 1:31). The hyperbolic scale of this judgment, which unlike the primordial deluge includes even the fish and birds, emphasizes that no element of creation – human, animal, or inanimate – will be able to escape it.[39]

If we are to understand the justification for such an action, we need to understand the significance of human beings and their actions in the Old Testament. According to Genesis 1, God created human beings "in his image" (Gen 1:27). This intrinsic resemblance distinguishes human beings from the rest of creation and entails specific roles and responsibilities.[40] For our purposes, it is sufficient to note that in the second creation narrative, Adam receives a focused divine prohibition that will test humanity's willingness

---

[39] Christoph Uehlinger, "Astralkultpriester und Fremdgekleidete, Kanaanvolk und Silberwäger: Zur Verknüpfung von Kult- und Sozialkritik in Zef 1," in *Der Tag wird kommen: Ein interkontextuelles Gespräch über das Buch des Propheten Zefanja*, ed. Walter Dietrich and Milton Schwantes, SBS 170 (Stuttgart: Verlag Katholisches Bibelwerk, 1996), 49–83 (50); similarly, C. J. Redelinghuys, "Creation Utterly Consumed? Toward an Eco-Critical Rereading of Zephaniah 1:2–6," *OTE* 30 (2017): 805–20. The phrase translated as "I will make the wicked stumble" (NJPS, similarly RSV) is difficult, and can also be translated as "the ruins along with the wicked" (NASB).

[40] See the helpful discussion in Gordon J. McConville, *Being Human in God's World: An Old Testament Theology of Humanity* (Grand Rapids, MI: Baker Academic, 2016), 11–29.

to remain in this role, particularly as it involves Yhwh's authority and trustworthiness. The motive clause that follows the serpent's invitation to the first couple to exercise epistemological and moral autonomy underlines the unparalleled importance of these issues: "you will be like God" (Gen 3:5). The first couple's acceptance of this invitation to quasi-divine status marks the entry of human autonomy into history. The twisted and erroneous nature of the knowledge of "good and evil" that their actions produce is evident in their subsequent expulsion from the garden and from life in Yhwh's presence. This sin–exile scheme reappears in Judah's history as interpreted by Zephaniah, who contends that departure from Yhwh's will has become characteristic of his chosen people just as it was of humanity at large long ago.[41] The backdrop for Act 1 is thus Edenic, with a direct (if lengthy) path starting in paradise, winding through history after sin enters the world, and terminating in late seventh-century Judah, where the prophet Zephaniah stands.

Act 1: Humanity's Imminent Destruction as Punishment for Sin (1:2–3, 17–18)
Act 1 begins abruptly: Yhwh will "totally remove ... everything from the face of the earth" (Zeph 1:2). God's destructive punishment is inevitable for the same reason that Genesis uses to explain the primeval flood: Divine justice and righteousness cannot let sin continue unchecked and unpunished. Since the relationship that human beings bear to their creator is all-determining, their

---

[41] Roy E. Ciampa argues that creation is the first point in the creation–sin–exile–restoration structure that spans the entire Old Testament in "The History of Redemption," in *Central Themes in Biblical Theology: Mapping Unity in Diversity*, ed. Scott J. Hafemann and Paul R. House (Grand Rapids, MI: Baker Academic, 2007), 254–308.

actions as volitional creatures are extremely significant, and bring with them consequences of the utmost importance. The mention of the "wicked" in 1:3 summarizes the moral grounds on which this punishment is based, and echoes the condemnation in Genesis 6:5 that precedes the flood account. Although it is "human beings" (*'ādām*, Zeph 1:3) that are threatened by God's justice, the effects of that divine intervention will spill over and affect representative categories of the animal kingdom. So, while only human beings may be guilty of sin, they are uniquely responsible for the effects that its punishment entails for the world around them. The repetition of "humanity" (*'ādām*) at the end of Zephaniah 1:3 reinforces this focus while emphasizing that there is no explicit limit (yet) to the destruction that YHWH will unleash. This global horizon reappears at the end of chapter 1, forming an *inclusio* around the Judah-focused material in 1:4–16.

A link between creation and righteousness is evident in numerous texts from the ancient Near East, and "the close connection between the cosmic and the ethical-social order" explains why God's intervention inevitably affects more than the human beings it will punish.[42] Importantly, the Old Testament's articulation of this link frequently asserts that "once the marred order is restored through punishment ... the world returns again to its order, it becomes whole and healthy."[43] The idea of a new beginning after sin and judgment first appears, canonically, after the flood, in Genesis 8–9. There the human race, preserved in the families that entered the ark, receives a divine mandate that echoes verbatim the one given to Adam and Eve (Gen 9:1, 7). The

---

[42] H. H. Schmid, "Creation, Righteousness, Salvation: 'Creation Theology' as the Broad Horizon of Biblical Theology," in *Creation in the Old Testament*, ed. Bernhard W. Anderson, IRT 6 (Philadelphia, PA: Fortress, 1984), 102–17 (105).

[43] Schmid, "Creation, Righteousness, and Salvation," 107.

reader of Genesis soon discovers, however, that the root problem of sin has not been resolved.

Although the global destruction at the opening of Zephaniah 1 receives some qualification by being limited to "the wicked," there is not the least hint that anything like a new world might eventually emerge from the cataclysm that is imminent.[44] Even with that qualification, this worldwide day of reckoning will be inescapable, and will remove any who disregards YHWH and his moral order. The delay until 2:1 of any mention of the possibility of escape creates a sense of danger that only grows through the extensive critique of Judah in 1:4–16 and the closing inclusion in 1:17–18.

A Subplot: The Punishment of (Some in) Judah (1:4-16)

Nestled within the larger worldwide judgment of Zephaniah 1 is an extensive critique of wide swaths of Judean society. This condemnation focuses on those who do not follow YHWH faithfully and exclusively (if they ever did; cf. 1:6a) and who worship other deities (especially Ba'al) instead of or alongside him. Ba'al's sphere of influence in the ancient Levant was wide, and was believed to involve especially rainfall and agricultural fertility as well as the sea and the underworld.[45] Despite the overall monotheistic tenor of the Old Testament, archaeology and the biblical record contend that worship of Ba'al was neither rare nor limited to non-Israelites.

---

[44] Similarly, Haraldo Reimer, "Sozialkritik und Zukunftsperspektiven in Zef 1-2," in *Der Tag wird kommen: Ein interkontextuelles Gespräch über das Buch des Propheten Zefanja*, ed. Walter Dietrich and Milton Schwantes, SBS 170 (Stuttgart: Verlag Katholisches Bibelwerk, 1996), 38–48 (43), sees in 1:14–16 "purification," not total destruction.

[45] See Wolfgang Herrmann, "Baal," *DDD* 132–39, whom I follow here.

The fundamental sin of turning away from Yhwh to follow some other authority or ultimate good – whether oneself or a deity other than Yhwh – is also evident in the religious practices of the Judean priests Zephaniah singles out. According to Zephaniah, these religious leaders worshiped the "host of heaven" (i.e., the sun, moon, and stars), so the rooftop location of these activities is not incidental.[46] Cults to the astral bodies were celebrated in a number of cultures outside Judah including Canaan, Babylon, and Assyria,[47] and would almost certainly have included divination as a means of discerning the future. As such, these religious pursuits reflect attempts to grasp control and power.[48]

The mention of "those who worship and swear [fealty] to Yhwh but [also] swear by Milcom," the primary Ammonite deity (this is the preferred reading of the Hebrew; a single vowel distinguishes this proper name from "their king"), likely adds syncretism to the growing list of illicit religious practices condemned here.[49] This practice involves worshiping Yahweh alongside one or more other gods, with the deities being essentially peers since the worshippers

---

[46] Herbert Niehr, "Host of Heaven," *DDD* 428–29.

[47] E. Theodore Muller Jr., "Hosts, Host of Heaven," *ABD* 3:301–4 (302–3).

[48] John J. Collins, "Cosmology: Time and History," in *Religions of the Ancient World*, ed. Sarah I. Johnston (Cambridge, MA: Belknap Press of Harvard University Press, 2004), 59–70 (63). The discovery of amulets and cylinder seals at Megiddo in Judah and at Shechem in Israel that depict the worship of astral bodies suggests that this practice was not uncommon in Israel and Judah during the Neo-Assyrian period. See the visual representations in Hubert Irsigler, *Zefanja*, HTKAT (Freiburg: Herder, 2002), 111–12, and Othmar Keel and Christoph Uehlinger, *Gods, Goddesses and Images of God in Ancient Israel*, trans. T. Trapp (Minneapolis, MN: Fortress, 1998), 320–21, as well as the related discussion in Jeffery L. Cooley, "Astral Religion in Ugarit and Ancient Israel," *JNES* 70 (2011): 281–87.

[49] Heath D. Dewrell, "'Swearing to Yahweh, but Swearing by Molek-Sacrifices': Zephaniah 1:5b," *VT* 69 (2019): 737–41, proposes that the Hebrew word in question refers to a type of sacrifice (often human) offered to Yhwh.

swear by them all. Whether one reads "Milcom" or "their king," the prophet alleges that Judeans were granting another entity the same importance that was reserved for Yhwh alone within the solemn context of taking an oath (cf. Deut 6:13–14).[50] In so doing, they rejected God's unique and universal kingship and "turned away" from him. This cannot end well, and Zephaniah commands his audience to be silent in anticipation of the judgment that will eventually fall upon these people (Zeph 1:7; cf. Hab 2:20).

The condemnation of officials and members of the royal family who wear foreign clothing (Zeph 1:8) may seem banal, but the wearing of foreign royal vestments by Judean royalty likely reflects political or trade arrangements with neighboring states and thus further evidence of lack of trust in God's commitment to care for his people.[51] The Day of Yhwh also spells disaster for those "leaping over thresholds" and engaging in violence and deceit in order to enrich their masters (1:9).[52] Stepping over a threshold appears to have been a superstitious practice by which the worshipper respected the presence of apotropaic statues buried near the doorways of royal or cultic sites and believed to ward off demons and

---

[50] Emile Puech, "Milcom," *DDD* 575–76, notes that Baal's very name means "lord" and his rule was thought to extend beyond this life to the underworld, while the name of Milkom, the highest god of the Ammonites, means "to rule."

[51] Uehlinger, "Astralkultpriester," 74–81, presents and discusses several iconographic representations of what are probably upper-class Judeans with Assyrian hairstyles and clothing. Walter Dietrich, *Nahum, Habakuk, Zefanja*, IEKAT (Stuttgart: W. Kohlhammer, 2014), 210, argues in favor of trading alliances. The focus on the court makes it likely that cultic activities are not in view.

[52] The plural "masters/lords" suggests that more than one "house" is in view, and could refer to the temple, the royal palace, and the homes of powerful Judeans among the general population. S. D. Snyman, "Violence and Deceit in Zephaniah 1:9," *OTE* 13 (2000): 89–102, thinks it refers to the palace (99), but also notes that the private homes in 1:13 are filled with wealth that is plundered (100).

other evil forces.⁵³ This practice manifested in the cultic domain an undue regard for illicit means for countering evil spirits, and so parallels the ruling class's readiness to affiliate itself with foreign powers to gain prestige or to curry political favor. Both activities involved putting one's trust in something other than Yhwh for safety or success. Violence within Judah, for its part, revealed that some Judeans treated others in ways that viewed them as nothing more than obstacles between them and material wealth, ignored Yhwh's covenantal stipulations to care for others, and flagrantly misused political, social, and personal power.

The outstretched divine hand of judgment in Zephaniah 1:4 is followed by two other images of judgment: a feast that Yhwh will hold to celebrate his victory over his enemies and the Day of Yhwh. The metaphorical feast that God is preparing appears first in 1:7. Feasts were not uncommon in the ancient Near East, and although their social significance varied,⁵⁴ they were at the most basic level "a central social event oriented toward abundant display and communal consumption with ritualizing tendencies."⁵⁵ At first glance, the feast here is a "patron-role" feast, involving a host (Yhwh) and guests (human beings) who benefit from the

---

[53] This is the view of Ben Zvi, *Zephaniah*, 96–97, and others. The practice is attested in Neo-Assyria and elsewhere; see Christopher A. Faraone, "Hephaestus the Magician and Near Eastern Parallels for Alcinous' Watchdogs," *Greek, Roman, and Byzantine Studies* 28 (1987): 257–80, esp. 268–72.

[54] Michael Dietler, "Theorizing the Feast: Rituals of Consumption, Commensal Politics, and Power in African Contexts," in *Feasts: Archaeological and Ethnographic Perspectives on Food, Politics, and Power*, ed. Michael Dietler and Brian Hayden, Smithsonian Series in Archaeological Inquiry (Washington, DC: Smithsonian Institute, 2011), 65–114 (75).

[55] Janling Fu and Peter Altmann, "Feasting: Backgrounds, Theoretical Perspectives, and Introductions," in *Feasting in the Archaeology and Texts of the Bible and the Ancient Near East*, ed. Peter Altmann and Janling Fu (Winona Lake, IN: Eisenbrauns, 2014), 1–32 (15).

host's "benefaction."⁵⁶ But this is no ordinary patron feast. Not only is it extremely rare for a deity to prepare the feast (in the Old Testament, Isa 25:6–8 and Ps 23 are perhaps the only parallels), but in this case the guests are not exactly invited. Rather, they are "consecrated," meaning "irrevocably dedicated to Yahweh," and so are *themselves* killed as part of the feast!⁵⁷ This is a feast that only Yhwh celebrates, and the event celebrated is his destruction of those who fail to respond appropriately to him as God.

The sins described in Zephaniah 1:9–12 lead to another perspective on punishment that is cast in terms of one's goods being plundered, one's house destroyed, and the stymying of efforts to lead a settled existence (planting vineyards and drinking the wine their harvests yield). Despite the claims by some Judeans that Yhwh neither blesses nor punishes, God's moral consistency is reflected in his commitment to maintain the deed–consequence link that is part of the covenant relationship (see, classically, the Book of Deuteronomy). The plundering and destruction of these naysayers' homes implies that Jerusalem will fall before an unnamed enemy, an event almost certainly to be followed by exile of the population. Not only does the fall of the nation's capital imply a major invasion, but the "futility curses" of building a house that one will not inhabit and planting vineyards from which one will not drink are drawn from a section of Deuteronomy 28 in which exile figures prominently (see Deut 28:30, 36, 37, 39, 41, etc.).⁵⁸

---

⁵⁶ Fu and Altmann, "Feasting," 22.
⁵⁷ This is clearly argued by John de Jong, "Sanctified or Dedicated? הקדיש in Zephaniah 1:7," *VT* 68 (2018): 94–101, who demonstrates that the Hifil of קדש is never used to describe the cultic or symbolic preparation of the guests for a feast.
⁵⁸ The theme of exile is examined from a number of perspectives in Mark J. Boda et al. (eds.), *The Prophets Speak on Forced Migration*, AIL 21 (Atlanta: SBL, 2015).

The complacency of those who think that God is unconcerned by matters of right and wrong (1:11–12) thus involves a tragic miscalculation. This futility curse blends into the "Day of Yhwh" in the following verses. This "day" appears frequently in the prophetic books of the Old Testament and refers to a variety of events that mark significant advances toward, or the final arrival of, "a new and ideal era in history."[59] While "the day" can involve both deliverance and judgment, here it is entirely negative, and is limited to the punishment and destruction of those who live contrary to Yhwh's will.

Act 2: Zephaniah Preaching: The Possibility of Escape for (Some) Judeans (2:1–3)

The looming global judgment at the end of Act 1 (1:17–18) is quite discontinuous with the very brief Act 2 (2:1–3), in which the prophet gives specific instructions to the rest of the Judeans so that they might avoid the worldwide judgment announced in Act 1. Since both the local and global dimensions of the Day of Yhwh are relevant to Zephaniah's Judean audience, the crucial question is whether they are among those who "have sinned" in chapter 1. In chapter 1, even if one thinks one is innocent of the specific sins it condemns, the repeated assertion that God's wrath will affect all of humanity leaves precious little reason to assume that escape is certain or even possible. As a prelude to the book's closing act and the artfully delayed description of deliverance found there, Zephaniah 2:1–3 stands out as the only other mention of a (qualified) possibility for Judeans to escape judgment. In terms of the

---

[59] Shimon Bakon, "The Day of the Lord," *JBQ* 38 (2010): 149–56 (156). Daniella Ishai-Rosenboim, "Is יום ה' (the Day of the Lord) a Term in Biblical Language?" *Bib* 87 (2010): 395–401, identifies some of the more common ways this "day" is referred to and the flexible meaning of the concept.

book's plot, this possibility is highly significant, because it begins to split what until now was a single plot, judgment, into two: *judgment and (or with) the possibility of deliverance.*

Advancing beyond the earlier commands to "Be silent!" in 1:7 and "Wail!" in 1:11, the prophet offers detailed advice on how to react to the threat that prompted those earlier imperatives. The path toward deliverance is simple, at least conceptually: "Gather ... Seek YHWH ... Seek righteousness, seek humility." The first command may call for a "ritual of penitence," but the emphasis lies on the following commands to radically (re)orient one's self and one's behavior to God and his will.[60] These imperatives call for "a religious devotion to Yahweh that involves the serious attempt to live righteously and humbly before him, and that is neither careless about obedience nor haughty in human self-sufficiency."[61] The urgency of the text is palpable. It employs no fewer than four imperatives, the last three of which (in 2:3) follow upon the heels of three uses of "before" in 2:2. The reason for this urgency is readily apparent: Apart from an authentic response along the lines indicated, Zephaniah's audience cannot hope to escape YHWH's wrath or anger, which this short speech mentions repeatedly.

Despite its brevity, this call to repentance corresponds closely to the critiques brought against the Judeans in Act 1, calling for the replacement of those actions and attitudes with their opposites. Worshiping gods other than YHWH, or trusting in other means of deliverance than those he provides, inevitably means abandoning

---

[60] This point is reinforced if the sense of לא נכסף is "who do not desire YHWH" rather than "undesired (by YHWH)," as suggested by Ben Zvi, *Zephaniah*, 140, and Lothar Perlitt, *Die Propheten Nahum, Habakuk, Zefanja*, ATD 25.1 (Göttingen: Vandenhoeck & Ruprecht, 2005), 119.
[61] J. J. M. Roberts, *Nahum, Habakkuk, Zephaniah: A Commentary*, OTL (Louisville, KY: Westminster/John Knox, 1991), 190.

him (1:6). Similarly, using violence and injustice to achieve one's goals, enrich oneself, and accumulate power and influence is a rejection of the righteous lifestyle that seeks the good of one's neighbor. Although it might seem odd to exhort the "humble of the land" to "seek humility," the logic here assumes that humility is not a permanent status but an attitude and a disposition that are continually expressed. It must therefore be constantly cultivated.[62]

All this puts enormous emphasis on humility. Only those who recognize their failure to live in conformity with Yhwh's righteous will and who trust that his grace will cover their inadequacy will turn from their present course to one oriented to and by Yhwh. Such individuals are the precise opposite of those condemned in chapter 1 – yet they may be the same people, since the identity of actors in this drama may change radically (see later in this chapter). Those who respond to Zephaniah's short exhortation do not act with impunity, doubting that God will act in history;[63] nor do they use whatever power they have to abuse others or ultimately trust in human institutions and plans. As a subgroup within Judah, these humble individuals prefigure the "remnant" and "survivors" of Judah later in the book, where the "may" that emphasizes the *possibility* of Yhwh's deliverance in 2:3 gives way to verbs in the indicative mood that assert his unqualified decision to save.

Zeph 2:1–3 introduces a dynamic of unsurpassed importance in the book: the possibility that someone might *move* from being guilty to being delivered from Yhwh's wrath. The extent to which that possibility will become a reality is apparent only later in the book and follows upon drastic divine intervention that produces

---

[62] For an analysis of humility in terms of contemporary theory, see Brendan I. McGroarty, "Humility, Contemplation and Affect Theory," *Journal of Religion and Health* 45 (2006): 57–72.

[63] Reimer, "Sozialkritik," 48.

personal, internal transformation. At this point in Zephaniah 2, however, the emphasis is only on these individuals' personal response to Zephaniah's command to seek YHWH.

Act 3: The Punishment of (Some) Non-Israelites (2:4–10, 12–15)
The element of punishing that is central to Act 3 corresponds to Act 1 and its subplot, with the qualification that Act 3 focuses on non-Israelites rather than the world as a whole or only Judeans. Act 3 clarifies the reasons for God's judgment against the whole world and demonstrates his justice in punishing nations that have slighted and harmed Judah, all the while ignoring God's unique deity and universal reign.

In the flow of the book, all non-Israelites were initially included in the descriptions of humanity that bracket chapter 1. The explicit inclusion of non-Israelites in the condemnations under consideration here shows how the primeval history, which weaves together the destinies of Israel and the nations before either group exists as such, continues to contribute to Zephaniah's theology. For example, Noah's curse of Canaan, one of his grandsons through Ham, also includes a blessing of Japheth's descendants according to which Shem's line would provide for and protect Japheth's (Gen 9:26–27). Further, one might infer that Ham's other descendants, in contrast to the Canaanites, are portrayed as being in a positive relationship with Shem's descendants.[64] The literary structure of the genealogies in Genesis 10 underlines Shem's prominence by placing Shem at the beginning and end of a concentric genealogical structure: "Shem, Ham, and Japheth" (10:1) is followed by the

---

[64] The latter point is advanced by Cain H. Felder, ed., *The Original African Heritage Study Bible* (Nashville, TN: James C. Winston, 1993), 15; I owe this reference to Edwin M. Yamauchi, "The Curse of Ham," *CTR* 6 (2009): 45–60 (48).

"sons of Japheth" (10:2), "the sons of Ham" (10:6), and the children of "Shem" (10:21). In a similar way, Judah is at the center of Zephaniah's literal geography, since the nations or people groups addressed in Zephaniah 2:4–15 (Philistia, Moab and Ammon, Cush, and Assyria) are located to the west, east, south, and north of Judah, respectively, and represent the non-Israelite world as a whole.[65] More importantly still, the future of these groups is inseparable from YHWH's action on behalf of his chosen people.

These and other features extend the horizon of 2:4–15 beyond the political context of the individual nations named, making it unlikely that the passage was composed primarily to advance Josiah's plans for national restoration in the late seventh century. The first people group mentioned, the Philistines, arrived in the Levant from the northeast Mediterranean basin in several stages, beginning already in the early twelfth century BCE. The Bible refers to the technical skills of the Philistines in metallurgy (1 Sam 13:19), and archaeology has revealed a number of Philistine bronze-working sites as well as bimetallic knives that suggest they introduced iron into their cultural milieu.[66] Biblical sources that treat Israel's early history depict the relationship between Israel and Philistia as characterized almost exclusively by friction, especially "from the period of the judges until the early monarchic age."[67] Later periods, however, are not described in such terms, and archaeological finds that bear on trade between Philistia

---

[65] It is difficult to limit the horizon and significance of these oracles to the seventh century as suggested by James D. Nogalski, "Zephaniah's Use of Genesis 1–11," *HBAI* 2 (2013): 351–72 (359–60).

[66] Trude Dothan, "Philistines," *ABD* 5: 332–33.

[67] Carl S. Ehrlich, "Philistia and the Philistines," in *The World around the Old Testament: The People and Places of the Ancient Near East*, ed. Bill T. Arnold and Brent A. Strawn (Grand Rapids, MI: Baker Academic, 2016), 353–77 (362).

and Judah from the ninth century onward, when both were fully fledged political and economic entities, suggest that "during times of economic prosperity, trade overpowered political contention."[68] This détente often coincided with increased Assyrian presence in the Levant, which made it more risky for smaller states to undertake violence against one another.[69]

The earlier Philistine antipathy toward the Israelites, rather than more recent confrontations or violence, presumably lies behind the judgment that is announced in Zephaniah 2 without any explicit accusations or elaboration. The testimony of other biblical books favors the conclusion that Yhwh's punishment is a response not only to Philistine opposition to Israel (e.g., their oppression of Israel during the time of the Judges) but also to Philistine indifference toward Israel's God (see 1 Sam 4–7; 16).

The next groups of non-Israelites that Yhwh will punish are Moab and Ammon, connected to Israel through Abraham's nephew Lot according to Genesis 19:30–38. Both groups settled to the east of the Jordan River and found themselves in occasional conflict with Israel, especially during the united monarchy and shortly afterward.[70] Despite their often adversarial relationship, Ammon probably had economic ties to Judah, since it controlled

---

[68] Itzhaq Shai, "Philistia and the Philistines in the Iron Age IIA," *ZDPV* 127 (2011): 119–34 (127, 129).

[69] In the late eighth century Assyria gained partial and temporary control of some Philistine territory, and Sennacherib V "recaptured Ashdod in 701 and went on to take Ashkelon, Ekron, and Gaza" in the same campaign (L. A. Sinclair, "Philistines," *EDB*, 1050–51). The Philistines remained vassals of Assyria until 604, when Nebuchadnezzar II destroyed Ashqelon and brought the rest of Philistia under Babylonian control; Ehrlich, "Philistia and the Philistines," 366–68.

[70] For Moab, see Num 21–24; Jdg 3:12–30; 11:26; 2 Sam 8:2–3; 2 Kgs 1:1; 3:4–27. For Ammon, see Jdg 3:12–14; 1 Sam 10:27–11:15; 2 Sam 12:26–31; 17:27–29; 1 Kgs 14:21, 31; Amos 1:13.

a large iron ore deposit at Mugharat Wardeh.[71] Moab's relationship with Israel was more difficult, at least during the reigns of the Israelite kings Omri (884–873) and Ahab (873–852), when Israel made Moab its vassal and appropriated its resources.[72]

Although the condemnation of Moab and Ammon does not mention a particular historical situation, their status as faithful vassals of Assyria may have led them to believe that their interests would be furthered by Assyria, which hardly had Judah's best interests at heart. These two nations' spiteful attitude may also have been fostered by the hope that when Egypt established control over Judah as Assyrian power waned, they would benefit from the new situation. Whatever the case, this section of Zephaniah charges these two states with showing spite for Judah and boasting of their own capabilities. These actions have profound consequences because Judah is "the people of Yhwh of Hosts" (2:10), and Yhwh's retribution on Moab and Ammon will parallel his total destruction of Sodom and Gomorrah (2:9; cf. Gen 19:24–25).

After an unexpected interlude that introduces a sharply contrasting plotline by foretelling the transformation of non-Israelites into worshippers of Yhwh (see the subplot, discussed later in this chapter), the rest of Act 3 continues to survey representative nations in their role as Yhwh's enemies, which includes their attachment to other deities. As noted earlier, the fall of Cush mentioned in Zephaniah 2:12 may refer to the collapse of

---

[71] Joel S. Burnett, "Transjordan: The Ammonites, Moabites, and Edomites," in *The World around the Old Testament: The People and Places of the Ancient Near East*, ed. Bill T. Arnold and Brent A. Strawn (Grand Rapids, MI: Baker Academic, 2016), 309–52 (316).

[72] An inscription by the Moabite king Mesha records that after Ahab's death in 853 he threw off the Israelite yoke. See Klaus A. D. Smelik (trans.), "The Inscription of King Mesha (2.23)," *COS* 2:137–38.

Cushite control of Egypt in 663, and would thus have preceded Zephaniah's time, or (less probably) to Judean participation in an Egyptian offensive against Cush during Josiah's reign. Contrary to the claim that "there was no relevance to an oracle of doom about an event which happened half a century before,"[73] Cush's fall as a *fait accompli* would testify to God's control over history and to his justice already having been realized with respect to Egypt's southern neighbor. These points, moreover, contribute to the argument of 3:6–7, which follows closely upon the oracles against the nations.

Zephaniah's focus on non-Israelite states concludes with Assyria, which by the time of Josiah had made its presence felt in Judah for over a century. This final unit is perhaps the most striking of the oracles against foreign nations in this section, not least because Assyria's fall would have appeared virtually unimaginable to the smaller powers of the ancient Near East until shortly before Nineveh's destruction in 612. Assyria's radically greater military superiority was also promoted by the Assyrian ideology that is summarized in Zephaniah 2:15. As noted earlier, Assyria's imperial ideology held that the empire enjoyed divine support and that its gods had conferred onto Assyria the mandate of world domination. Not surprisingly, these beliefs inflated Assyria's self-image, especially on the part of its kings, who often referred to themselves as the "great king, mighty king, king of the world," "who with the help of the gods Aššur, Sîn, Šamaš, Nabû, Marduk, Ištar of Nineveh, (and) Ištar of Arbella"[74] marched against their "brazen, rebellious," and "perfidious" enemies, treating them with

---

[73] So Kahn, "The Historical Setting," 448.
[74] Erle Leichty, *The Royal Inscriptions of Esarhaddon, King of Assyria (680–669 BC)*, RINAP 4 (Winona Lake, IN: Eisenbrauns, 2011), 28.

disdain and egregious violence.⁷⁵ "I am, and there is no one beside me" (2:15) well captures Assyria's understanding of its geopolitical role, therefore, but its pride and self-determination ironically justify its imminent destruction. God's judgment of Assyria will leave it like a desert, uninhabited except for wild animals, equivalent to a non-place, wiped out of existence (2:13–14).⁷⁶ The implosion of Assyria's inflated self-evaluation and self-serving, violent ideology will leave onlookers astonished and filled with disdain for it (cf. Nah 3:7, 19).

As a selective overview of the world outside Judah, this part of Zephaniah provides a detailed condemnation of these nations' motivations and actions, announcing judgment against them on that basis. It is almost a mirror image of the central section of chapter 1, which did the same with Judah. Taken together, these two units demonstrate YHWH's commitment to establishing justice worldwide, irrespective of ethnicity, nationality, or even membership in the covenant that bound him to Israel. Also common to both passages is the focus on the destruction of power structures, whether political or ideological, rather than the total annihilation of the states mentioned.⁷⁷ This careful targeting of the guilty also appears in the oracle of salvation in 2:11, which makes clear that YHWH's transforming deliverance is not limited to his chosen people but will reach groups far and wide when he completes the reestablishment of his kingdom.

---

⁷⁵ Victor A. Hurowitz (trans.), "Assurbanipal's Rassam Prism(A) (4.41)," *COS* 4:189.
⁷⁶ Heinz-Josef Fabry, "'Gewalt über Gewalt!' Die dunkeln Seiten Gottes im Zwölfprophetenbuch," in *The Books of the Twelve Prophets: Minor Prophets, Major Theologies*, ed. Heinz-Josef Fabry, BETL 295 (Leuven: Leuven University Press, 2018), 3–32 (22).
⁷⁷ Reimer, "Sozialkritik," 46.

A Subplot: The Transformation and Deliverance of (Some) Non-Israelites (2:11)

In sharp contrast to the rest of Act 3, the brief interlude in 2:11 lacks any punitive element. Although the first phrase's "them" connects what follows to Moab and Ammon, the rest of the verse expands this group of non-Israelites to include "all the coasts of the nations," a phrase that encompasses the most distant non-Israelite locations.[78] God's intervention will "starve" or "make lean" the divinities that "all the earth" worships. Whether this is achieved directly in the spiritual realm or indirectly as the former worshippers of these gods stop supplying the "daily meals allotted to cult images," these non-Israelites realize that these deities are not to be compared with Yhwh.[79] God's superiority inevitably leads to worship, an essential element of a right relationship with him.

Act 4: The Condemnation and Sentencing of Judeans and Non-Israelites (Acts 1 and 3 Reprise)

The placement of 3:1–8 immediately after the oracles against non-Israelite nations (2:4–10, 12–15) invites the reader to consider in what ways Judah and the nations are similar or different. The Judean focus of 3:1–8 also connects this unit to the call for Judah's repentance in 2:1–3, although the two passages give very different evaluations of the possibility of repentance. As in 2:1–3, pride is especially prominent in 3:1–8;[80] 3:1–8 is also closely related to the critique of Judah in 1:4–13, but exchanges that passage's focus on

---

[78] See the exploration of this passage in Timmer, *Nations*, 158–60. The phrase itself occurs elsewhere only in Gen 10:5, where it describes the dispersion of Japheth's descendants.

[79] The latter option is suggested by Rudman, "A Note on Zephaniah," 112.

[80] This point is helpfully explored by Nathan Hays, "Humility and Instruction in Zephaniah 3.1–7," *JSOT* 44 (2020): 472–89.

external religious practices for a focus on Judean attitudes, priorities, and injustice.

Zephaniah 3:1–8 begins by announcing woe against an unnamed city that the reader quickly understands must be Jerusalem. The activities that motivate this critique read like a diagnosis of narcissism: "a grandiose sense of self-importance" and "a sense of entitlement" characterize an individual who "takes advantage of others" and "lacks empathy."[81] These people, perhaps especially prominent among the city's elite (3:3–4), reject Yhwh's authority, oppress the vulnerable, act autonomously, reject correction, and refuse to trust or draw near to God (3:1–2). The predatory nature of their actions leads the author to describe Jerusalem's social and religious leaders as roaring lions and wolves that prowl during the night, consuming all that they capture or find (3:3). Such attitudes and behavior show no respect for what Yhwh declares holy and are as much a violent attack on God's law (3:4, using the verb ḥāmās) as they are on other Judeans.

The abruptly introduced description of Yhwh as "righteous," uncontaminated by "injustice," and continually exercising "justice" (3:5) reveals his utter incompatibility with the immorally defined Judean subgroup here, which is further characterized as "unjust" and without shame. The punishment of non-Israelite nations for their pride (2:4–10, 12–15) is relevant here, because before punishing Judah for its own pride and covenant infidelity, Yhwh gave clear proof that other nations would suffer if they did not abandon their proud, violent, and self-serving projects. Unfortunately, such warnings, far from bringing rebellious Judeans to their senses,

---

[81] American Psychiatric Association, *Diagnostic and Statistical Manual of Mental Disorders IV-TR*, rev. ed. (Washington, DC: American Psychiatric Publishing, 2000), 301.81.

were interpreted as permission to continue business as usual (3:7). It is this state of affairs that has brought Judah to the same point as the non-Israelite nations. "All the earth" (*kol-hāʾāreṣ*), that is, Judah and the nations, are the objects of divine wrath (3:8; cf. 1:18). By using this phrase, Zephaniah evokes chapter 1's opening salvo against all creation, but now the reader knows in much more detail the reasons for God's condemnation. This "day" of 3:8 overlaps with Yhwh's feast and the "Day of Yhwh" in 1:7–16 as well as with God's gathering of the earth's inhabitants to pour out his fury on them and consume the earth itself (1:18). The juxtaposition of these images underlines for the last time in Zephaniah the inescapable nature of Yhwh's punitive and purifying justice.

Act 5: Deliverance from Punishment (3:9–20)
But suddenly punishment *is* escapable, after all. The radically positive nature of 3:9–20 with respect to the preceding material in Zephaniah makes the book's final act seem like a beautiful, serene sunrise after a cold and terrifying night. Even though 2:1–3 and 2:11 hinted that deliverance is possible for some Judeans and some non-Israelites, this final act in Zephaniah's drama is by far the most developed presentation of the *deliverance* plotline. Here, in the end, the prophet describes God's deliverance in ways that are no less powerful than the somber descriptions of judgment that predominate in chapters 1–2. In terms of the causes of divine deliverance, while justice was the necessary and sufficient cause for punishment, Yhwh's mercy and grace are necessary to any explanation of why he should agree to renew his relationship with those who repent (2:1–3) or should transform and purify those who, like the two groups in 3:9–10, were formerly unable or unwilling to serve him acceptably.

The complex drama (*both* judgment *and* deliverance) that finally comes fully into view here is driven by God's actions, which elicit direct human responses. These human subjects are described above all in terms of their transformed relationship to YHWH. In the case of Judah, they are explicitly distinguished from other Judeans, thereby forming a remnant or subgroup within the larger group. An equivalent internal transformation distinguishes the non-Israelites in view here from those who oppose YHWH and his people (cf. 2:4-10, 12-15). Indeed, the transformation of non-Israelites in 3:9 is essentially identical to the description of Judah's transformation in 3:10-13. Even though some distinctions remain between these radically changed non-Israelites and the Judean remnant (e.g., in 3:20), they share the definitive criterion of identity of having been transformed by God, and now showcase attitudes and actions that are radically oriented toward and normed by him. Those who are not transformed, Israelite or otherwise, are either already gone following the judgments of chapters 1-2, or are removed in this last act.[82]

Not surprisingly, the renewed relationship between these groups and YHWH is described in ways that contrast markedly with the punishment plot. The punishment of Judah by means of exile (cf. 1:13), for example, is reversed in the gathering of the remnant (3:20); and the cataclysmic judgment that opens the book (1:2-3) gives way to a world at peace with YHWH (3:15-17). The removal of divine condemnation (3:15) is essential to these reversals, and the description of God's now fully realized rule over a renewed world as "the King of Israel" transcends even the most remarkable moments of Israel's history. In short, this final act presents the same world as earlier acts but with a radically transformed cast and with the world itself enjoying peace. Some actors

---

[82] Greg A. King, "The Remnant in Zephaniah," *BSac* 151 (1994): 414-27, offers a thorough treatment of the topic.

are gone, while those who remain are profoundly different; the discontinuity of before and after produces an idyllic stability.

The (Re)new(ed) Cast: Some Non-Israelites (3:9) and Some Judeans (3:10–20)

The first group that is part of this transformed cast of characters is composed of non-Israelites. In 3:9, Yhwh promises to change the language of the "peoples" to a pure language, with the result that "all of them" will call on his name and serve him together. What comes out of one's mouth expresses what is in one's heart (cf. Hos 2:17; Isa 6:5–7; Matt 15:11), so this linguistic change affects (and reflects) these people's deepest commitments and desires. Whereas formerly they served other gods, these people now invoke Yhwh as worshippers in relationship with him. They are also at peace with one another rather than preying upon one another as before (cf. Zeph 2:4–9, 12–15). This change is thus much more than a reversal of the linguistic confusion that Genesis 11 ties to the Tower of Babel. It is also more focused than Genesis 11, since not all non-Israelites experience this change. The profound change that remakes these non-Israelites is continuous with the changes that 3:10–20 predicted will take place among some Judeans. A common commitment to Yhwh outweighs the other features which distinguish these groups, so that they form a diverse unity that paves the way for harmony and peace in God's fully established kingdom.[83]

The description of the Judean remnant's renewal that follows 3:9 is considerably more elaborate. First, their worship will be directed exclusively to Yhwh and will not be impeded even by great distances (3:10). The internal changes that drive this radically new

---

[83] Adele Berlin, *Zephaniah: A New Translation with Introduction and Commentary*, AB 25A (New York: Doubleday, 1994), 13–14.

behavior amount to the systematic undoing of the dispositions that had characterized Judah's earlier destructive and rebellious behavior (3:1–7). The newly created "humble" and "lowly" dispositions express themselves in terms of trust in God rather than autonomy and self-sufficiency.[84] This produces a correspondingly radical turn toward truth and goodness in speech and action as well as new security and well-being under Yhwh's protection and blessing (3:13).[85]

The unprecedented and total renewal of Judah's remnant, entirely purged of pride and the proud, demands a jubilant response of praise to God for his gracious salvation. No fewer than four imperatives in 3:14 call the Judean remnant to celebrate what has just been announced: Yhwh's pardon, the elimination of Judah's enemies, and God's protective presence. Moreover, this new, ideal situation is *permanent*, with Zion being sustained and satisfied by the ongoing reality of Yhwh's presence and goodness in full measure. Yhwh's title "The King of Israel" elegantly connects the royal roles of protection and provision, but also emphasizes that this new situation is the now fully established divine kingdom, a new creation that exhibits both continuity and discontinuity with the original creation.[86]

First, the new world that God's saving actions create is in continuity with the pristine world of the first two biblical creation

---

[84] Hays, "Humility," 482.
[85] "We invent lies because, for whatever reason, we want to invent reality. And the false reality we invent ... has one great advantage for us: It makes no claims upon us. It demands nothing." John Webster, *Confronted by Grace: Meditations of a Theologian*, ed. D. Bush and B. Ellis (Bellingham, WA: Lexham, 2014), 5.
[86] Rainer Albertz, "Exile as Purification: Reconstructing the 'Book of the Four,'" in *Thematic Threads in the Book of the Twelve*, ed. Paul L. Redditt and Aaron Schart, BZAW 325 (Berlin: de Gruyter, 2003), 232–51 (250), argues that Zephaniah presents "a radical new start" that goes far beyond "restoring the pre-exilic conditions."

accounts, since it is without sin or evil. In Genesis 1–2, "[a]ll fits into his dominion and purposes, and the King, as the ultimate arbiter of value, declares it is good."[87] Yhwh's celebration in Zephaniah 3 of his successful intervention against his enemies in favor of those who trust in him has the same significance. In both texts, the world is Yhwh's domain, although his uninterrupted presence among his people and the permanence of this remade world in Zephaniah 3 are points of discontinuity with the world of Genesis 1–2 prior to sin.[88]

The superiority of the world described in Zephaniah 3:9–17 compared with the world as initially created is even more striking in light of what the world had become after sin. "East of Eden," our world is ravaged by the effects of human autonomy and rebellion. But God creates something new via a complex movement of destruction, transformation, and purification. This new world is free of hegemony and the abuse of power, and the absence of sin guarantees the presence of peace, justice, and stability on all levels.[89]

A final perspective on the formation of the Judean remnant under the image of return from exile situates them with respect to the rest of the world (3:18–20). This last element in the deliverance plotline maintains a distinction between the Judean remnant and the non-Israelites who have become worshippers of Yhwh, but not an overly sharp one: They are not separated;

---

[87] Bruce R. Reichenbach, "Genesis 1 as Theological-Political Narrative of Kingdom Establishment," *BBR* 13 (2003): 47–69 (60).

[88] Cf. Colin Gunton, *The Triune Creator: A Historical and Systematic Study* (Grand Rapids, MI: Eerdmans, 1998), 167: "There must be redemption if creation is to be itself."

[89] These and other political features of Zephaniah are explored in Daniel C. Timmer, "Political Models and the End of the World in Zephaniah," *BI* 24 (2016): 310–31.

neither do they have fundamentally different identities. God's reign cannot be limited to Zion (cf. 2:11), and therefore his kingdom includes non-Israelites "among" whom Israel is honored (3:20). Both remnants, Israelite and non-Israelite, are now in an idealized world. The Judean remnant has been purified of sin and sinners (3:11–13); the non-Israelite remnant recognizes Yhwh as its God (cf. 3:9) and rejoices over Judah's new status – even praises it (3:20). The two groups' common religious identity does not remove the other differences between them, but that identity takes precedence over other characteristics and constitutes their essential unity.

The drama traced by the Book of Zephaniah finds its endpoint in restored Zion as the center of the world, "a peaceful place in a peaceful human world in which all the peoples will serve YHWH."[90] Zion's prominence is due above all to Yhwh's presence, as it is there that he reigns and enjoys his perfected relationship with his multiethnic people. This happy reversal of fortunes captures, at the very end of the book, God's honoring of the humble and deconstruction of human pride.[91] Further, the universalism that is the culmination of Yhwh's acts in history brings order out of disorder, (re)establishes justice, and restores the human community as worshippers of God without erasing its ethnic, cultural, and geographical diversity. Zephaniah's vision invites its readers to hope for nothing less than a world that is fully, permanently perfected. This is all the more stunning when we remember the dire circumstances in which Judah found itself, whether by its own fault (chapter 1) or the fault of others (chapter 2). This drama puts the spotlight on God's wisdom, power, justice, and grace, and

---

[90] Ben Zvi, *Zephaniah*, 345.
[91] Dietrich, *Nahum, Habakuk, Zefanja*, 250.

ends with his worship and his worshippers' overflowing satisfaction and joy in him and the consummated world he has brought into being.[92]

Zephaniah's Audiences

Like any text, Zephaniah includes features that bring its message to bear on its audience. A fruitful way of exploring this dimension of the book's message is to trace the different ways in which it addresses the audiences that are part of its discourse, not least because the audience seems to change in keeping with the plotlines examined earlier. Although we could include third-person descriptions, this feature will be clearer if we consider only second-person speech, already highlighted in Wendland's work referenced earlier (see Tables 4.1–4.3).[93] The variety of addressees and their stated or proposed emotional states guides reception of the book's message by a wide variety of readers, whether by means of feeling present at the events described, identifying with the characters' emotions, or sensing how the characters are located within the work's viewpoint.[94]

The first words aimed directly at the audience are the imperatives in 1:7 ("Be silent!") and 1:11 ("Wail!"), both part of the judgment plotline. Both commands are presented as suitable responses to the announcement of the terrifying Day of YHWH, and conjoin *stupefaction* at God's awe-inspiring arrival in judgment with the *profound perturbation* that those affected will feel as wealth, stability, and life itself come under threat.

---

[92] Irsigler, *Zefanja*, 435.
[93] See Wendland, "The Drama of Zephaniah."
[94] Kobie van Krieken, Hans Hoeken, and José Sanders, "Evoking and Measuring Identification with Narrative Characters: A Linguistic Cues Framework," *Frontiers in Psychology* 8 (2017), article 1190 (2, 4).

The next use of second-person address also involves direct commands (2:1–3), but these are quite different because they are in the deliverance plotline. The addressees here are not insouciant sinners but those who can take seriously the warnings spelled out in chapter 1. The Day of Yhwh is still the immediate motivation for the response, but the holistic changes urged upon the addressees (seeking Yhwh and pursuing humility) are potential ways to escape that judgment. This call to repent, therefore, assumes that the audience is threatened by God's judgment but also that it is *aware of its dangerous situation and is able to change.*

The first pair of oracles against the nations in 2:4–11 includes more direct speech, now addressed to non-Israelites. Following the identification of the speaker proposed by Wendland (see Table 4.2), both Yhwh and the prophet pronounce woes to non-Israelites because of their past or present mistreatment of Israel and Judah. These verses describe rather than command, and their announcement of destruction either precludes the possibility of repentance or assumes that there is no interest in repenting. This is even more true of the Cushites mentioned in 2:12 if, as suggested earlier, the verse describes their defeat in the recent past.[95]

The next direct address is to Zion in 3:7, prior to its being judged. Here Yhwh quotes himself as he explains to Judah that it should respond to the divine punishment of other nations with humble repentance. God goes on to recount that not only was such a response not forthcoming, but the divine actions outside Judah were misconstrued as permission to commit even more acts

---

[95] Kevin Burrell, *Cushites in the Hebrew Bible: Negotiating Ethnic Identity in the Past and Present*, BibInt 181 (Leiden: Brill, 2020), 272–73, 287.

of oppression, self-advancement, and violence. This last description of the Judean audience is perhaps the most negative in the book, bypassing the existence of those who might repent (2:1–3) and emphasizing the audience's inability to learn from the punishment of others for similar sins.

The second-person address in the book's closing section appears in the contrasting deliverance plotline and so strikes a very different tone as it addresses the radically changed remnant. First, the "you" in 3:11–12 is defined as Judah newly separated from its own pride and the "proudly exultant ones" that were among its members. The remnant is humble and lowly, and trusts in Yhwh for deliverance and vindication. Referred to as Daughter Zion (3:14), this group is exhorted to celebrate God's removal of his condemnation and of her enemies and his subsequent taking up residence in Zion. This address asserts that the remnant *has recognized its sin and trusts that yhwh can and will remove it*. Further, Yhwh takes for granted that the remnant *understands the significance of God's permanent, unveiled presence*, with the unequaled love and perfect protection that entails.

This short overview shows that the use of direct address in Zephaniah serves the same purpose as the discourses in which it appears, but does so in a precise way. The second-person grammar adds specific force to the more general approach of referring to a number of named audiences in the same work. The descriptions of these various groups and how they respond to Yhwh's word and works in specific contexts are an effective way for the author to make these speeches relevant to the audience. If Habakkuk's first-person grammar invites its reader to ask "are Habakkuk's words and attitudes mine?" Zephaniah's second-person addresses encourages its readers to ask "is Zephaniah speaking to me?" Even on the most general level, such a question seems inescapable, since readers find themselves in the same world that Zephaniah asserts will be profoundly affected by God's judgments. Even so, by locating its audiences in relation to specific events, evoking emotions, and presenting negative and positive evaluations of the addressees, the Book of Zephaniah makes it quite difficult for readers to avoid pondering their relation to the book's message and to Yhwh, its ultimate source.

A THEOLOGY OF ZEPHANIAH

The following themes summarize the main features of Zephaniah's theology, with a focus on their development, interrelation, and relevance to readers. Each is connected to the meta-theme of the establishment, contestation, and reestablishment of God's kingdom.

Yhwh and Creation: Initial Order

The backdrop for Zephaniah's depiction of a cataclysmic worldwide judgment is the world in its pristine state, as God initially created it. God's initial creation was "very good" (Gen 1:31), and all that humanity needed to thrive in harmony with God, with each other, and with the rest of creation was available in abundance (Gen 2:5–25). God's absolute authority and goodness stand alongside the call for humanity to exercise its role as vice-regent over creation, and makes humanity both free and responsible to him (Gen 1:28–30; 2:15–17).

Life without Yhwh: Disorder

The decision, recounted in Genesis 3, of the primeval couple to pursue autonomy rather than submit to Yhwh's will, is paralleled by Zephaniah's presentation of Judah and of the world at large in the late seventh century. Human beings and the political entities and ideologies they form pursue their own interests at the expense of others, with the result that all that the world and humanity *should be* is ignored, threatened, or attacked outright. The rejection of God's authority leads human beings to grasp for their own and to pursue autonomy, glory, and permanence on an almost divine scale.[96] While the sin of idolatry also characterizes empires according to Nahum and Habakkuk, Zephaniah contends that it is no less evident in the lives of individuals, Judean or otherwise. Life lived in that way is oriented toward self rather than toward God and others; the result is that such a person's deepest desires are profoundly "disordered" and they pursue what is not good.[97] Zephaniah's repeated critiques of pride and exhortations to humility suggest that pride is inseparable from this disorder. The theological and moral nature of this critique reveals that it is only incidentally social, and thus not against the elites as such. Zephaniah condemns these proud individuals' "entanglement with foreign practices, their failure to worship Yhwh exclusively, and – the cause of both of these – their failure to trust in YHWH."[98] Zephaniah's goal is thus not "the total eradication of the government ... but rather its reformation, in alignment with recognition of YHWH as the ultimate power and source of justice in the world."[99]

---

[96] Andrew Bowie, *Introduction to German Philosophy: From Kant to Habermas* (Cambridge: Polity, 2003), 114, sees the "need for self-transcendence via devotion to something higher" in the rising power of nationalism from the nineteenth century onward.

[97] See William Wood, *Blaise Pascal on Duplicity, Sin, and the Fall: The Secret Instinct*, Changing Paradigms in Historical and Systematic Theology (Oxford: Oxford University Press, 2013), 29.

[98] Crouch, "Nahum, Habakkuk, and Zephaniah," 378.

[99] Crouch, "Nahum, Habakkuk, and Zephaniah," 378.

The Consequences of Life without Yhwh

The negative outcomes of life without and against God are the primary means by which Zephaniah presses his audience toward change. Living in Yhwh's world while flouting his explicit moral directives and the value of other human beings inevitably leads to divine judgment intended (among other things) to prevent the total ruin of humanity and the world it inhabits. In some cases the prophet or Yhwh announces a punishment that, while severe, is still limited to a particular group such as individual nations (2:4–10, 12–15 and 3:6) or certain groups in Judah (1:4–6). These outcomes are significant and foreshadow the coming Day of Yhwh that is announced in 1:7–18, but several features distinguish the final manifestation of this "day" from the lesser judgments that precede it. Most notably, the full realization of the Day of Yhwh in Zephaniah focuses not on nations as such but on morally defined groups within them, such as the violent (1:9) or otherwise guilty individuals *regardless of political affiliation* (1:17). No less importantly, the Day of Yhwh in the fullest sense involves punishment that surpasses even exile and entails the total extermination of its targets (1:18).

Remnants in Judah and among the Nations: Worshippers of Yhwh in a Disordered World

Nearly all the prophetic books of the Old Testament distinguish between those Israelites that the authors believes are faithful to Yhwh and those who are not. This distinction is fundamental to Zephaniah's theology and is much clearer in this book than in Nahum and Habakkuk, as it appears in every chapter. Interestingly, Zephaniah also makes the same distinction among non-Israelites, with some remaining God's enemies and others turning to the Lord in worship and obedience. Because a restored relationship with YHWH is the defining characteristic of both subgroups (remnants), Zephaniah's vision of a future consummation includes *both* Israelites *and* non-Israelites, providing an elegant solution to the tension sometimes perceived between particularism (Israel is God's chosen people) and universalism (God will bless all nations through Israel).[100]

A Return to Life with YHWH: Order Fully Established, Human Thriving

While the political context of Zephaniah and the political ramifications of his message are important, they do not constitute the book's ultimate horizon. Our exploration of the book has shown that it promotes much more than "seek[ing] YHWH by supporting Josiah's reform" or political independence from Assyrian and Egyptian domination.[101] The problem that Zephaniah critiques, and that the deliverance he promises will resolve, is at root *anthropological*. As such, it affects human beings in their relationships with other persons, with God, and with their environment. Zephaniah's condemnation of those who worship other gods, or YHWH alongside other gods, suggests that human beings inevitably orient their lives toward a value, good, or goal regardless of whether it is formalized as a deity, accompanied by a worldview or moral code, or held by a large number of individuals.[102]

---

[100] See Jon D. Levenson, "The Universal Horizon of Biblical Particularism," in *Ethnicity and the Bible*, ed. Mark Brett, BibInt 19 (Leiden: Brill, 1996), 143–69; Timmer, *Nations*, 167–68, 243–44.

[101] Sweeney, "Zephaniah: A Paradigm," 135, proposes the first of these; Anselm Hagedorn, "When Did Zephaniah Become a Supporter of Josiah's Reform?" *JTS* 52 (2011): 453–75, the second.

[102] Roger Scruton reflects on some contemporary examples of this widespread human disposition in *The Soul of the World* (Princeton, NJ: Princeton University Press, 2014). Iain Provan, "To Highlight All Our

Zephaniah presents worship of and life with Yhwh as superior to all other options and as a relationship freely given to humans who have been delivered from the sin that separated them from God. The love of God for his people that leads God himself to sing (3:15) captures this amazing reality with great power.

Zephaniah gives only fleeting glimpses of the process by which human beings move from being autonomous and oriented toward other (pseudo-)deities to being faithful worshippers of Yhwh who orient their lives, desires, and values in light of his character and will. The first, in 2:1–3, calls sinful Judeans to "seek Yhwh" by radically aligning their will with his and recognizing their dependence upon and obligation to him as creator, covenant suzerain, and deliverer. The second, in 3:9–13, emphasizes Yhwh's initiative (3:9, 3:11, not least because the call to repent in 2:1–3 has apparently not born fruit) that produces sweeping changes in belief and behavior in those whom he changes. Despite the book's focus on the punitive aspect of the Day of Yhwh, this salvific side is also part of that day (3:8–9).[103]

Ecology

Ironically, the destruction of animal life in the hyperbolic description of a future judgment in Zephaniah 1:2–3 underlines the importance of animals and their habitats in Zephaniah's theology and as part of creation. Beyond judgment, images of restoration include bucolic scenes in which the remnant's flocks will pasture peacefully and the remnant itself will also be satiated, protected, and at rest (2:6–7).

Idols: Worshipping God in Nietzsche's World," *ExAud* 15 (1999): 19–38, presents an incisive critique of common idols in our modern age, including the state, material possessions, and self.

[103] This dual movement is explored by Mark Seifrid, "Righteousness, Justice, and Justification," *New Dictionary of Biblical Theology*, ed. T. Desmond Alexander and Brian S. Rosner (Downers Grove, IL: InterVarsity, 2000), 740–45.

Even the calls of birds are heard in images that depict the tranquility of a world without abusive, violent, self-glorifying empires such as Assyria (2:14). These scenes include not only domesticated animals but all kinds of beasts, a faint echo of the harmonious animal world as initially created. Despite the bold colors in which the destruction of the created order is portrayed in Zephaniah, it is not absolute, since the book's descriptions of judgment and salvation presuppose fundamental continuity between that situation and the restored world that follows. The purification of the existing cosmos will produce a world that is home to human beings, but which ultimately serves its creator, not any abusive human master.

Yhwh, Humanity, and Response-Ability
In the late seventh century, the Book of Zephaniah presents a clear understanding of what human beings are and the place they have in Yhwh's world. To begin with the cultic offenses described in 1:4–6, worshiping other gods than Yhwh or lowering him to their level cuts persons off from him as creator, sustainer, source of justice, and redeemer. Such individuals put themselves in a box from which they cannot escape and in which they cannot survive. Such persons fail to fulfill their human vocation of knowing, loving, and serving Yhwh. Similarly, those who use violence and injustice to achieve their goals, enrich themselves, or to satisfy their will to power (1:7–13) make themselves liable to God's judgment by usurping divine supremacy, ignoring his moral order, and violating the dignity and worth of others made in his image.[104]

---

[104] Humans as those made in the image of God arguably reflect God in relational, functional, and ontological ways. See, respectively, Richard Lints, *Identity and Idolatry: The Image of God and Its Inversion*, NSBT 36 (Downers Grove, IL: Intervarsity, 2015); Michael Horton, "Image and Office: Human Personhood and the Covenant," in *Personal Identity in Theological*

Trusting in powers other than God is the characteristic error of those seeking security, identity, or self-advancement in an immanent framework: that is, one limited to material things in which humans exist and know autonomously.[105] These "powers" most frequently appear as empires in the prophetic books, but the ideology, values, and goals that they promote are not dependent upon a particular political structure. Contemporary cults focused on a charismatic individual, a group of "initiated" or "aware" people, and many other kinds of networks and associations all promise well-being (defined differently in each case). The same is true of individuals who make themselves the source of ultimate norms, value, and meaning, as did some of the religious and civic leaders in Zephaniah's day (3:1-5).

Against such proposals, Zephaniah locates human value and significance in one's identity as created by YHWH for loving, obedient worship and service. On this view, each human has inherent value that is not dependent upon performance by some measure such as physical attractiveness, material wealth, power, or social status. At the same time, the significance of human actions is so great that it inevitably affects one's well-being and destiny in relation to YHWH, to others, and to the world. Living in harmonious relation with God brings unparalleled security in this life and beyond, whereas exercising autonomy in the

---

Perspective, ed. Richard Lints, Michael S. Horton, and Mark R. Talbot (Grand Rapids, MI: Eerdmans, 2006), 178-203; Colin Gunton, "In the Image and Likeness of God," in Colin Gunton, *Christ and Creation* (Eugene, OR: Wipf & Stock, 2005), 99-116.

[105] For a contemporary description of this phenomenon, see Charles Taylor, *A Secular Age* (Cambridge, MA: Harvard University Press, 2007). Thomas Pfau, "Religion," in *The Oxford Handbook of European Romanticism*, ed. Paul Hamilton (Oxford: Oxford University Press, 2016), 730-51, helpfully traces the rise of immanence in much nineteenth-century European thought.

independent pursuit of self-determined wholeness and good will inevitably fail.[106] The binary outcomes of God's final intervention in the world could not be more different: destruction or consummation. Negatively, the world is purified of those who are unwilling to live with God as their highest authority and who use other human beings for their own ends. Positively, God radically changes those who humbly submit to his rule and realize their vocation as human beings in obedience to him and in relationship with him and with others. This twofold description of humanity's "Paradise Lost" and the possibility of regaining that paradise invites readers to respond in such a way as to escape punishment and to enjoy reconciliation by relinquishing self-determination and taking up humanity's original vocation of life in covenant with YHWH.

ZEPHANIAH'S CONTRIBUTION TO JEWISH AND CHRISTIAN TRADITIONS

The Old Testament and Related Literature
Historically and literarily, the Book of the Twelve is arguably the most proximate context for appropriation of Zephaniah's theology. Walter Dietrich suggests that when read in their current sequence, Nahum, Habakkuk, and Zephaniah show that while God was committed to destroying the "great northern empire" (Assyria, in the case of Nahum), "God decided to give it a free

---

[106] For a contemporary argument along these lines, see Henri de Lubac, *The Drama of Atheist Humanism* (San Francisco: Ignatius, 1995). Nietzsche's classic case against this view and in favor of a moral system that elevates the strong and the transcending (i.e., rejection) of all moral categories is discussed in Anthony Kenny, *A New History of Western Philosophy*, vol. 4, *Philosophy in the Modern World* (Oxford: Clarendon, 2007), 237–42.

hand" for some time (Babylon, in Habakkuk) before finally destroying it (Assyria again, in Zephaniah).[107] He explains the location of Zephaniah, which may be slightly older, after the possibly younger Book of Habakkuk as the result of the earlier joining of Nahum and Habakkuk.[108] Julia M. O'Brien more boldly suggests that Zephaniah is "a summary of Hosea through Nahum," concluding that "the fall of Israel, Judah, and the nations was YHWH's doing; YHWH also promised restoration for Judah (and perhaps, too, the remnant of the nations)."[109] O'Brien also argues that Zephaniah was in turn used by Zechariah, especially in the latter's post-exilic assurance that "YHWH the Warrior will intervene as in the past, restoring monarchy and sovereignty to Judah."[110] Tchavdar S. Hadjiev, an important dissenting voice in the context of current study of the Book of the Twelve, moves in another direction, concluding that there is little evidence of an attempt to integrate Zephaniah in the Book of the Twelve on a literary level.[111] While this may be true, the earlier discussion has revealed numerous points at which Zephaniah's theology contributes to or aligns well with other books of the Twelve. To note but one such example, the singling out in Malachi of those

---

[107] Walter Dietrich, "Three Minor Prophets and the Major Empires: Synchronic and Diachronic Perspectives on Nahum, Habakkuk, and Zephaniah," in *Perspectives on the Formation of the Book of the Twelve: Methodological Foundations – Redactional Processes – Historical Insights*, ed. Rainer Albertz, James D. Nogalski, and Jakob Wöhrle, BZAW 433 (Berlin: de Gruyter, 2012), 147–56 (149).

[108] Dietrich, "Three Minor Prophets," 154.

[109] Julia M. O'Brien, "Nahum – Habakkuk – Zephaniah: Reading the 'Former Prophets' in the Persian Period," *Int* 61 (2007): 168–83 (177).

[110] O'Brien, "Nahum – Habakkuk – Zephaniah," 179.

[111] Tchavdar S. Hadjiev, "Zephaniah and the 'Book of the Twelve' Hypothesis," in *Prophecy and the Prophets in Ancient Israel*, ed. John Day, LHBOTS 531 (New York: T & T Clark, 2010), 325–38.

Israelites who "fear Yhwh" sharpens Zechariah's development of the remnant motif in Judah, especially by locating it in the present. Malachi also presents some non-Israelites in very positive terms, announcing that they will serve Yhwh wherever they are (Mal 1:11, 14). Malachi contrasts these non-Israelites with unfaithful Israelites, something that considerably sharpens Malachi's tone (Mal 1:10–11, 14) but which is at most implicit in Zephaniah.

Outside the Minor Prophets, William L. Holladay has argued that Jeremiah adapted a number of phrases from Zephaniah (cf. Jer 8:13 and Zeph 1:2; Jer 12:4 and Zeph 1:3; Jer 19:13 and Zeph 1:5; Jer 46:10 and Zeph 1:7; Jer 5:27 and Zeph 1:9, etc.).[112] These correspondences lead him to conclude that Jeremiah drew on Zephaniah to support his critique of Judah's "lapses from the law of Deuteronomy" and that Zephaniah itself is heavily dependent on earlier prophetic books.[113] Striking use is made of Zephaniah 3:16b in 2 Chronicles 15:7, which applies God's encouragement to (eschatologically) restored Judah in Zephaniah 3:16 to the Judean king Asa as an encouragement to continue the religious reforms he undertook out of fidelity to Yhwh.[114] Ezekiel 22:24–28 seems to model its critique of Judah's religious and civil leaders on Zephaniah 3:1–4, and mentions the same groups of prophets, priests, and leaders/princes (the judges in Zeph 3:3 are absent). Fishbane concludes that Ezekiel's condemnation of (false) prophets for presenting their own ideas as God's word elaborates upon Zephaniah's charge that Jerusalem does not listen to or heed

---

[112] William L. Holladay, "Reading Zephaniah with a Concordance: Suggestions for a Redaction History," *JBL* 120 (2001): 671–84.
[113] Holladay, "Reading Zephaniah," 672, 684.
[114] Ben Zvi, *Zephaniah*, 29 n. 44; Sara Japhet, *I and II Chronicles: A Commentary*, OTL (Louisville, KY: Westminster/John Knox, 1993), 721.

God's word, and is a creative reuse of an earlier biblical text in the production of a newer one.[115]

Early Judaism and the Dead Sea Scrolls
The translation of the Minor Prophets into Greek near the middle of the second century BCE in what became the Septuagint (LXX) made Zephaniah accessible to a Greek-speaking audience. Through a discernible pattern of translation choices (e.g., "earth" for the Hebrew ʾereṣ, which can mean "land" or "earth"), minor additions (e.g., "of all the nations" following "gods" in 2:11) and possible omissions (e.g., of "daughters of my dispersed ones" in 3:10), the translator seems to have subtly stressed the "universalistic" aspect of the book.[116] Perhaps most interestingly, the use of imperative verbs in place of indicative verbs in 2:3 ("do his commands" rather than "who do his commands") and 3:7 ("Fear me ... Accept correction" in place of "Surely you will fear ... will accept correction") and other word choices give the book a more pronounced "pedagogical, ethical movement."[117]

---

[115] Michael Fishbane, *Biblical Interpretation in Ancient Israel* (Oxford: Clarendon, 1985), 461–63, discusses this reuse in more detail. Irsigler, *Zefenja*, 50–52, provides a lengthy list of "analogous" Old Testament texts that are mostly clustered in Genesis 1–11; key sections in Deuteronomy and the Deuteronomistic history (e.g., Deut 28; 2 Kgs 23); several prophetic books, especially Isaiah; and a few scattered psalms and proverbs.

[116] Jong-Hoon Kim, "Sophonias/Zephaniah," in *Introduction to the Septuagint*, ed. Siegfried Kreuzer, trans. D. A. Brenner and P. Altmann (Baylor: Baylor University Press, 2019), 483–86 (485); on Zeph 3:10, see Cécile Dogniez, "La Bible d'Alexandrie II: Select Passage: Sophonie (Zephaniah) 3,8–11," in *X Congress of the International Organization for Septuagint and Cognate Studies: Oslo, 1998*, ed. Bernard A. Taylor, SCS 51 (Atlanta, GA: SBL, 2001), 199–216 (205–6).

[117] Kim, "Sophonias/Zephaniah," 486, quoting Hans Schmoll and Gottfried Seitz, "Sophonias/Zefanja," in *Septuaginta Deutsch: Erläuterungen und*

Somewhat later than the LXX, the *Apocalypse of Zephaniah* attributes to the seventh-century prophet a series of apocalyptic visions. Dated loosely to the period between 100 BCE and 175 CE, and only partially preserved, the text recounts that Zephaniah received a vision consisting of various episodes, usually in otherworldly settings. Although the vision's source ties it to Zephaniah, its content more frequently (but still indirectly) parallels that of the post-exilic Book of Zechariah.[118] Angels figure largely in many episodes, as when 5,000 angels torment the soul of a "lawless" person who died without repenting.[119] In another episode, the prophet reads a full and complete list of "all [the] sins" that he had done that was held by the accusing angel at the gate of Hades. He then prays: "May your mercy reach me and may you wipe out my manuscript because your mercy has [co]me to be in every place and has filled every [pl]ace." To this an angel responds: "Triumph, prevail because you have prevailed and have triumphed over the accuser, and you have come up from Hades and the abyss."[120] The text's alternation between judgment and deliverance resembles the Book of Zephaniah's bifocal message, but any significant dependence on Zephaniah is unlikely.

Roughly half a dozen (often damaged and very partial) manuscripts from Qumran and Wadi Murabbaʿat preserve a few verses of Zephaniah.[121] Among these, the *pesharim* (interpretations that apply older texts to the present) are the most interesting from the

---

Kommentare zum griechischen Alten Testament, Band II, *Psalmen bis Daniel,* ed. Martin Karrer and Wolfgang Kraus (Stuttgart: Deutsche Bibelgesellschaft, 2011), 2429–39 (2429).

[118] O. S. Wintermute, "Apocalypse of Zephaniah," *OTP* 1:497–515 (499), whom I follow in this section.
[119] Wintermute, "Apocalypse," 508.
[120] Wintermute, "Apocalypse," 513.
[121] See the list in Irsigler, *Zefanja,* 74–75.

perspective of Zephaniah's theological contribution. Although 1QpZeph (1Q15) comments on Zephaniah 1:18–2:2 and 4QpZeph (4Q170) on Zephaniah 1:12–13, their regrettably poor state of preservation only reveals, as is de rigueur with *pesharim*, that the "interpretation" has to do with the "land of Judah" near the end of the present era (so 1Q15 line 5).¹²²

Rabbinic Judaism
Centuries later, the Babylonian Talmud explains the future conversion of some Gentiles to Judaism by referring to Zephaniah 3:9.¹²³ In Tractate *Avodah Zarah*, Rav Yosef asks and answers the following question: "What is the verse from which it is derived that they will convert?" After citing Zephaniah 3:9, he continues:

> This verse indicates that all nations will worship God. Abaye said to him: "But perhaps it is only from idol worship that they will withdraw, while they will still engage in forbidden sexual relations...." Rav Yosef said to him, "That cannot be, as it is written at the conclusion of the verse, 'To serve him with one consent,' which indicates that the Gentiles will accept all of God's mitzvoth [commands]."¹²⁴

This quotation asserts that non-Israelites can become worshippers of Yhwh on a par with Jews, but also that such a conversion entails full acceptance of Yhwh's torah. This is already a notable position within rabbinic literature, for some rabbis "saw all Gentiles as inevitably idolatrous" while others allowed for some

---
¹²² Florentino G. Martínez, *The Dead Sea Scrolls Translated: The Qumran Texts in English*, 2nd ed. (Grand Rapids, MI: Eerdmans; Leiden: Brill, 1996), 202.
¹²³ A comprehensive list of references to Zephaniah in the rabbinic corpus can be found in Caleb T. Friedman (ed.), *A Scripture Index to Rabbinic Literature* (Peabody, MA: Hendrickson Academic, 2021), 404.
¹²⁴ *William Davidson Talmud*, Avodah Zarah 24a:16, www.sefaria.org/Avodah_Zarah.24a.16?lang=bi. I owe this reference to Irsigler, *Zefanja*, 78.

"Gentile relationship with God that was not idolatrous, even if not as intense as that of Judaism."[125] The openness of Zephaniah to the conversion of non-Israelites of any ethnicity is consonant with, if not a contributor to, the later widespread belief that "all peoples were to be judged by moral, not racial, criteria."[126] Zephaniah's condemnation of various non-Israelite polities for contravening God's will and its inversion of that reality among those who turn to worship him are likewise very closely connected to the "great innovation of rabbinic Judaism in this area, ... the new insistence that the prohibition of idolatry is universal."[127]

The New Testament and Early Christianity
A wide swath of early Jewish and Christian interpretation proceeded on the assumption that "all the prophets spoke, to a large extent, in one voice and in accordance with their entire corpus of sacred literature, be it the Hebrew Bible and the Oral Law or be it a Christologically-oriented Old Testament, the New Testament and the traditions of the Church."[128] This allowed early interpreters to make connections across the Old Testament by borrowing phrases and expressions or by making connections at the level of content and theme.[129] To begin with the former, Zephaniah is cited or alluded to in a few New Testament texts.[130] It is possible

---

[125] David Novak, "Gentiles in Rabbinic Thought," in *The Cambridge History of Judaism*, vol. 4, *The Late Roman-Rabbinic Period*, ed. Steven T. Katz (Cambridge: Cambridge University Press, 2006), 647–62 (652).
[126] Novak, "Gentiles in Rabbinic Thought," 651.
[127] Novak, "Gentiles in Rabbinic Thought," 652.
[128] Ben Zvi, *Zephaniah*, 24.
[129] This phenomenon is carefully considered by Ian Turner, "Going Beyond What Is Written or Learning to Read? Discovering OT/NT Broad Reference," *JETS* 61 (2018): 577–94.
[130] Possible allusions and echoes may include Zeph 1:3 in Matt 13:41; Zeph 1:14, 18 in Rev 6:17; Zeph 3:8 in Rev 16:1; Zeph 3:9 in Rom 15:6; Zeph 3:13 in Rev 14:5; Zeph 3:15 in John 12:13; Zeph 3:16 and Zech 9:9 in John 12:15.

that the Greek translation of Zephaniah 1:18b ("in the fire of his jealousy all the earth will be consumed") lies behind the similar expression in Hebrews 10:27, although Isaiah 26:11 may be the more likely source.[131] It is more likely that Zephaniah 3:13 has informed Jesus's description of Nathanael as "an Israelite in whom there is no deceit" in John 1:47, since only that text combines the absence of deceit "with the name Israel."[132] The same verse from Zephaniah is probably also cited in Rev 14:5: "And there was not found in their mouth [a deceitful tongue]."[133] Notably, both texts use a feature from Zephaniah's description of Judah's remnant, that of truthfulness, to identify a faithful Israelite in the first century CE (John 1:47) or those redeemed by the Lamb (Rev 14:5). Finally, Zephaniah 3:14–17 (or Isa 40:9–11) has probably contributed (possibly after first being integrated with Zech 9:9) to John's exhortation: "Do not be afraid, Daughter Zion. Look! Your king is coming sitting on a donkey's colt" (John 12:15).[134]

Thematic continuity between Zephaniah's affirmation of God's sovereignty and the New Testament can be found in Jesus's power over demons in the Gospels (cf. Zeph 2:11)[135] and in Revelation's insistence that no spiritual powers will ultimately be able to resist

---

[131] Radu Gheorghita, "The Minor Prophets in Hebrews," in *The Minor Prophets in the New Testament*, ed. Maarten J. J. Menken and Steven Moyise, LNTS 377 (London: T & T Clark, 2009), 115–33 (132); Paul Ellingworth, *The Epistle to the Hebrews*, NIGTC (Grand Rapid, MI: Eerdmans, 1993), 534

[132] Maarten J. J. Menken, "The Minor Prophets in John's Gospel," in *The Minor Prophets in the New Testament*, ed. Maarten J. J. Menken and Steven Moyise, LNTS 377 (London: T & T Clark, 2009), 79–96 (92).

[133] NA[28].

[134] Menken, "The Minor Prophets in John's Gospel," 83. Additional allusions are suggested by Kim, "Sophonias/Zephaniah," 486.

[135] Graham H. Twelftree documents this theme in the New Testament and early Christian writings in *In the Name of Jesus: Exorcism among Early Christians* (Grand Rapids, MI: Baker Academic, 2007).

the coming of God's kingdom (Rev 17:1–19:10, etc.).[136] The Book of Acts develops at length the twin themes of the renewal of Israel and the inclusion of some non-Israelites in the salvation that God brings to his people in Jesus Christ.[137] Zephaniah's redemptive-historical paradigm, in which YHWH's original creation is purified and fully restored and Israelites and non-Israelites both enter a right relationship with God, corresponds closely to Paul's theology of the new creation, in which Jesus Christ's life, death, and resurrection make possible full reconciliation between God and human beings (2 Cor 5:17–18) and between formerly estranged groups or individuals (especially Jews and non-Jews; Gal 6:15; Eph 2:11–22; Col 3:10–11). Interestingly, Pauline moral teaching related to the new creation, which in Pauline thought has begun but is not yet consummated, condemns "greed, slander, and abuse" (e.g., Col 3:5–9; Eph 4:25–30), attitudes that largely define the groups Zephaniah inveighs against.[138] Paul's teaching on the Day of the Lord as the "Day of the Lord Jesus Christ" (1 Cor 5:5) emphasizes Christ's glorious return (1 Cor 15:23, etc.) for the dual purposes of judgment (1 Thess 5:3–4) and salvation (Phil 1:9–10),[139] and thus closely corresponds to the twofold plot in Zephaniah.

Early Christian preachers were sensitive to Zephaniah's ethical implications. Cyprian (ca. 200–258) cites Zephaniah's

---

[136] Allan J. McNicol, *The Conversion of the Nations in Revelation*, LNTS 438 (London: T&T Clark, 2011), 97–99.

[137] Robert Wall, "Israel and the Gentile Mission in Acts and Paul: A Canonical Approach," in *Witness to the Gospel: The Theology of Acts*, ed. I. Howard Marshall and David Peterson (Grand Rapids, MI: Eerdmans, 1998), 437–57.

[138] John R. Levison, "Creation and New Creation," in *Dictionary of Paul and His Letters*, ed. Gerald F. Hawthorne and Ralph P. Martin (Downers Grove, IL: InterVarsity, 1993), 189–90 (190).

[139] Larry J. Kreitzer, "Eschatology," in *Dictionary of Paul and His Letters*, ed. Gerald F. Hawthorne and Ralph P. Martin (Downers Grove, IL: InterVarsity, 1993), 253–69 (259).

condemnation of excessive or misused wealth (Zeph 1:13) in his warning that "[t]he lust of possessions and money are not to be sought for."[140] Zephaniah's exhortation to repent (Zeph 2:1–3) prompts Cassiodorus (ca. 485–ca. 585) to write: "What is more beneficial and farsighted for the person who could have no hope in his own deserts because of the sins which he has committed than to decide to pray to God's fatherly love while in this world, while there is opportunity for repentance?"[141] As a final example, Cyril of Alexandria (ca. 376–444 CE), commenting on the call to rejoice in Zephaniah 3:14–15, asserts that:

> As far as the factual account goes, he clearly promises them peace after the return from Babylon, when their former faults are forgotten and God promises to accompany and protect them. On the other hand, as far as the deeper meaning goes, he necessarily ordered them to *rejoice exceedingly,* and as well to *be glad with their whole heart* at the removal of their sins – through Christ, obviously.[142]

Cyril thus applies to "the church, the holy multitude of believers" what Zephaniah predicts concerning God's renewed people. Interestingly, he interprets the promise that God's people will "*witness troubles no longer*" as a guarantee of the church's protection by Christ, who "repels war waged by the spiritual Assyrians and annuls the schemes of the demons.[143]

---

[140] "To Quirinus, Testimonies against the Jews," 12.3.61, cited in Alberto Ferreiro (ed.), *The Twelve Prophets*, ACCS 14 (Downers Grove, IL: InterVarsity, 2003), 210.

[141] "Exposition of the Psalms 6.1," cited in Ferreiro, *The Twelve Prophets*, 210.

[142] *St. Cyril of Alexandria: Commentary on the Twelve Prophets*, vol. 3, trans. Robert C. Hill, Fathers of the Church 124 (Washington, DC: Catholic University of America Press, 2012), 53.

[143] *St. Cyril of Alexandria*, 53.

PAST AND PRESENT RECEPTION OF ZEPHANIAH

As is the case with the other prophetic books treated in the present volume, the Book of Zephaniah's poetry, imagery, and themes have been taken up in myriad ways outside the context of biblical exposition and commentary. As a first example, *Dies irae* (Day of Wrath) is a "rhymed sequence" whose text is based on a poetic medieval elaboration of Zephaniah 1:15 later included in the Requiem Mass by the Council of Trent (1545–63).[144] Comprising eighteen verses, it begins with the phrase that is its title: "Day of wrath / that woeful day / Shall the world in ashes lay / David and the Sibyl say." However, the text focuses less on Zephaniah's paired dynamics of salvation and judgment in world history than on the specter of the final judgment:

> What a trembling, what a fear,
> When the dread Judge shall appear,
> Strictly searching far and near. …
> Lo, the Book of ages spread,
> From which all the deeds are read,
> Of the living and the dead.[145]

The first-person response of the author to this awesome moment dominates the majority of the poem, much as Zephaniah urges his hearers to "Be silent!" and "Wail!" (1:7, 11) in response to the announcement that the Day of YHWH is coming. Due as much to its musical power as its lyric beauty, *Dies irae* was adapted to other liturgical compositions and was also taken up in literature, film,

---

[144] Don Michael Randel, "Dies Irae," in *The Harvard Dictionary of Music*, 4th ed., ed. Don Michael Randel (Cambridge, MA: Belknap, 2003), 241.

[145] The text is from *Hours at Home: A Popular Monthly of Instruction and Recreation* 7 (1868): 39–40; cited from Terence Bailey, "A Syllabic and Metrical Dies irae? Variations on This Most-Famous Text and Melody," *Sacred Music* 143 (2016): 22–34 (22).

and theater, including Goethe's *Faust*, Harriet Beecher Stowe's *Uncle Tom's Cabin* (1851), and the Jewish Haftarah in which Genesis 11 is followed by Zephaniah 3:9–17, 20.[146] The song "La vie bohème" in Jonathon Larson's 1996 musical *Rent* sees Collins and Roger respond to the death of Benny's dog, and symbolically to the death of the Bohemian ideal, with "Dies irae, dies illa," ("That day is a day of wrath"), followed by the Greek liturgical refrain "Lord, have mercy" and the Hebrew opening line of the Jewish Kaddish (a doxology often offered in response to the death of another), "Yitgadal v'yitkadash" ("Glorified and sanctified [be God's great name…"]).[147]

Creation, Stewardship, and Ecology
In his eco-critical reading of Zephaniah, C. J. Redelinghuys brings to the foreground several dimensions of the relationship between YHWH, the created world, and humanity. These include especially the "interconnectedness" of the humans who are the object of divine punishment and their material surroundings, which are radically undone and ruined as a result.[148] Redelinghuys's observation that humanity is dependent upon the same creation that human wrongs inevitably degrade or destroy can be strengthened by the recognition that creation does not depend upon humanity as much as humanity depends upon it.[149] Although some of ancient Israel's theological traditions hold that humanity was indeed

---

[146] Ben Zvi, *Zephaniah*, 24–25.
[147] Jonathon Larson, *Rent: The Complete Book and Lyrics of the Broadway Musical* (New York: Applause Theatre and Cinema Books, 2008), 72. On the Kaddish, see Robert M. Seltzer, *Jewish People, Jewish Thought: The Jewish Experience in History* (New York: Macmillan, 1980), 305.
[148] Redelinghuys, "Creation," 810.
[149] Redelinghuys, "Creation," 810.

given mastery over creation (e.g., Gen 1), the account in Genesis 2 emphasizes the care and investment of the primordial couple in their garden-home.[150] Since the created world is the setting in which humanity served and obeyed God, its stewardship is not anthropocentric but ethically theocentric.[151] This point is captured well by Colin Gunton's conclusion that human custodianship of creation is "a calling to be and to act in such a way as to enable the created order to be itself as a response of praise to its maker."[152]

Other elements of an eco-critical reading intersect Zephaniah in suggestive ways, especially by connecting with a number of the book's themes. The "voice" of creation in the Old Testament is a faithful witness to human violence (Gen 4:10; Job 31:38–39; Jer 12:4; Mic 6:2, etc.), and it bears eloquent if silent witness to "human choice and its effects."[153] Much past and present human use of creation is grossly irresponsible, showing "that the elemental tension between the 'good' design of divine creation and what humans have made of it, [has] almost meant the end of this creation."[154] The worth of creation – animate and inanimate – is evident in YHWH's decision not to destroy it as he destroys his human enemies, but to preserve and renew it as the site for his permanent presence with his people (Zeph 3:13). This means that the purpose of creation is not to be trodden under foot, as it were, by an insouciant and self-centered humanity, nor to be worshiped as if it were supreme (1:5), but ultimately to be (re)made as the material environment for a renewed humanity that will not jeopardize its

---

[150] Cf. Redelinghuys, "Creation," 811.
[151] Similarly Rolf Rendtorff, *The Canonical Hebrew Bible: A Theology of the Old Testament*, trans. D. E. Orton, Tools for Biblical Study 7 (Leiden: Deo, 2005), 429.
[152] Gunton, *The Triune Creator*, 12.
[153] John Kessler, *Old Testament Theology: Divine Call and Human Response* (Waco, TX: Baylor University Press, 2013), 139.
[154] Rendtorff, *Canonical Hebrew Bible*, 16.

flourishing "whether directly or indirectly."¹⁵⁵ God's judgment of sinful humanity and his deliverance of the penitent run roughly parallel to his purifying and remaking of the world. Thanks to his restoring and purifying intervention, the world will again take up its original role as the perfected, enjoyed, and fruitful environment in which a God-oriented, creation-stewarding humanity enjoys uninterrupted well-being.

Poverty, Social Justice, and Spiritual Virtues of Zephaniah in Contemporary Settings

Zephaniah's powerful condemnation of social injustice and the misuse of power continues to resonate with contemporary readers. Walter Houston contends that in Zephaniah 3:11–13 the prophet "appears to envisage the removal of an existing hierarchy, and the takeover of governing functions (since this is the main function of the city) by a group identified as 'the humble and poor.'"¹⁵⁶ On his view, Zephaniah defines a just society as one in which equals are "living in harmony and taking no advantage of one another."¹⁵⁷ I have argued along similar lines that the radically renewed world that Zephaniah foresees is global in scope and populated by those whose fundamental characteristic is worship of Y H W H.¹⁵⁸ The absence of a Judean monarch from the new Jerusalem by itself suggests that socio-political hierarchy is likewise absent, something emphatically affirmed by God's presence with his people as an undifferentiated collective.¹⁵⁹ Finally, the

---

[155] Redelinghuys, "Creation," 812.
[156] Walter Houston, *Contending for Justice: Ideologies and Theologies of Social Justice in the Old Testament*, LHBOTS 428 (London: T & T Clark, 2008), 166.
[157] Houston, *Contending for Justice*, 167.
[158] Timmer, "Political Models," 324–26.
[159] Timmer, "Political Models," 325–26.

complete removal of violence (Zeph 3:9) and sin from God's multicultural people (3:10-12) sees them realize the purpose for which they were created: worshiping God and living in his glorious presence (3:15-17).[160]

The liberation theologian Gustavo Gutiérrez argued from the same passage, and from Zephaniah 2:1-3, that poverty, understood as the opposite of "pride, [and] an attitude of self-sufficiency," is in fact "synonymous with faith, with abandonment, and [with] trust in the Lord."[161] Consequently, "those who awaited the liberating work of the Messiah were 'poor.'"[162] This idea reaches "its highest expression," according to Gutiérrez, in the New Testament beatitude that pronounces happiness on "the poor (in spirit)," those who are "totally at the disposition of God."[163] The salvific advancement of the Kingdom of God in history involves spiritual liberation from sin as well as economic, social, and cultural liberation from oppression, individualism, and exploitation.[164]

Although the economic aspect is noticeably more muted in Zephaniah, the book's emancipating vision is indeed inseparable from divine justice, human beings' loving obedience to their creator and redeemer, and the prospect of eschatological deliverance from divine judgment. This makes Zephaniah's theology eminently worthy of reflection in a world where power, justice,

---

[160] John Webster, *Christ our Salvation: Expositions and Proclamations*, ed. Daniel Bush (Bellingham, WA: Lexham, 2020), 99, asserts that "praise of God is the supremely normal activity of human life."
[161] Gustavo Gutiérrez, *Theology of Liberation*, 15th anniversary ed., trans. C. Inda and J. Eagleson (Maryknoll, NY: Orbis, 1988), 169.
[162] Gutiérrez, *Theology of Liberation*, 169.
[163] Gutiérrez, *Theology of Liberation*, 169.
[164] Luis R. Rodríguez, "Gutiérrez, Gustavo," *The Westminster Dictionary of Theologians*, ed. Justo L. González, trans. S. E. Hoeferkamp Segovia (Louisville, KY: Westminster John Knox, 2006), 163-64.

and human flourishing often seen to be mutually incompatible. Zephaniah's confidence in Yhwh's gracious commitment to intervene supernaturally to restore fellowship with his people, purge the world of the effects of sin, and save his people requires just that: confidence that Yhwh is who he says he is.[165] In that name, his people will find refuge (Zeph 3:12) – and much more.

---

[165] Pfau, "Religion," 739, identifies Kant as a prominent source of the rejection of "grace – transcendently given, unaccountably received" in favor of "an exclusively human-engineered salvation."

CHAPTER 5

Conclusion
The Prophetic Message as Paradigm for Change

One of the primary goals of this volume is to help readers see in the theologies of Nahum, Habakkuk, and Zephaniah a multifaceted but coherent perspective on reality that challenges, inspires, and potentially transforms them. To read these books as mere repositories of defunct religious reflection or dry historical data would be to miss badly the prophets' communicative intent. Further, since this volume is explicitly theological in orientation, it is committed to seeing God, first of all, and, thereafter, "all things in relation to God."[1] This final chapter briefly summarizes the main lines of these prophets' theologies in order to sketch the nature of the response they seek to elicit as well as that response's primary dynamics and significance.

THE HUMAN DRAMA: ON THE WAY TO...

The God-oriented perspective evident in the three prophetic books examined here is grounded in Yhwh's creation of all

---

[1] Martin Westerholm, "Webster on the Theology of the University," in *A Companion to the Theology of John Webster*, ed. Michael Allen and R. David Nelson, foreword by Kevin J. Vanhoozer (Grand Rapids, MI: Eerdmans, 2021), 88–101 (89). William P. Brown's questions, mentioned in the Introduction, provide the same orientation.

things. As the sole creator, he brings into existence a cosmos that is "very good" even though not unchangeably so.[2] YHWH delegates stewardship of the creation to human beings, who as those made in his image are in a unique relationship to him. "Human life is of a particular kind, not simple animal life but life characterized by knowledge and love. Knowledge and love are essential to fellowship, whether with other creatures or, supremely, with the creator himself."[3] Human life is thus to be radically oriented to God and lived in fellowship with him and with other human beings. This fellowship, perfected and made permanent, is central to the goal toward which these books see God directing the world.

But the real world the prophets know is quite different. Their condemnations of sin, their distress due to its effects, and their announcements of judgment reveal that the originally pristine world has gone badly wrong, almost intolerably so. The reader repeatedly hears the claim that life lived in opposition or indifference to YHWH inevitably separates a person from him and from others, and destroys rather than benefits the one who lives that way. This negative assessment of many in the prophets' audiences and the related calls or incitements to change reflect another central claim in these books: the sinful nature of human beings. As Mary Midgley writes: "Unless evil is to be seen as a mere outside enemy, totally external to humanity, it seems necessary to locate

---

[2] Arguments for the "telic character" of the seventh day of the creation week and the unconsummated nature of the world as created are offered in Daniel C. Timmer, *Creation, Tabernacle, and Sabbath: The Sabbath Frame of Exodus 31:12–17; 35:1–3 in Exegetical and Theological Perspective*, FRLANT 227 (Göttingen: Vandenhoeck & Ruprecht, 2009), 70.

[3] John Webster, "Biblical Reasoning," *AThR* 90 (2008): 733–51 (736–37).

some of its sources in the unevenness of this original equipment [i.e., original human nature]."[4]

Although Scripture does not assert that sin is original to humanity as created, the biblical storyline does trace a radical downward trajectory from the point at which the primordial couple asserted its epistemological and moral autonomy by rejecting God's guidance and doubting his goodness.[5] The prophets' calls for and pressures toward repentance assume this deficiency or corruption of humanity as well as the divine desire to see human beings turn from their sin and live (Ezek 18:32; 33:11; cf. 1 Tim 2:4; 2 Pet 3:9). Further, although these insistent encouragements aim at radical change, they are accompanied by promises that God will be at work in those who turn to him (Nah 1:7; Zeph 3:9, 11–14), empowering and effecting the very change they participate in when they accept his word as authoritative divine speech and respond accordingly.[6]

The view of the human being in these books is thus complex: created for fellowship with God and others; corrupted by deeply rooted sin; but capable of being renewed, changed, and even perfected by YHWH. YHWH's word finds them in this liminal situation and accentuates it by challenging hearers to reckon with the fact that God will continue to pursue his purposes in this world, in justice and mercy, until the cosmos reaches the goal set for it. God's actions present both danger and opportunity, and Nahum, Habakkuk, and Zephaniah press the reader to escape the danger of judgment by seizing the opportunity to repent and seeking YHWH.

---

[4] Mary Midgley, *Wickedness: A Philosophical Essay*, with a new preface, Routledge Classics (Routledge: London, 2001), 16.
[5] Mark J. Boda, *A Severe Mercy: Sin and Its Remedy in the Old Testament*, Siphrut 1 (Winona Lake, IN: Eisenbrauns, 2009), 18–19.
[6] Cf. Webster, "Biblical Reasoning," 737.

THE ESSENCE OF THE CHANGE FOR WHICH THE PROPHETS CALL

Perhaps the most fundamental dimension of repentance is epistemological, and involves changes in the person's knowledge of herself, the world, and God.[7] In the early twenty-first century, the prophets' call collides with a number of dominant discourses. Rather than being self-determined in a world whose history and future are dependent primarily on human self-improvement and initiative (the promise of modernism), the prophets invite their hearers to recognize their imperfection and inability to bring about lasting, internal change in themselves (and others) or to remake their relationship with God (if the divine realm is even an issue for these moderns).[8] Instead of the postmodern self as "multiplicity, heterogeneity, difference, and becoming, bereft of origin and purpose"[9] in a world that has been "dispersed into a non-sequential, non-developmental, non-utopian, non-eschatological scatter of elements,"[10] the prophets put before the reader's imagination – and propose for his belief – a profoundly meaningful world in

---

[7] See Oliver O'Donovan, *Resurrection and Moral Order*, 2nd ed. (Grand Rapids, MI: Eerdmans, 1993), 81: "The exercise of knowledge is tied up with the faithful performance of man's task in the world, and ... his knowing will stand or fall with his worship of God and his obedience to the moral law."

[8] William Desmond asserts that modernism "turns to the human being as its own measure of self-determination uncoupled from any mysterious God who cannot be quite univocally factored into any equation of immanent autonomy." See his "The Metaphysics of Modernity," in *The Oxford Handbook of Theology and Modern European Thought*, ed. Nicholas Adams, George Pattison, and Graham Ward (Oxford: Oxford University Press, 2013), 543–63 (549–50).

[9] Calvin O. Schrag, *The Self after Postmodernism* (New Haven, CT: Yale University Press, 1997), 8, cited in John Webster, "Eschatology, Anthropology and Postmodernity," *IJST* 2 (2000): 13–28 (24).

[10] Webster, "Eschatology, Anthropology and Postmodernity," 17.

which God brings order out of what seems to be chaos and deep value and meaning out of apparent purposelessness.[11]

Changes in one's epistemology and knowledge lead to changes in identity and action – or, better, progressive transformation. The prophets valorize an identity that Yhwh graciously *gives* to those who take him at his word rather than an identity that is self-constructed or so malleable and ethereal that it lacks weight and continuity. Still more crucially, the prophets invite their audiences into a radically different life *with Yhwh*. Rather than leaving human beings "trapped within one or another form of natural determinism"[12] and so limited by their own abilities to resist changeless laws of cause and effect, the prophets underline God's ability and delight in breaking into the so-called natural order to deliver, transform, and perfect.[13] This intervention establishes a harmonious relationship between God and individuals, replacing alienation with fellowship and dullness with spiritual vigor.

In Christian theology, the reconciliation that the prophets announce is ultimately dependent on the obedient life, sacrificial death, and resurrection of Jesus Christ (Rom 5:11), which are appropriated by faith and applied to those who believe by God's Spirit (Rom 8:1–17). Their subsequent identity "in Christ" is rooted in the fundamental reality of God and his unchanging

---

[11] Barry Harvey argues that "[t]he absolute relativism and romantic nihilism that often characterize postmodernism as a cultural style should be viewed as inverted images of modern culture's arrogant longing for godlike power"; Barry Harvey, "Anti-postmodernism," in *Handbook of Postmodern Biblical Interpretation*, ed. A. K. M. Adam (St. Louis, MO: Chalice, 2000), 1–7 (5).

[12] O'Donovan, *Resurrection and Moral Order*, 82.

[13] Roland Deines, "God's Role in History as a Methodological Problem for Exegesis," in *Acts of God in History*, ed. Christoph Ochs and Peter Watts, WUNT 317 (Tübingen: Mohr Siebeck, 2013), 1–26.

love, and so is permanent. Yet their lives with God are far from static, as God progressively transforms and renews them. This means that as persons, they increasingly know, both cognitively and experientially, *life with God*. In John Webster's words, "in the economy of grace, God remakes human creatures precisely by taking from them the evil self-existence which devastates creaturely flourishing."[14] Liberated to pursue obedience, love of God, and love of others, their lives are now part of and contribute to God's project of cosmic renewal, and are therefore immensely significant. As Christopher Watkin observes, this reality should have a "galvanizing effect" on our service in this world, no matter how miniscule the results may appear to be: "Even the most transient good is worth achieving in the here and now for its own sake because nothing done in creation will be lost or forgotten on the final day."[15]

Yet living by faith in God's word does not spell the end of challenges and difficulties. Like the seventh-century BCE world that Nahum, Habakkuk, and Zephaniah describe, the world of the twenty-first century has not reached the goal God has set for it. Far from it. It would be superfluous (because they are obvious) and tedious (because they are legion) to mention even a fraction of the environmental, political, social, economic, and personal problems that beset us, our societies, and our world. Be that as it may, the worldview that these three prophetic books build on and enrich not only recognizes these evils and wrongs, it diagnoses them and proposes a holistic, progressive solution whose roots are solidly planted in God's history with his people

---

[14] Webster, "Biblical Reasoning," 746.
[15] Christopher Watkin, *Biblical Critical Theory* (Grand Rapids, MI: Zondervan Academic, 2022), 556, drawing on Richard Bauckham, *The Bible in the Contemporary World* (Grand Rapids, MI: Eerdmans, 2015), 33.

in the Old and New Testaments. The prophetic message is thus one of profound *hope* based on Yhwh's absolutely reliable word (Hab 3:16–19) and focused on the eschatological, perfected world God is making.

Finally, in keeping with the relational nature of the human being made in God's image, Nahum, Habakkuk, and Zephaniah present the new creation – already begun, in Christian thought, in the resurrection of Jesus Christ – in ways that underscore the profoundly relational nature of life at all points along this storyline. In Yhwh's world, his justice and saving actions enable those whom he delivers to "know him," a reality that is intimately personal (Hab 2:14) and decidedly unconstrained by the "Modernist ideal of detached, objective" knowledge.[16] In Zephaniah 3:15–17, the fear, danger, and evil that spoil and ultimately destroy human life are replaced with purification and the experience of God's jubilant love for his people. Even Nahum, despite its very rough edges, forcefully encourages the reader to escape the threatened divine judgment by finding safety in Yhwh himself (1:7) and to celebrate the defeat and destruction of evil (1:15[2:1]; 3:7, 19). Nahum, Habakkuk, and Zephaniah put before us a kaleidoscope of grace, reconciliation, peace, justice,

---

[16] Murray Rae, "'Incline Your Ear So That You May Live': Principles of Biblical Epistemology," in *The Bible and Epistemology: Biblical Soundings in the Knowledge of God*, ed. Mary Healy and Robin Parry (Milton Keynes: Paternoster, 2007), 161–80. Esther L. Meek, *Loving to Know: Introducing Covenant Epistemology* (Eugene, OR: Cascade, 2011), 21–22, draws attention to the work of Michael Polanyi, who argued that "for every truth claim to which we are giving our attention at a certain time, there are several truth claims which we cannot even specify and yet must rely on in trust. It is not possible to doubt or question all our commitments simultaneously and offer foolproof justification for the lot. All knowing, he said[,] was either wholly, or at its root, subsidiary, tacit, and anticipative."

purpose, and confidence rooted in God as the only way to live. It is not too much to hope that their words will challenge, inspire, and transform those who read them and that as a result our world will be brought that much closer to the eschatological horizon to which they point us.

Further Reading

COMMENTARIES ON NAHUM, HABAKKUK, AND ZEPHANIAH

Among the commentaries listed below, I distinguish between those that are intended primarily for academic use ("extensive") and shorter ones that are more accessible to a wider readership even though these, too, provide careful analysis of the text and engage with a wide range of secondary literature ("concise"). Those that are historical-critical typically integrate to varying degrees the author's reconstructions of the book's literary development or redaction in their explanation of the book as we have it.

Ben Zvi, Ehud. *A Historical-Critical Study of the Book of Zephaniah*. BZAW 198. Berlin: de Gruyter, 1992. Extensive, wide-ranging, moderately historical-critical, attends to the conceptual and theological features of the book.

Berlin, Adele. *Zephaniah: A New Translation with Introduction and Commentary*. AB 25A. New York: Doubleday, 1994. Extensive, thorough, moderately historical-critical.

Christiansen, Duane. *Nahum: A New Translation with Introduction and Commentary*. AYB 24F. New Haven, CT: Yale University Press, 2009. Extensive, theologically oriented, with a strong emphasis on the poetic nature of the text.

Coggins, Richard J., and Jin H. Han. *Six Minor Prophets through the Centuries*. Blackwell Bible Commentaries. Chichester: Wiley-Blackwell, 2011. A fascinating history-of-reception treatment for Nahum to Malachi; the only commentary of its kind for these books.

Fabry, Heinz-Josef. *Nahum*. HTKAT. Freiburg: Herder, 2006. Thorough, moderately historical-critical work with a strong historical and theological focus; discusses history of interpretation and much more.

Floyd, Michael H. *Minor Prophets Part 2*. FOTL 22. Grand Rapids, MI: Eerdmans, 2000. Gives particular attention to literary forms and their contribution to each book; less attention is paid to historical or theological dimensions.

Irsigler, Hubert. *Zefanja*. HTKAT. Freiburg: Herder, 2002. Extensive, thorough, gives significant attention to redactional reconstructions, but with historical and theological focus; discusses history of interpretation, and so on.

McComisky, Thomas, ed. *The Minor Prophets: An Exegetical and Expository Commentary*. 3 vols. Grand Rapids, MI: Baker, 1993. Very good attention to historical, literary, and theological elements, with some practical reflections in Old Testament and New Testament contexts as well.

Nogalski, James D. *The Book of the Twelve: Micah-Malachi*. Smyth & Helwys Bible Commentary 18b. Macon, GA: Smyth & Helwys, 2011. Balances attention to each book's diachronic formation with reflection on its contribution to the Twelve.

Renaud, Bernard. *Michée, Sophonie, Nahum*. Sources Bibliques. Paris: J. Gabalde et Cie, 1987. Gives some attention to redactional reconstructions, but with a strong theological focus.

Renz, Thomas. *The Books of Nahum, Habakkuk, and Zephaniah*. NICOT. Grand Rapids, MI: Eerdmans, 2021. Very thorough, gives significant attention to literary, textual, and exegetical details as part of a theologically-oriented interpretation. Includes brief surveys of each book's reception history.

Roberts, J. J. M. *Nahum, Habakkuk, Zephaniah: A Commentary.* OTL. Louisville, KY: Westminster/John Knox, 1991. Concise, mildly critical, good theological and historical focus.

Spronk, Klaas. *Nahum.* HCOT. Kampen: Kok Pharos, 1997. Excellent, concise yet thorough.

Sweeney, Marvin A. *The Twelve Prophets.* Volume Two. Berit Olam. Collegeville, MN: Liturgical Press, 2000. Concise, balanced treatment of Micah to Malachi.

Sweeney, Marvin A. *Zephaniah: A Commentary.* Hermeneia. Minneapolis, MN: Fortress, 2003. Extensive, detailed, moderately critical, ample treatment of many issues and questions surrounding the interpretation of Zephaniah.

Tidiman, Brian. *Nahoum, Habaquq, Sophonie.* CEB. Vaux-sur-Seine: Edifac, 2009. Concise, well-balanced exegesis of literary, historical, and theological features in Old Testament and New Testament contexts.

Timmer, Daniel C. *Nahum: A Discourse Analysis of the Hebrew Bible.* ZECOT. Grand Rapids, MI: Zondervan Academic, 2020. Gives equal attention to literary, historical, and theological features in Old Testament and New Testament contexts.

STUDIES ON NAHUM, HABAKKUK, AND ZEPHANIAH

The last few decades have witnessed a steady flow of publications dedicated to interpreting Nahum, Habakkuk, and Zephaniah from a variety of perspectives. Those presented here range widely over literary, historical, and theological issues. Studies that focus on the Twelve as a collection appear in the next section.

Studies on Nahum

Ball, Edward. "'When the Towers Fall': Interpreting Nahum as Christian Scripture." Pages 211–30 in *In Search of True Wisdom: Essays in Old Testament Interpretation in Honour of Ronald E. Clements.* Edited by E. Ball. JSOTSup 300. London: T & T Clark, 1999.

Becking, Bob. "Passion, Power and Protection: Interpreting the God of Nahum." Pages 1–20 in *On Reading Prophetic Texts: Gender-Specific and Related Studies in Memory of Fokkelien van Dijk-Hemmes.* Edited by B. Becking and M. Dijkstra. BibInt 18. Leiden: Brill, 1996.

Johnston, G. H. "Nahum's Rhetorical Allusions to the Neo-Assyrian Lion Motif." *BSac* 158 (2001): 287–307.

Timmer, Daniel C. "'Ah, Assyria Is No More!' Retribution, Theodicy, and Hope in Nahum." Pages 157–72 in *Theodicy and Hope in the Book of the Twelve.* Edited by G. Athas, B. Stovell, D. C. Timmer, and C. Toffelmire. LHBOTS 705. London: T & T Clark, 2021.

Timmer, Daniel C. "Nahum's Representation of and Response to Neo-Assyria: Imperialism as a Multifaceted Point of Contact in Nahum." *BBR* 24.3 (2014): 349–62.

Wendland, Ernst R. "What's the 'Good News' – Check Out the 'Feet'! Prophetic Rhetoric and the Salvific centre of Nahum's 'Vision.'" *OTE* 11 (1998): 154–81.

Wessels, Wilhelm J. "Reading Nahum with the Oppressed: Power as a Social Justice Issue." Pages 313–26 in *Postcolonial Commentary and the Old Testament.* Edited by H. Gossai. London: Bloomsbury/T & T Clark, 2018.

Woods, Julie. "The West as Nineveh: How Does Nahum's Message of Judgement Apply to Today?" *Them* 31 (2005): 7–37.

Studies on Habakkuk

Legaspi, Michael C. "Opposition to Idolatry in the Book of Habakkuk." *VT* 67 (2017): 458–69.

Moseman, R. David. "Habakkuk's Dialogue with Faithful Yahweh: A Transforming Experience." *PRS* 44 (2017): 261–74.

Prinsloo, G. T. M. "Life for the Righteous, Doom for the Wicked: Reading Habakkuk from a Wisdom Perspective." *SK* 21 (2000): 621–40.

Renz, Thomas. "Habakkuk and Its Co-Texts." Pages 13–36 in *The Book of the Twelve – An Anthology of Prophetic Books or The Result of Complex Redactional Processes*. Edited by H. Wenzel. OSJCB 4. Göttingen: Vandenhoeck & Ruprecht, 2017.

Watts, James W. "Psalmody in Prophecy: Habakkuk 3 in Context." Pages 209–23 in *Forming Prophetic Literature: Essays on Isaiah and the Twelve in Honor of John D. W. Watts*. Edited by J. W. Watts and P. R. House. JSOTSup 235. Sheffield: Sheffield Academic, 1996.

Whitehead, Philip. "Habakkuk and the Problem of Suffering: Theodicy Deferred." *JTI* 10 (2016): 265–81.

Studies on Zephaniah

Hays, Nathan. "Humility and Instruction in Zephaniah 3.1–7." *JSOT* 44 (2020): 472–89.

King, Greg A. "The Day of the Lord in Zephaniah." *BSac* 152 (1995): 16–32.

King, Greg A. "The Remnant in Zephaniah." *BSac* 151 (1994): 414–27.

Melvin, David P. "Making All Things New (Again): Zephaniah's Eschatological Vision of a Return to Primeval Time." Pages 269–81 in *Creation and Chaos: A Reconsideration of Hermann*

Gunkel's Chaoskampf Hypothesis. Edited by J. Scurlock and R. H. Beal. Winona Lake, IN: Eisenbrauns, 2013.

Timmer, Daniel C. "Political Models and the End of the World in Zephaniah." *BI* 24 (2016): 310–31.

Wendland, Ernst R. "The Drama of Zephaniah: A Literary-Rhetorical Analysis of a Proclamatory Prophetic Text." Pages 497–530 in idem, *Prophetic Rhetoric: Case Studies in Text Analysis and Translation*. 2nd ed. Dallas, TX: SIL International, 2014.

THE BOOK OF THE TWELVE AND ITS INTERPRETATION

The sense in which is Book of the Twelve is a book, like the status of the twelve books it includes, remain debated questions. The literature surveyed here touches on the theoretical and literary facets of these questions (see especially Landy), but more often undertakes interpretation of part or all of the collection and handles hermeneutical questions as part of that task.

Fabry, Heinz-Josef (ed.). *The Books of the Twelve Prophets: Minor Prophets – Major Theologies*. BETL 295. Leuven: Leuven University Press, 2019. An extensive collection of essays on many theological features of the Twelve from various points of view.

House, Paul R. "The Character of God in the Book of the Twelve." Pages 125–45 in *Reading and Hearing the Book of the Twelve*. Edited by J. D. Nogalski and M. A. Sweeney. SBL SymS 15. Atlanta: Scholars Press, 2000.

Landy, Francis. "Three Sides of a Coin." *JHS* 10 (2010): article 11. Evaluates the positions of J. D. Nogalski and Ehud Ben Zvi on the Book/s of the Twelve and stakes out his own position.

Menken, M. J. J., and S. Moyise (eds.). *The Minor Prophets in the New Testament.* LNTS 377. London: T & T Clark, 2009. Chapters discuss the Twelve in Paul, Hebrews.

O'Brien, Julia M. "Nahum – Habakkuk – Zephaniah: Reading the 'Former Prophets' in the Persian Period." *Int* 61 (2007): 168–83.

O'Brien, Julia M. (ed.). *The Oxford Handbook of the Minor Prophets.* Oxford: Oxford University Press, 2021. A wide-ranging survey of themes, approaches, and issues related to the Twelve.

Rae, Murray. "Theological Interpretation and Historical Criticism." Pages 94–109 in *A Manifesto for Theological Interpretation.* Edited by Craig G. Bartholomew and Heath A. Thomas. Grand Rapids, MI: Baker Academic, 2016.

Scheffler, Eben. "Various Views on Peace in the Twelve Minor Prophets." Pages 501–17 in *The Books of the Twelve Prophets: Minor Prophets, Major Theologies.* Edited by H.-J. Fabry. BETL 295. Leuven: Leuven University Press, 2018.

Thomas, Heath. "Hearing the Minor Prophets: The Book of the Twelve and God's Address." Pages 356–79 in *Hearing the Old Testament: Listening for God's Address.* Edited by C. G. Bartholomew and D. J. H. Beldman. Grand Rapids, MI: Eerdmans, 2012.

Timmer, Daniel C. "The Twelve." Pages 321–40 in *A Biblical-Theological Introduction to the Old Testament: The Gospel Promised.* Edited by M. V. Van Pelt. Wheaton, IL: Crossway, 2016.

Tucker, Gene M. "The Law in the Eighth-Century Prophets." Pages 201–16 in *Canon, Theology, and Old Testament Interpretation: Essays in Honor of Brevard S. Childs.* Edited by G. M. Tucker et al. Philadelphia, PA: Fortress, 1988.

Van Seters, John. "Editing the Bible: The Romantic Myths about Authors and Editors." *HBAI* 3 (2014): 343–54.

Watson, Francis. "The Scope of Hermeneutics." Pages 65–80 in *The Cambridge Companion to Christian Doctrine*. Edited by C. E. Gunton. Cambridge: Cambridge University Press, 1997.

Select Bibliography

Albertz, Rainer, James D. Nogalski, and Jakob Wohrle (eds.). *Perspectives on the Formation of the Book of the Twelve: Methodological Foundations – Redactional Processes – Historical Insights.* BZAW 433. Berlin: de Gruyter, 2012.

Arnold, Bill T., and Brent A. Strawn (eds.). *The World around the Old Testament: The People and Places of the Ancient Near East.* Grand Rapids, MI: Baker Academic, 2016.

Athas, George, Beth Stovell, Daniel C. Timmer, and Colin Toffelmire (eds.). *Theodicy and Hope in the Book of the Twelve.* LHBOTS 705. London: T & T Clark, 2021.

Bauckham, Richard. "Babylon IV: New Testament." *EBR* 3: 269–73.

Bauckham, Richard. *The Bible in the Contemporary World.* Grand Rapids, MI: Eerdmans, 2015.

Becking, Bob. "Divine Wrath and the Conceptual Coherence of the Book of Nahum." *SJOT* 9 (1995): 277–96.

Bekkum, Koert van. "'Is Your Rage Against the Rivers, Your Wrath Against the Sea?' Storm-God Imagery in Habakkuk 3." Pages 55–76 in *Playing with Leviathan: Interpretation and Reception of Monsters from the Biblical World.* Edited by Koert van Bekkum et al. Themes in Biblical Narrative. Leiden: Brill, 2017.

Bernat, David A., and Jonathan Klawans (eds.). *Religion and Violence: The Biblical Heritage*. Recent Research in Biblical Studies 2. Sheffield: Sheffield Phoenix, 2007.

Brisch, Nicole (ed.). *Religion and Power: Divine Kingship in the Ancient World and Beyond*. OIS 4. Chicago, IL: Oriental Institute of the University of Chicago, 2008.

Brueggemann, Walter. *Theology of the Old Testament: Testimony, Dispute, Advocacy*. Minneapolis, MN: Fortress, 1997.

Carroll, R. (Rodas), M. Daniel, and J. Blair Wilgus (eds.). *Wrestling with the Violence of God: Soundings in the Old Testament*. BBR Sup 10. Winona Lake, IN: Eisenbrauns, 2015.

Castelo, Daniel. *Theological Theodicy*. Cascade Companions. Eugene, OR: Cascade Books, 2012.

Chapman, Stephen B. "What Are We Reading? Canonicity and the Old Testament." *WW* 29 (2009): 334–47.

Crouch, Carly L. *War and Ethics in the Ancient Near East: Military Violence in Light of Cosmology and History*. BZAW 407. Berlin: de Gruyter, 2009.

Deines, Roland. "God's Role in History as a Methodological Problem for Exegesis." Pages 1–26 in idem, *Acts of God in History*. Edited by Christoph Ochs and Peter Watts. WUNT 317. Tübingen: Mohr Siebeck, 2013.

Di Pede, Elena, and Donatelle Scailoa (eds.). *The Book of the Twelve – One Book or Many?* FAT 91. Tübingen: Mohr Siebeck, 2016.

Fabry, Heinz-Josef. *The Books of the Twelve Prophets: Minor Prophets, Major Theologies*. BETL 295. Leuven: Leuven University Press, 2018.

Gordon, Robert P. "'Comparativism' and the God of Israel." Pages 45–67 in *The Old Testament and Its World*. Edited by J. C. de Moor and Robert P. Gordon. OtSt 52. Leiden: Brill, 2005.

Gordon, Robert P. "'Where Have All the Prophets Gone?': The 'Disappearing' Israelite Prophet against the Background of Ancient Near Eastern Prophecy." *BBR* 5 (1995): 67–86.

Gunton, Colin. *The Triune Creator: A Historical and Systematic Study*. Grand Rapids, MI: Eerdmans, 1998.

Hafemann, Scott J., and Paul R. House (eds.). *Central Themes in Biblical Theology: Mapping Unity in Diversity*. Grand Rapids, MI: Baker Academic, 2007.

Harrisville, Roy A. *Pandora's Box Opened: An Examination and Defense of Historical-Critical Method and Its Master Practitioners*. Grand Rapids, MI: Eerdmans, 2014.

House, Paul R. *The Unity of the Twelve*. JSOTSup 97. Sheffield: Almond, 1990.

Johnston, Sarah I. (ed.). *Religions of the Ancient World*. Cambridge, MA: Belknap Press of Harvard University Press, 2004.

Jones, Barry. "The Seventh-Century Prophets in Recent Research." *CurBR* 14 (2016): 129–75.

Kelle, Brad. "The Phenomenon of Israelite Prophecy in Contemporary Scholarship." *CurBR* 12 (2014): 275–320.

LeCureux, Jason T. *The Thematic Unity of the Book of the Twelve*. HBM. Sheffield: Sheffield Phoenix, 2012.

Legaspi, Michael C. "Opposition to Idolatry in the Book of Habakkuk." *VT* 67 (2017): 458–69.

Levenson, Jon D. *Creation and the Persistence of Evil: The Jewish Drama of Divine Omnipotence*. Princeton: Princeton University Press, 1988.

Lim, Timothy H. *The Earliest Commentary on the Prophecy of Habakkuk*. Oxford Commentary on the Dead Sea Scrolls. Oxford: Oxford University Press, 2020.

Lints, Richard. *Identity and Idolatry: The Image of God and Its Inversion*. NSBT 36. Downers Grove, IL: Intervarsity, 2015.

Liverani, Mario. *Assyria: The Imperial Mission*. Translated by A. Trameri and J. Valk. Winona Lake, IN: Eisenbrauns, 2017.

Magary, Dennis, and James K. Hoffmeier (eds.). *Do Historical Matters Matter to Faith? A Critical Appraisal of Modern and Postmodern Approaches to Scripture*. Foreword by John Woodbridge. Wheaton, IL: Crossway, 2012.

McConville, J. Gordon. *God and Earthly Power: An Old Testament Political Theology, Genesis-Kings*. London: T & T Clark, 2006.

Menken, Maarten J. J., and Steve Moyise (eds.). *The Minor Prophets in the New Testament*. LNTS 377. London: Bloomsbury Academic, 2009.

Miller, Patrick D. *The Religion of Ancient Israel*. LAI. Louisville: Westminster John Knox, 2000.

Nissinen, Martti. *Prophets and Prophecy in the Ancient Near East*. 2nd ed. With contributions by C. L. Seow, Robert K. Ritner, and H. Craig Melchert. WAW 41. Atlanta, GA: SBL, 2019.

Noble, Paul. "Synchronic and Diachronic Approaches to Biblical Interpretation." *Journal of Literature & Theology* 7 (1993): 130–48.

Nogalski, James D., and Ehud Ben Zvi. *Two Sides of a Coin: Juxtaposing Views on Interpreting the Book of the Twelve / the Twelve Prophetic Books*. Edited by Thomas Römer. Analecta Gorgiana 201. Piscataway, NJ: Gorgias, 2009.

Nogalski, James D., and Marvin A. Sweeney (eds.). *Reading and Hearing the Book of the Twelve*. SBL SymS 15. Atlanta, GA: Scholars, 2000.

O'Brien, Julia M. (ed.). *The Oxford Handbook of the Minor Prophets*. Oxford: Oxford University Press, 2021.

Parpola, Simo. *Assyrian Prophecies*. SAA 9. Helsinki: Helsinki University Press, 1997.

Person, Raymond F., and Robert Rezetko (eds.). *Empirical Models Challenging Biblical Criticism*. AIL. Atlanta, GA: Society of Biblical Literature, 2016.

Pfau, Thomas. "Religion." Pages 730–51 in *The Oxford Handbook of European Romanticism*. Edited by Paul Hamilton. Oxford: Oxford University Press, 2016.

Rae, Murray. "Creation and Promise." Pages 267–99 in *"Behind" the Text: History and Biblical Interpretation*. Edited by Craig Bartholomew et al. SHS 4. Grand Rapids: Zondervan, 2003.

Rae, Murray. "'Incline Your Ear So That You May Live': Principles of Biblical Epistemology." Pages 161–80 in *The Bible and Epistemology: Biblical Soundings in the Knowledge of God*. Edited by Mary Healy and Robin Parry. Milton Keynes: Paternoster, 2007.

Renz, Thomas. "Habakkuk and Its Co-Texts." Pages 13–36 in *The Book of the Twelve – An Anthology of Prophetic Books or The Result of Complex Redactional Processes*. Edited by Heiko Wenzel. OSJCB 4. Göttingen: Vandenhoeck & Ruprecht, 2017.

Reventlow, Henning Graf, Yair Hoffman, and Benjamin Uffenheimer (eds.). *Politics and Theopolitics in the Bible and Postbiblical Literature*. JSOTSup 171. Sheffield: JSOT, 1994.

Rollston, Christopher A. (ed.). *Enemies and Friends of the State: Ancient Prophecy in Context*. University Park, PA: Eisenbrauns, 2018.

Sals, Ulrike. "Babylon II." *EBR* 3: 259–65.

Sanders, Seth L. "Why Prophecy Became a Biblical Genre." *HBAI* 6 (2017): 26–52.

Schart, Aaron. "Twelve, Book of the: History of Interpretation." Pages 806–17 in *Dictionary of the Old Testament: Prophets*. Edited by Mark J. Boda and J. Gordon McConville. Downers Grove, IL: IVP Academic, 2012.

Sommer, Benjamin. "Dating Pentateuchal Texts and the Perils of Pseudo-Historicism." Pages 85–108 in *The Pentateuch: International Perspectives on Current Research*. Edited by Thomas B. Dozeman, Konrad Schmid, and Baruch W. Schwartz. FAT 78. Tübingen: Mohr Siebeck, 2011.

Stangor, Charles, and Mark Schaller. "Stereotypes as Individual and Collective Representations." Pages 3–40 in *Stereotypes and Stereotyping*. Edited by C. Neil Macrae, Charles Stangor, and Miles Hewstone. New York: Guilford, 1996.

Stavrakopoulou, Francesca, and John Barton (eds.). *Religious Diversity in Ancient Israel and Judah*. London: T & T Clark, 2010.

Sweeney, Marvin A. "Twelve, Book of the." Pages 788–806 in *Dictionary of the Old Testament: Prophets*. Edited by Mark J. Boda and J. Gordon McConville. Downers Grove, IL: IVP Academic, 2012.

Taylor, Charles. *A Secular Age*. Cambridge: Harvard University Press, Belknap Press, 2007.

Teeter, D. Andrew, and William A. Tooman. "Standards of (In) coherence in Ancient Jewish Literature." *HBAI* 9 (2020): 94–129.

Tiemeyer, Lena-Sofia, and Jakob Wöhrle (eds.). *The Book of the Twelve: Composition, Reception, and Interpretation*. VTSup 184. Leiden: Brill, 2020.

Timmer, Daniel C. "Prophetic Literature: Book of the Twelve." In *The State of Old Testament Studies*. Edited by H. H. Hardy II and M. Daniel Carroll R. (Rodas). Grand Rapids: Baker Academic, forthcoming.

Vanderhooft, David J. *The Neo-Babylonian Empire and Babylon in the Latter Prophets*. HSM 59. Atlanta: Scholars, 1999.

Webster, John. "Biblical Reasoning." *AThR* 90 (2008): 733–51.

Webster, John. "Eschatology, Anthropology and Postmodernity." *IJST* 2 (2000): 13–28.

Wendland, Ernst R. "The Drama of Zephaniah: A Literary-Rhetorical Analysis of a Proclamatory Prophetic Text." Pages 497–530 in idem, *Prophetic Rhetoric: Case Studies in Text Analysis and Translation*. 2nd ed. Dallas, TX: SIL International, 2014.

Scripture Index

OLD TESTAMENT

Genesis
1	183, 188, 235
1–2	211
1–3	211
1:26–28	136
1:27	188
1:28–30	216
1:31	188, 216
2	235
2:5–25	216
2:15–17	216
3	216
3:5	189
4:10	235
6–8	188
6:5	188, 190
6:7	188
7:4	188
7:23	188
8–9	190
9:1–7	190
9:26–27	199
10	199
10:1	199
10:2	200
10:5	205
10:6	200
10:21	200
11	209, 234
12:3	6, 64
16:4–5	49
18:22–32	168
19:30–38	201
29:24–25	202
32	64
33	64
34:2	61
35:1–15	64
49:3	131

Exodus
9:3	152, 158
14:22	152, 158
19–24	63
19:4–6	64
19:5–6	63
19:16–18	152, 158
20:5	84
23:10–12	149
28:30	4
32–34	84, 85
32:11	39, 84
33:19	41, 84
34	41
34:5	41
34:6	84
34:6–7	41, 80
34:7	84
34:14	84
32	94

Leviticus
18:8	60
26	63

Numbers

21–24	201
27:12–23	4

Deuteronomy

4:37	39
6:13–14	193
9:29	39
12:15–18	147
13:1–5	4
17:14–20	49
17:15	129
18	3
18:18	4
22:28	61
28	63, 226
28:1–14	129
28:15–69	129
28:30	195
28:36	195
28:37	195
28:39	195
28:41	195
30:1–10	63

Joshua

2:10	42
4:23	42
5:1	42
10:12–14	152

Judges

3:12–14	201
3:12–30	201

1 Samuel

2:30	49
4–7	201
10:27–11:15	201
13:19	200
16	201

2 Samuel

8:2–3	201
12:26–31	201
13:12	61
13:14	61
17:27–29	201

1 Kings

14:21	201
14:31	201

2 Kings

1:1	201
3:4–27	201
8:7–15	7
14:8–14	34
14:25	79
15:28–29	34
16:18	185
17:1–5	35
17:36	39
18:13	36
18:25	47
18:33	49
18:35	49
19:19	49
21:1–18	36
23	226
23:1–20	185
23:3	185
23:6	185
23:15–20	186
23:29	120
24:10–16	106
24:10–17	120

2 Chronicles

15:7	225
33:10–17	36

Nehemiah

1:10	39

Job

13:11	131
31:23	131
31:38–39	235
40:4	49
41:17	131

Psalms

1:1	128
1:4	128
2	49
10:2–3	128
23	195
26:5	128
29:10	43
37:12	128
37:14	128
44:1	135

Psalms (cont.)			52:1	83
62:5	131		52:7	83
74:12	134	Jeremiah		
77:12	135		5:27	225
104:15	147		8:13	225
104:16	148		12:4	235
104:17–18	148		13:22	60–61
143:5	135		13:26	61
147:5	39		19:13	225
Proverbs			27:5	39
1:11	39		30:7–15	84
1:16	39		32:17	39
1:18	39		46:2–12	84
Isaiah			46:10	225
1	36, 128		51:58	146
5:25–30	83, 88	Ezekiel		
6:5	4		16:36	60
6:5–7	209		18:21–23	18
7	34		18:32	241
10:5–11	96		22:24–28	225
10:5–19	7	Daniel		
10:5–34	85		9:21	159
11	158		11:27	159
13–23	158	Hosea		
13:19	89		1:2	41
14	18		2:17	209
14:3–23	89		4:3	82
14:13–14	131		14:1	41
14:32	7	Joel		
19:18–25	7		2	41
21:1–10	89		2:13	41
21:11–12	7		2:32	82
25:6–8	195		4:2	81
26:11	230	Amos		
36:4–20	47		1:2	82
36:10	47		1:2–2:3	7
36:18	49		1:13	201
36:20	49		2:13–16	128
37:11–13	47		3:2	18
37:20	49		3:10–11	128
40:9–11	230		4:1–4	128
41	18		5	18
45:12	135		5:18	175
46–47	89		5:20	175
47:8	131		6:1–7	128
51:9	134		7:1–6	6

SCRIPTURE INDEX

7:2	4	1:12–14	30
7:5	4	1:13	51
7:6	6	1:14	47, 49–50, 88
7:7–9	6	1:15	47, 63, 71, 72, 77, 83, 88, 245
Obadiah			
12	81	2:1	63
14	81	2:1–2	93
Jonah		2:1–3	93
3:10	41	2:2	63, 64
4:2	80	2:3–10	16, 51
Micah		2:3–3:19	30
1:3	82	2:7	68
2–3	128	2:10	68
3	36	2:11	51, 86
6:2	235	2:11–13	51–54
7:7	41	2:13	32, 68
7:18–20	41, 82	3	93
Nahum		3:1	88
1	93	3:1–3	93, 161
1:1	30	3:1–4	39
1:1–11	30	3:4	60
1:2	84	3:4–7	55–63
1:2–3	43	3:5	32, 60–62
1:2–5	71	3:6–7	93
1:2–8	27, 29, 30, 37–44, 54, 69, 74–77, 80, 82, 84–86, 89, 91, 97	3:7	64, 71, 161, 204, 245
		3:8–11	73
		3:12–15	73
1:3	39, 71, 84, 85	3:13	59
1:3–5	18, 42, 43	3:15–17	73
1:4	42	3:18–19	73
1:5	43, 71	3:19	46, 64, 71, 77, 88, 204, 245
1:6	39, 71, 77, 85, 88		
1:7	75, 77, 81, 84, 90, 241, 245	Habakkuk	
		1–2	158
1:8	75	1:1	107, 110
1:9–10	30, 39, 46, 47, 88	1:2	126–27, 131, 133
1:9–14	30	1:2–4	37, 110, 114, 126–30
1:9–15	51	1:2–2:5	110, 115
1:9–2:2	27, 29, 30	1:3	127, 131
1:9–3:19	45–74	1:4	127–28, 133, 135, 141, 163
1:10	30		
1:11	30, 88	1:5	106, 130
1:11–13	47	1:5–10	140
1:11–14	62	1:5–11	114, 130–39, 160, 164
1:12	36, 63, 65	1:6	131, 163
1:12–13	63	1:6–11	132

Habakkuk (cont.)		3:6	153
1:7	131, 135	3:8	153
1:8	169	3:8–15	151
1:9	127, 131, 133	3:10	152, 158
1:11	131, 133	3:11	152, 158
1:12	18	3:12	153
1:12–2:1	110, 114, 135, 140, 150	3:12–15	81
1:13	128, 133	3:13	153, 161
1:14	106, 136	3:16	4, 81, 151, 160
1:15	136	3:16–17	153–54
1:15–17	108	3:16–19	110, 140, 154, 245
1:16	137	3:18	154
1:17	138	3:18–19	153
2:1	139, 162, 168	Zephaniah	
2:2	108, 110	1:1	181
2:2–5	114	1:1–2:3	175
2:2–20	139–50	1:2	188, 189, 225
2:3	139, 159, 160, 168	1:2–3	18, 183, 189–91, 208, 220
2:3–4	165		
2:4	141, 164, 165, 167, 168	1:2–6	179
2:4–5	115	1:2–19	180
2:5	141, 145	1:2–3:8	176
2:5–6	144	1:3	190, 225, 229
2:6	167	1:4	194
2:6–8	145	1:4–5	37, 184
2:6–20	110, 115, 140, 144	1:4–6	218, 221
2:8	127, 145, 159	1:4–14	205
2:9–11	145	1:4–16	190–96
2:10	145	1:5	225, 235
2:12–14	146	1:6	191, 198
2:13	146	1:7	175, 179, 193, 194, 197, 225, 233
2:14	145, 151, 158, 165, 245		
2:15	162	1:7–13	221
2:15–17	146	1:7–16	207, 213
2:17	127, 149, 160	1:7–18	218
2:18–20	149	1:8	184, 193
2:20	145, 151, 164, 165, 193	1:8–10	179
3:1	107, 110	1:9	193, 218, 225
3:1–19	83, 110, 114, 150–54, 168	1:9–12	195
3:2	110, 116, 141, 151	1:11	179, 197, 213, 233
3:3	152	1:11–12	196
3:3–7	151–52, 162	1:12–13	179, 228
3:3–15	80, 108, 110, 115, 140, 151, 165	1:13	208, 232
		1:14	229
3:4	152, 158	1:14–16	175, 179
3:5	152, 158	1:15	81, 233

1:17	179, 218	3:3	206, 225
1:17–18	189–91, 196	3:3–4	206
1:18	179, 181, 207, 218, 229	3:4	206
		3:5	206
1:18–2:2	228	3:6	218
2	41	3:6–7	179, 203
2:1–3	18, 156, 180, 181, 196–98, 205, 207, 214, 220, 232, 237	3:7	179, 204, 207, 214, 226
		3:8	207, 229
2:1–5	179	3:8–9	220
2:1–7	180, 184	3:8–13	179, 181
2:2	197	3:9	208, 209, 212, 220, 228–29, 237, 241
2:3	41, 197–98, 226		
2:4	180		
2:4–7	177	3:9–10	207
2:4–9	209	3:9–13	220
2:4–10	181, 199–206, 208, 218	3:9–17	211, 234, 241
		3:9–20	83, 209–13, 234
2:4–11	214	3:10	209, 226
2:4–15	200	3:10–12	237
2:4–3:5	181	3:10–13	208
2:5	179	3:10–20	209
2:5–7	180	3:11	220
2:6–7	179, 221	3:11–12	215
2:8–9	177, 179	3:11–13	212, 236
2:8–15	184	3:11–14	241
2:8–18	180	3:12	238
2:9	202	3:13	210, 229, 230, 235
2:10	202	3:14	210, 215
2:10–11	179	3:14–15	232
2:11	177, 178, 204–5, 207, 212, 226, 230	3:14–17	179, 230
		3:15	208, 229
2:12	177, 179, 182, 202, 214	3:15–17	208, 237, 245
		3:16	225, 229
2:12–15	199–204, 206, 208–9, 218	3:18–20	179, 211
		3:19	204
2:13–14	204	3:20	208, 212
2:13–15	177, 179, 182	Haggai	
2:14	221	1:12	162
2:15	203–4	Zechariah	
3:1–2	206	1:15	96, 159
3:1–4	225	2:6–9	159
3:1–5	128, 179, 222	9:9	229, 230
3:1–7	37, 210	14:3	81
3:1–8	205–7	Malachi	
3:1–20	180, 184	1:10–11	225

Malachi (cont.)
- 1:11   225
- 1:14   225
- 4:1–3   81

NEW TESTAMENT

Matthew
- 13:41   229
- 15:11   209
- 24–25   90

Mark
- 1:15   90

John
- 1:47   230
- 12:13   229
- 12:15   229, 230

Acts
- 10:36   88
- 13:41   164

Romans
- 1   165
- 1:17   165, 167
- 5:11   243
- 6:17   88
- 8:1–17   243
- 10:15   88
- 15:6   229

1 Corinthians
- 5:5   231
- 15:23   231

2 Corinthians
- 5:17–18   231

Galatians
- 3:11   165
- 6:15   231

Ephesians
- 2:11–22   231
- 4:25–30   231
- 6:15   88

Philippians
- 1:9–10   231

Colossians
- 3:5–9   231
- 3:10–11   231

1 Thessalonians
- 5:3–4   231

1 Timothy
- 2:4   241

Hebrews
- 10:27   230
- 10:37–38   165

2 Peter
- 3:9   156, 241

Revelation
- 6:17   229
- 14:5   229, 230
- 16:1   229
- 16–19   89
- 17:1–6   89
- 17:1–19:10   231
- 17:2   166

Author Index

Abusch, Tvzi, 60
Aḥituv, Shmuel, 152
Albertz, Rainer, 7, 184, 210
Allen, Leslie, 61
Al-Rawi, F. N. H., 111
Alter, Robert, 64
Altmann, Peter, 194, 195
American Psychiatric Association, 206
Andersen, Francis I., 106, 114, 140, 149
Armgardt, Matthias, 158, 183
Arnold, Bill T., 119, 120, 200
Augustine, 167
Averbeck, Richard E., 135

Baden, Joel, 185
Bailey, Terence, 233
Bakon, Shimon, 168, 196
Ball, Edward, 70, 91
Ball, Ivan J., Jr., 180, 184
Banister, Jamie A., 151
Barker, Joel D., 81
Barker, L. S., Jr., 158
Barr, James, 31
Barthélemy, Dominique, 113, 114
Barton, John, 7, 113

Bauckham, Richard, 55, 89, 166, 244
Baumann, Gerlinde, 82
Beasley-Murray, G. R., 90
Beaulieu, Paul-Alain, 55, 123, 124, 143
Beck, Martin, 11
Becking, Bob, 27, 46
Bekkum, Koert van, 153, 154, 157
Ben Zvi, Ehud, 11, 12, 177, 194, 197, 212, 225, 229, 234
Benun, Ronald, 28
Bergland, Kenneth, 158
Bergmann, Claudia, 62
Berkowitz, Beth A., 149
Berlejung, Angelika, 26, 52, 73, 105
Berlin, Adele, 178, 209
Berrin, Shani L., 87
Bienkowski, Piotr, 136
Billig, Michael, 67
Bird, Phyllis, 60
Boda, Mark J., 159, 195, 241
Boer, Roland, 23
Bosman, Jan P., 41
Bottéro, Jean, 118, 133
Bowie, Andrew, 217
Brett, Mark G., 132

Brody, Samuel H., 1
Brooks, David, 59
Brown, William P., 15, 239
Brueggemann, Walter, 2, 15–17, 21, 40, 187
Bryan, Steven M., 90
Burrell, Kevin, 214
Bussmann, H., 31
Butler, Judith, 51

Campbell, Anthony J., 32
Capps, Walter H., 20
Carroll R., M. Daniel, 157
Carter, Warren, 122
Cassin, Elena, 52
Castelo, Daniel, 95
Cathcart, Kevin J., 127, 135, 140
Chapman, Cynthia R., 62
Chapman, Stephen B., 14, 96
Charlesworth, James H., 87
Childs, Brevard, 80
Christiansen, Duane, 32
Ciampa, Roy E., 189
Cifarelli, Megan, 57
Clancier, Philippe, 147
Clendenen, E. Ray, 165
Clifford, Richard J., 109
Clines, David J. A., 16
Cogan, Mordechai, 119, 185
Coggins, Richard J., 92, 93, 99, 168, 169, 171
Collins, John J., 161, 192
Consultation on Texts, 93
Cook, Gregory, 61
Cook, John A., 152
Cooley, Jeffery L., 192
Cornell, Colin, 5
Craigie, Peter C., 61

Crouch, Carly L., 43, 96, 112, 152, 182, 217
Cyril of Alexandria, 232

Da Riva, Rocío, 125
Dalley, Stephanie, 89
Dangl, Oskar, 107
Dawkins, Stephen, 16
Day, John, 43, 135
de Lubac, Henri, 223
De Vries, Simon, 46
Deines, Roland, 23, 243
Delorme, Jean-Philippe, 143
Desjarlais, Robert, 72
Desmond, William, 242
Dewrell, Heath D., 192
Dick, Michael B., 53
Dickhaut, Kirsten, 187
Dietler, Michael, 194
Dietrich, Walter, 83, 107, 133, 140, 146, 193, 212, 224
Dines, Jennifer M., 86
Dogniez, Cécile, 22
Dooley, Robert A., 112
Dothan, Trude, 200
Dozeman, Thomas B., 84
Duby, Steven J., 97
Duff, R. Antony, 57, 98, 147

Ehrenberg, Erica, 125
Ehrlich, Carl S., 200, 201
Ellingworth, Paul, 230
Emerton, J. A., 61
England, Emma, 91

Fabry, Heinz-Josef, 61, 83, 85, 86, 161, 164, 204
Fales, Frederick Mario, 34

Faraone, Christopher A., 194
Felder, Cain H., 199
Fischer, Georg, 185
Fishbane, Michael, 159, 226
Fitzmeyer, Joseph A., 62
Floyd, Michael, 28, 30, 48, 104, 128, 144
Forepaugh, Adam, 101
Forg, Florian, 109
Forsyth, Neil, 109
Foster, Benjamin R., 43, 118, 153
Freddoso, Alfred J., 95
Fretheim, Terence E., 96, 97
Frey, Christofer, 57
Friedman, Caleb T., 87, 168, 228
Fu, Janling, 194, 195
Fuller, Russell E., 79

Galter, Hannes D., 119
Gamberoni, Johann, 40
Garber, David G., Jr., 94
Gelston, Anthony, 141
George, Andrew R., 111, 122
Getz, Trevor R., 25
Gheorghita, Radu, 230
Girard, René, 172
Glenny, W. Edward, 79
Gnuse, Robert, 4
Goldstein, Jonathon, 118, 119
Gordon, Robert P., 5, 8, 18, 91
Grabbe, Lester, 36, 184, 185
Grayson, A. Kirk, 33, 124, 131, 132, 137, 138
Grimal, Nicolas, 183
Gulker, Jill L., 66
Gunneweg, A. H. J., 108
Gunton, Colin, 171, 211, 222, 235
Gutiérrez, Gustavo, 237

Hadjiev, Tchavdar, 176, 224
Hagedorn, Anselm, 28, 29, 219
Hamilton, Victor P., 64
Hamori, Esther J., 3
Han, Jin H., 92, 93, 99, 168, 169, 171
Haring, James W., 139, 140
Harré, Rom, 69
Harris, Rivkah, 60
Harrisville, Roy A., 109
Harvey, Barry, 243
Hayes, John H., 7
Hays, Christopher M., 156
Hays, Nathan, 205, 210
Heal, Bridget, 92
Helmer, Christine, 22, 23
Hendel, Ronald, 27
Herrmann, Wolfgang, 191
Hess, Richard, 37, 121
Heywood, Andrew, 58
Hiebert, Theodore, 50, 107
Hilber, John, 107, 182
Hill, Robert C., 90, 91, 232
Hinton, Perry R., 67–69
Hoeken, Hans, 213
Holladay, William L., 107, 225
Holloway, Steven W., 50
Horton, Michael, 171, 221
House, Paul R., 11, 187
Houston, Walter, 236
Hurowitz, Victor A., 204
Hutton, Jeremy M., 36, 70, 121

Irsigler, Hubert, 192, 213, 226–28
Ishai-Rosenboim, Daniella, 196

Jacobs, Mignon, 113
Janzen, J. Gerald, 141
Johnson, Paul, 25

Johnson, Steven G., 34
Johnston, G. H., 26, 50
Jones, Barry, 11
Jong, John de, 195
Joosten, Jan, 27

Kahn, Dan'el, 182, 183, 203
Kalmin, Richard, 167
Kamionkowski, Tamar, 94
Keel, Othmar, 136, 137, 153, 192
Keen, Suzanne, 117
Kelle, Brad, 8, 33, 35
Kenny, Anthony, 223
Kessler, John, 235
Kessler, Rainer, 80, 82, 108, 158
Kilchör, Benjamin, 158, 183
Kim, Jong-Hoon, 226
King, Charles, 145
King, Greg A., 208
Kipling, Rudyard, 100
Kissine, Mikhail, 17
Ko, Grace, 107, 140
Krakowczyk, Piotr, 104
Kreitzer, Larry J., 231
Krieken, Kobie van, 213

Landy, Francis, 11, 112
Lange, Armin, 86, 162
Larson, Jonathon, 234
Laytner, Anson, 169
LeCureux, Jason T., 41
Lee, Won W., 31
Legaspi, Michael C., 137, 142, 150
Leichty, Erle, 47, 52, 119, 203
Lemke, W. E., 15
Levenson, Jon D., 6, 19, 219
Levin, Christoph, 175, 176, 182
Levinsohn, Stephen H., 112, 113

Levison, John R., 231
Lewis, Theodore J., 46
Leyens, Jacques-Philippe, 66
Lim, Timothy H., 87, 162, 163
Lints, Richard, 171, 221
Liverani, Mario, 24, 48, 49, 121
Lohfink, Norbert, 185
Long, Burke O., 101
Long, V. Philips, 181, 185
Longman, Tremper III, 181, 185
Lowth, Robert, 92
Lyons, William J., 91

Maré, Leonard, 94
Markl, Dominik, 108, 185
Marr, Andrew, 24
Martin of Brage, 166
Martínez, Florentino García, 86, 163, 228
Masotti, Felipe A., 158
McConville, J. Gordon, 5, 44, 97, 98, 129, 188
McGarty, Craig, 66
McGoeugh, Kevin M., 100
McGroarty, Brendan I., 198
McKane, William, 61
McNicol, Allan J., 231
Mears, Steve D., 170
Meek, Esther L., 245
Melugin, Roy, 109
Melville, Sarah C., 50, 52
Menken, Maarten J. J., 230
Midgley, Mary, 241
Millard, Alan R., 95, 135, 186
Miller, Daniel, 149
Miller, Patrick D., 36, 50, 72, 121
Mizrahi, Noam, 183
Moberly, R. W. L., 23, 64

Monteith, Margo, 66
Moon, Joshua, 62
Moore, Carey A., 88
Moseman, R. David, 116
Moyise, Steve, 88, 165
Mudge, Ronald R., 62
Muller, E. Theodore, Jr., 192
Müller, Reinhard, 11
Mulroney, James A. E., 160

Naudé, Jackie A., 135
Neef, Heinz-Dieter, 177
Neusner, Jacob, 167
Niditch, Susan, 183
Niehr, Herbert, 192
Nissinen, Martti, 2, 3, 6
Nitzan, Bilhah, 163
Noble, Paul, 31
Nogalski, James D., 11, 80, 82, 200
Nordlie, Johanna, 16
Novak, David, 229

Oates, Joan, 120
O'Brien, Julia M., 10, 60, 224
Oded, Bustaney, 48, 143, 144
O'Donovan, Oliver, 242, 243
O'Dowd, Ryan, 4
Olyan, Saul M., 149
Oppenheim, A. Leo, 148
Oshima, Takayoshi, 111
Otto, Eckart, 108

Paganini, Simone, 185
Pakkala, Juha, 11
Pardee, Dennis, 140
Parker, Bradley J., 48
Parpola, Simo, 50, 111
Peckham, Brian, 144

Peels, H. G. L., 38
Perdue, Leo G., 122
Perlitt, Lothar, 29, 106, 110, 135, 142, 150, 197
Person, Raymond F., 13
Peterson, David L., 11, 29
Pfau, Thomas, 22, 222, 238
Plantinga, Alvin, 22
Pongratz-Leisten, Beate, 118, 133
Porter, Barbara N., 118
Premnath, D. N., 102
Prinsloo, Gert T. M., 105, 116, 127, 142, 152, 158
Propp, William H. C., 84
Provan, Iain, 181, 185, 219
Puech, Emile, 193

Raabe, Paul, 29
Rae, Murray, 20–22, 245
Randel, Don Michael, 233
Redelinghuys, C. J., 188, 234–36
Rehg, William, 171
Reichenbach, Bruce R., 211
Reimer, Haraldo, 191, 198, 204
Reiser, Markus, 110
Rendtorff, Rolf, 81, 235
Renz, Thomas, 28, 56, 60, 184
Reuter, Eleonore, 38
Rezetko, Robert, 11
Rieff, Philip, 172
Roberts, J. J. M., 136, 140, 141, 145–47, 158, 197
Roberts, Richard H., 59
Rodriguez, Luis R., 237
Rollston, Christopher A., 4
Rosenbloom, Joseph, 1
Roth, Martha, 62
Roux, Georges, 33

Rudman, D., 205
Runions, Erin, 170
Ryou, Daniel H., 177

Saggs, H. W. F., 33, 185
Samely, Alexander, 16
Sanders, José, 213
Sanders, Seth L., 2, 3, 107, 182
Sandt, Huub van de, 165
Schadron, Georges, 66
Schaller, Mark, 67
Schart, Aaron, 9
Schmid, H. H., 42, 190
Schmoll, Hans, 226
Schrag, Calvin O., 242
Schwemer, Anna Maria, 162
Scoralick, Ruth, 82
Scruton, Roger, 97, 219
Seifrid, Mark, 220
Seitz, Christopher R., 9, 79
Seitz, Gottfried, 226
Serfontein, Johan, 94
Seybold, Klaus, 28
Shai, Itzhaq, 201
Sheriffs, Deryck, 125
Sherman, Philip M., 149
Sinclair, L. A., 201
Skornik, Jordan E., 92
Smelik, Klaus A. D., 202
Smith, Anthony D., 58, 59
Smith, John, 25
Smith, Mark S., 43
Snyman, S. D., 193
Solomon, Norman, 168
Sommer, Benjamin D., 13, 109
Spears, Russell, 66
Spronk, Klaas, 30, 50, 61, 79
Stangor, Charles, 67

Steinmetz, Devora, 168
Stendahl, Krister, 17
Stökl, Jonathan, 5
Strawn, Brent A., 33, 35, 52–54, 84
Streets-Salter, Heather, 25
Studevent-Hickman, Benjamin, 124
Stump, Eleonore, 157
Sweeney, Marvin A., 10, 11, 79, 139, 149, 184, 219
Swindell, Anthony, 169, 170

Tadmor, Hayim, 185
Taylor, Charles, 22, 58, 222
Teeter, D. Andrew, 111
Ten, C. L., 95
Tidiman, Brian, 146, 150
Tiemeyer, Lena-Sofia, 10
Timmer, Daniel C., 10, 13, 19, 25, 27, 46, 72, 79, 83, 84, 134, 152, 154, 178, 205, 211, 219, 236, 240
Tooman, William A., 111
Tremblay, Hervé, 13
Trepp, Leo, 169
Tsumura, David T., 140
Tucker, Gene M., 7
Tull, Patricia K., 9
Turner, Ian, 229
Twelftree, Graham H., 230

Uehlinger, Chrisoph, 188, 192, 193
Ulrich, Eugene, 161
Unger, Christoph, 108

Van De Mieroop, Marc, 121, 122
Van Dijk, T. A., 16
Van Langenhove, Luk, 69
Van Seters, John, 11, 111

Vanderhooft, David S., 116–18, 122, 124, 125, 130–32, 137, 138, 158
Vanderkam, James C., 163
Verderame, Lorenzo, 55
Vogt, Peter, 185

Waerzeggers, Caroline, 122
Wall, Robert, 231
Walzer, Michael, 5
Watanabe, Kazuko, 50
Watkin, Christopher, 244
Watts, James W., 140, 151, 153, 154
Webster, John, 210, 237, 240–42, 244
Weigl, Michael, 16
Weissert, Elnathan, 53
Wells, Rahel, 158
Wendland, Ernst, 32, 40, 114, 115, 179, 213
Wengst, Klaus, 166
Wenyi, Jacob O., 78
Werse, Nicholas R., 177, 181
Westbrook, Raymond, 117
Westerholm, Martin, 239

Whitehead, Philip, 115, 116
Whitekettle, Richard, 106
Widmer, Michael, 40
Wiederblank, Netanel, 22
Wiesel, Elie, 169
Wilckens, Ulrich, 110
Wintermute, O. S., 227
Wiseman, D. J., 106, 125, 132
Woelfel, Craig, 20
Wöhrle, Jakob, 10, 29, 79, 115
Wood, Charles M., 22
Wood, William, 217
Woodcock, Anna, 66
Woods, Julie, 102

Yamauchi, Edwin M., 199
Younger, K. Lawson, Jr., 35
Yzerbyt, Vincent, 66

Zapff, Burkard M., 82
Zehnder, Markus, 48, 57, 158, 183
Zevit, Ziony, 37
Ziemer, Benjamin, 13

Subject Index

1QpZeph (1Q15), 228
4QpZeph (4Q170), 228

Ambrose of Milan, 167
Ammon, 201–2
Apocalypse of Zephaniah, 227
Assurbanipal
  prophecy, 6
  royal ideology, 52–53
Assyria
  condemnation of, 203–4
  fall, 83
  gods and imperialism,
    47–48, 50
  relations with Israel/Judah,
    33–36
  royal ideology, 47–54
  violence, 55
Augustine, 167

Ba'al, 43, 191
Ba'al Epic, 42–43
Babylon
  condemnation of, 136–50
  empire, 64–65, 88–89, 95–97,
    106, 132, 154, 159–60,
    166, 182

  history of, 117–21, 132–33
  means of divine punishment,
    130–34
  religious significance of city,
    121–22
  symbol of empire, 166
Bel and the Dragon, 161
Book of Common Prayer, 93
Book of the Twelve (Minor
    Prophets)
  nature and unity, 10–12
  recent research, 9–14
  themes, 13

Cassiodorus, 232
Code of Hammurabi, 117
Creation
  and history, 21–22, 169
  and judgment/order, 19, 103,
    134, 153, 169, 188, 190,
    207, 216
  renewal, 210–11, 231, 240,
    244–46
Ctesias, 101
Cush, 183, 202–3
Cyprian, 231–32
Cyril of Alexandria, 232

SUBJECT INDEX

Day of YHWH, 81–82, 89–90, 174, 175, 180, 193–97, 207, 213, 214, 218, 220, 231, 233
Deuteronomy, book of, 128–29, 185, 225
Dies irae, 233

Ecology/environment, 147–49, 190, 220–21, 234–36, 240
Enlightenment, xiii, 20, 22
Enuma Elish, 43, 118, 136
Esarhaddon
 and Babylon, 119
 and prophecy, 6
 royal ideology, 52, 111
 self-description, 47
Exile
 divine punishment, 6
 foreshadowed, 189
 return from, 211
 threatened, 195, 208

Gender, 59–63

Habakkuk
 in Jewish and Christian tradition, 158–69
 reception, 169–72
 unity and diversity, 107–16
Habakkuk Pesher (1QpHab), 113, 162–64
Hezekiah, 35, 181
Human beings
 in image of God, 98, 136, 171, 221, 222
 moral agency, 19, 95–96, 155, 188–90

moral imperfection, 77, 105, 156, 174, 192, 217, 219, 240–41
 relation to YHWH, 39–40, 44–45, 69, 71, 76, 91, 141, 153, 171, 189, 218–23, 228, 240
 value, 56, 136, 145–46, 171, 218, 222, 240

Imperialism
 Babylonian, 81, 88–89, 122–25, 131–34, 136–38, 142, 144–50
 modern, 24–25, 98–100, 172
 Neo-Assyrian, 47, 55–56, 73–74, 88–89, 203–4
Israel (northern kingdom)
 annexed by Assyria, 34
 conquered by Assyria, 35

Jerome, 91
Jerusalem
 fall to Babylon, 106, 108
 under Hezekiah, 35, 182
 prophetic critique of, 195, 205–7, 214–15
 restored, 212, 235
Jesus Christ, 90, 165, 166, 230–32, 243, 245
Josiah, 120, 127, 129, 181–85
Judah (southern kingdom)
 annexed by Assyria, 34
 fall to Babylon, 120
 prophetic critique of, 126–30, 191–96, 206–7
 religious practice, 36–37, 185
 remnant of, 180, 208–11, 215, 218–19

SUBJECT INDEX

Judah (southern kingdom) (cont.)
  restoration by YHWH predicted, 63–65, 207–13
  vassal of Assyria, 35

Kant, Immanuel 22, 238

Literary coherence, 12, 16, 31–32, 112–15
Literary cohesion, 27, 31–32, 113
Literary genre, 108–11, 113, 115, 175–76
The Lives of the Prophets, 162
Lowth, Robert, 91–92
Ludlul Bēl Nēmeqi, 110

Marduk, 43, 110, 118–19, 122–25, 132–33, 138, 143, 148, 153, 203
Martin of Brage, 166
Moab, 201–2
MurXII (Mur88), 114

Nabopolassar, 120, 122–24, 131, 138
Nahum
  in Jewish and Christian traditions, 78–91
  reception, 91–103
  unity and diversity of, 26–33
Nahum Pesher (4QpNah = 4Q169), 86–87
Nationalism
  Babylon, 125
  Judah, 44, 74, 125
  modern, 58–59, 100, 217
  rejected in Habakkuk, 151
  rejected in Nahum, 100
  rejected in Zephaniah, 218

Nations (non-Israelite)
  moral accountability, 7, 96–97
  relation to Israel, 6, 64, 200, 201, 205
  relation to YHWH, 132, 151, 177–78, 199–204
  remnant of, 212, 218–19
Nebuchadnezzar II, 121, 123–25, 131, 137, 138, 145, 147–49
Nineveh
  fall, 33, 101–2, 203
  prophetic condemnation of, 55–56, 60, 73–74
  survivors of its fall, 68
  symbol for Assyria, 80

Pesharim of Zephaniah, 228
Philistines, 200–1
Prayer, 111, 116–17, 140, 150–54, 168
Prophet, prophecy
  concerning foreign nations, 6–7, 199–205
  contemporary relevance, 1, 17, 19–23, 77–78, 116–17, 171–72, 215–16, 239–46
  covenant conversation, 4–5, 8, 63, 77, 94, 129–30, 220
  critique of political leaders, 4, 8, 36, 67, 192, 206, 225
  distant future (eschatology), 6, 10, 19, 21, 71, 75, 80–81, 97, 105, 150–54, 176, 196, 205, 209–13, 218–21, 225, 237, 243–46
  diverse views on authority, 2–3
  divination, 3–4, 55, 192
  Israelite, distinctive features, 3
  Israelite, theology of, 14–19

judgment and salvation, 7–8, 13, 19, 81, 96, 102, 153, 176, 180, 186–87, 221, 231, 233
Mari, prophecy in, 3
metaphor, 55–56, 109, 136–37, 145–47, 194
spokesperson for deity, 2

Race, ethnicity, 1, 68–69, 204, 219, 229
"Recessional" (Rudyard Kipling, 1897), 98–100
Remembering Babylon (David Malouf, 1993), 170
Rent (Jonathon Larson, 1996), 234
Repentance, 79, 81, 90, 102, 156, 197–98, 205, 214, 218, 220, 232, 241–43
Revised Common Lectionary, 93
Roman Catholic Lectionary (1969), 93

Sennacherib, 36, 46, 47, 49, 89, 119
Septuagint, 85–86, 114, 160–61, 165, 226
Sirach, Book of, 78
Stereotypes
  Assyria, 66–70
  Judah, 66–70
  limits, 76
  and social identity theory, 67
  theory, 65–66
The Sublime Historic Bible Spectacle, Fall of Nineveh (Forepaugh, 1892), 100–1

Talmud, 167–68, 228–29
The Task (William Cowper 1784), 170
Thebes, 26, 33, 36, 73, 74

Theodore of Mopsuestia, 90–91
Tiamat, 43, 118, 136, 153
Tobit, Book of, 87–88
Transformation (personal), 6, 8, 18–20, 105, 177–78, 198–99, 205, 207–10, 220, 239, 241–44

Violence
  end, 146, 236–37
  gender, 59–63
  im/morality of, 37, 59–63, 93–103, 127, 131–34, 137, 141, 145–47, 157, 166, 172, 193–94, 204, 221, 235
  purposes, 25, 51–55, 93–94, 146, 198, 215, 221

Yahweh
  acting in the world, 19, 21, 23, 29, 38, 42–44, 63–64, 70, 72, 105, 106, 150
  character and attributes, 38, 41–42, 54, 55, 71, 75, 76, 80, 84–85, 106, 135, 141, 154, 212, 238, 243, 244
  covenant partner with Israel, 5, 63, 77, 120–21, 128, 155, 185, 195
  creator, 18–19, 21, 40, 97, 134–35, 148, 153, 155, 169, 172, 174, 240, 241
  and eschatology, 21, 71, 81, 97, 105, 150, 154, 156, 157, 164, 174, 210, 215, 244
  and forgiveness, 156, 210, 215
  judge, 39–40, 43, 50, 54, 56–58, 70, 75, 81, 84–85, 93–103, 144, 153, 155, 172, 174, 180, 186–87, 189, 194–95, 197, 204, 218, 236

Yahweh (cont.)
  praise of, 71–72, 77–78, 152–54, 210, 213, 235, 237
  reconciler, 39–40, 44, 71–72, 75, 81, 84–95, 105, 153, 154, 157, 172, 174, 180, 187, 197, 209–13, 237

Zephaniah
  in Jewish and Christian tradition, 223–32
  reception, 233–38
  unity and diversity of, 174–78

Milton Keynes UK
Ingram Content Group UK Ltd.
UKHW010156090424
440733UK00009B/46